Andrew Eliot

Twenty Sermons on the Following Subjects

Andrew Eliot

Twenty Sermons on the Following Subjects

ISBN/EAN: 9783337114336

Printed in Europe, USA, Canada, Australia, Japan

Cover: Foto ©Lupo / pixelio.de

More available books at **www.hansebooks.com**

TWENTY SERMONS

ON THE FOLLOWING

SUBJECTS,

VIZ.

I. The Folly and Danger of Duplicity in Religion.

II. The Excellency of the human Soul.

III. Jesus Christ the only Source of Rest and Happiness.

IV. The Dominion of an Omnipotent Deity a Reason for Joy and Praise.

V.
VI. } Charity more excellent than Faith or Hope.
VII.

VIII. Christ preaching to the Spirits in Prison.

IX. Redemption by the Blood of Christ.

X. } The Connection between the Du-
XI. } ties and Comforts of Religion.

XII. The Obligations to Family-Religion.

XIII. The Usefulness and Importance of Religious Education.

XIV.
XV. } The Table of the Lord rendered contemptible.
XVI.

XVII. } Practical Observations on the
XVIII. } History of Judas and his tragical End.

XIX. Man doomed to return to the Dust from whence he was taken.

XX. The Blessedness of those who have not seen and yet have believed.

BY

ANDREW ELIOT, D. D.

Pastor of a CHURCH in BOSTON.

BOSTON:
by JOHN BOYLE in Marlborough-Street.
MDCCLXXIV.

TO THE

CHURCH AND CONGREGATION

To which the AUTHOR stands in a

PASTORAL RELATION.

My Dear Christian Friends,

IT is now more than Thirty-two Years since I devoted myself to the Service of your Souls. From that Time my Studies and Endeavors have been employed to promote your best Interests.

The mutual Affection there hath been between us during the Time of
my

my Miniſtry, the Harmony and Peace which have ſubſiſted among yourſelves, and your kind Acceptance of my Labors, have been no ſmall Support and Encouragement to me, amidſt the many Difficulties and Trials which unavoidably attend the Paſtoral Charge.

In the Courſe of my Preaching, I have not meddled with abſtruſe Speculations: And, as far as Miniſterial Fidelity would allow, have avoided Subjects of Controverſy. I have rather deſired to impreſs on your Hearts and my own a deeper Senſe of thoſe great and important Truths, in which good Men are agreed, and which are at the Foundation of all Religion. Being fully perſuaded, that the Pulpit was not deſigned to be a School of Diſputation, or to diſplay a Miniſter's Acquaintance with Science falſly ſo called. My

DEDICATION. v

My chief Aim hath been to be a useful Preacher-----To be an Instrument of building you up in Faith and Holiness unto eternal Life-----Blessed be God ! I have Reason to hope my Labors have not been wholly in vain.--------I do not mean by this, to boast of any peculiar Fidelity or Success. I am conscious I have not done the good I might and ought to have done.----The Imperfections which have attended my Life and Ministry are a constant Source of Humiliation and Grief-----My only Hope is in the Mercy of God through Jesus Christ. May He forgive the Defects both of Preacher and Hearers !

The earnest and repeated Desire of a great number of you, hath brought the following Discourses into public View. It was a sufficient Reason with me, and I hope it will be thought so by by others, that I should by the Publication gratify a kind and obliging People. At the same Time, I am not without hopes, that these Sermons which I present you, as a Mark of my Affection and Gratitude, may, by the Blessing of God, promote your spiritual Advantage, as well as afford you some Instruction and Entertainment. Very few of them were chosen by myself. Several were desired for the Press immediately after the Delivery. It was more agreable to collect them into a Volume than to publish them separately.

I am very sensible they will not bear a critical Inspection, and ask the Candor of those who shall vouchsafe to give them the Perusal. I pretend to no great Skill in Composition; and some Allowance will be made for the
almost

almoſt innumerable Avocations to which I am continually expoſed.

I the more readily complied with your Requeſt, as I am aware my Life is upon the Decline, and that I muſt ſhortly put off this Tabernacle.

I have only to requeſt for myſelf, that you would ſhew me the ſame Tenderneſs, while I abide with you, which I have hitherto experienced. And that you would continue to favor me with your Prayers, that I may be faithful to God and to your Souls, and may not, when I have preached to others, be myſelf a Caſt-away.

God forbid! that I ſhould ceaſe to pray for you, that your Love may abound yet more in Knowledge, and in all Judgment. That ye may approve things

things that are excellent; that ye may be sincere, and without Offence till the Day of Christ: Being filled with the Fruits of of Righteousness, which are by Jesus Christ unto the Glory and Praise of God.

I am,

With sincere respect,

Your Affectionate Friend,

And Servant in the Gospel,

ANDREW ELIOT.

Boston, May 20:h, 1774.

THE CONTENTS.

SERMON I.

The Folly and Danger of Duplicity in Religion.
JAMES I. 8.
A double-minded man is unstable in all his ways.
Page 1

SERMON II.

The Excellency of the human Soul.
GENESIS II. 7.
And man became a living soul. 27

SERMON III.

Jesus Christ the only Source of Rest and Happiness.
JOHN VI. 68.
Then Simon Peter answered him, Lord, to whom shall we go? Thou hast the words of eternal life. 57

The CONTENTS.

SERMON IV.

The Dominion of an Omnipotent Deity a Reason for Joy and Praise.

REVELATION XIX. 6.

Alleluia: *for the Lord God omnipotent reigneth:* 79

SERMON V. VI. VII.

Charity more excellent than Faith or Hope.

1 CORINTHIANS XIII. 13.

And now abideth faith, hope, charity, these three; but the greatest of these is charity. 105

SERMON VIII.

Christ preaching to the Spirits in Prison.

1 PETER III. 19, 20.

By which also he went and preached unto the spirits in prison; which sometimes were disobedient, when once the long suffering of God waited in the days of Noah, while the ark was a preparing, wherein few, that is eight souls, were saved by water. 177

SERMON IX.

Redemption by the Blood of Christ.

REVELATION V. 9.

Thou wast slain and hast redeemed us to God by thy blood. 205

SERMON X. XI.

The Connection between the Duties and Comforts of Religion.

ACTS IX. 31.

———*Walking in the fear of the Lord, comfort of the Holy Ghost.*

SERMON XII.

The Obligations to Family-Religion.

JOSHUA XXIV. 15.

———*But as for me and my house we will serve the Lord.* 271

SERMON XIII.

The Usefulness and Importance of Religious Education.

GENESIS XVIII. 19.

For I know him, that he will command his children and his houshold after him, and they shall keep the way of the Lord to do justice and judgment. 295

SERMON XIV. XV. XVI.

The Table of the Lord rendered contemptible.

MALACHI I. 7.

Ye say the Table of the Lord is contemptible. 323

SERMON XVII. XVIII.

Practical Observations on the History of Judas and his tragical End.

MATTHEW XXVII. 3, 4, 5.

Then Judas, which had betrayed him, when he saw that he was condemned, repented himself, and brought again the thirty pieces of silver to the chief priests and elders, saying, I have sinn'd, in that I have betrayed innocent blood. And they said, What is that to us? see thou to that. And he cast down the pieces of silver in the temple, and departed, and went and hanged himself. 387

SERMON XIX.

Man doomed to return to the Dust from whence he was taken.

GENESIS III. 19.

Dust thou art, and unto dust shalt thou return. 435

SERMON XX.

The Blessedness of those who have not seen and yet have believed.

JOHN XX. 29.

Jesus saith unto him, Thomas, because thou hast seen me, thou hast believed. Blessed are they that have not seen, and yet have believed. 459

SERMON I.

The Folly and Danger of Duplicity in Religion.

JAMES I. 8.

A double minded man is unstable in all his ways.

IF we look around and take a view of mankind; we find multitudes sunk into the lowest state of degeneracy; either immersed in vicious pleasures, or engaged in unworthy pursuits; wholly negligent of God and their most important interests.—We find a few, a very few, acting a wise and rational part, attentive to the truths of religion, and making the will of God the rule of their conduct.—Besides these, we find a third sort; who attempt to divide their hearts between God and the world; or as our Saviour expresses it, to serve God and mammon. They desire to have their good things here and hereafter too; to enjoy the pleasures of sin, and practice the duties of religion at the same time. In consequence of this divided state of mind, they are uncertain and inconstant; sometimes for God, and sometimes for Baal: sometimes they seem to be men of religion and virtue, at other times they devote themselves to worldly cares and pleasures, as if there was no God, or they had no connection with him.

"A double-minded man is unstable in all his ways."

In discoursing on this subject I shall endeavour

First, To explain to you the character of a double-minded man.

Secondly, I shall consider the instability of conduct which is the consequence of such a state of mind.

Thirdly, I shall set before you the folly and danger of such a temper and conduct.

I shall then conclude with a serious exhortation to all to devote themselves to God, entirely and without any reserve.

First, I am to shew what it is to be double-minded.

We

We call that man double-minded, in our transactions with each other, who at one time professes a warm regard and friendship; at another, when perhaps we most need his help, is distant and lukewarm, discovers no concern for our interest, nor disposition to serve us; or if he can gain any advantage to himself, forsakes his friend and betrays his cause. Such absolute deceit and hypocrisy, argues a mind proof against every virtuous consideration. There are others who make a fair appearance, and would do some things to serve us, but are easily led away by an opposite interest. They do not intend to deceive us in their professions of friendship; but when they are in a different company, or there is a change of circumstances, their disposition alters; their mind is divided; they are wavering and uncertain; not knowing how to determine, or how to act. It is in this latter sense the apostle speaks of a double-minded man in the text. He doth not intend persons who are guilty of direct prevarication and falshood in their professions of religion, and who assume a character which they know doth not belong to them, with a design to deceive and impose on the world: but he speaks of those who are distracted and divided in their thoughts; who feel at some times a warmth and zeal for God and the cause of virtue; but at other times are languid and indifferent, give themselves no concern, whether religion prevails in their own souls or the souls of others.—There is,

as

as critics observe, an antithesis, or opposition between this temper and what was before said of the blessed God ; God giveth *simply*, or with a *single mind*—but the other is *double-minded*, and destitute of that simplicity and steady goodness which God approves and enjoins ; one while resolving upon this and another upon that. The expression intimates, that we profess a regard to God, and do some things in religion ; but that there is some other interest which we prefer to him, or which hath at least an equal place in our hearts, and which we cannot give up for his sake. It implies, that God is at times in our thoughts, and that we have some faint desires to secure his favor and approbation : but that our regard is not sufficient to carry us to that entire devotedness to him which we profess to have, and which christianity requires ; that there are some things, some difficult duties, in the omission of which we hope the Lord will pardon his servants, and make some kind allowance for our particular circumstances, connections, and temptations.

If we had not the clearest evidence of this criminal duplicity, we should be ready to think it impossible such a divided state of mind should ever exist. Religion, a conformity to the whole will of God, is so much our duty and interest, that if our minds were in a right state, we could not have the least hesitation about any part of christian practice. The blessed God is so infinitely superior to every other

ther object, that we ought not to defire any thing in comparifon with him. Jefus Chrift is fo good a friend, and hath done fo much for us, that we fhould never think any thing too much to do for him. We fhould account his yoke to be eafy and his burden light: and rejoice in every opportunity to teftify our gratitude and efteem. But fo it is; there are double minded men; fcripture and experience make it too evident to be denied. It will be well, if this character doth not in fome degree belong to us. 'Tis true, God deferves all our love, and if we faw things in their juft light, and had no wrong bias, we fhould not judge or act amifs in this or any other inftance. But the cafe is far otherwife, our minds are weak and ignorant, there is in us an evil propenfity, fomething which makes it difficult to confider religious truths with that attention and impartiality they deferve. Our natural fondnefs for earthly and fenfual objects darkens our underftanding, perverts our judgment, and often makes things appear quite different from what they are; or quiets our minds when we know we do amifs.

The bounds which God hath fixed to the gratification of our natural inclinations are not merely arbitrary conftitutions, they are fixed by infinite wifdom, and by them God defigns our advantage, as well as his own honor. The law of God is the rule by which we are to govern ourfelves; this law
is

is holy, juſt, and good. Reaſon and conſcience therefore urge us to comply with it's requirements; they dictate to us, theſe things ye ought to do and thoſe to leave undone; but our fleſhly appetites and inclinations too often prevail againſt reaſon and conſcience; they either ſilence this ſtill ſmall voice, or perſuade us to diſregard it.

God who is perfectly acquainted with the weakneſs and perverſeneſs of the human heart, knowing that we ſhould be likely to diſregard naked precepts, though founded in the higheſt reaſon, hath enforced his law by the moſt powerful ſanctions; ſanctions moſt wiſely adapted to operate on our hopes and fears, thoſe leading paſſions in human nature, and which if ſuitably attended to, could not fail of producing their genuine effect; but men are awfully inattentive to theſe weighty and intereſting conſiderations, they put far away the evil day, and forget God amidſt the cares and amuſements of life. They do not at once become wholly negligent of the things that belong to their peace, nor ſink into a ſtupidity ſo diſhonorable to their reaſonable nature. Conſcience gives many alarms, and ſometimes they have a lively ſenſe of the power and wrath of God; they conſider and are afraid of him.—There are none, at leaſt none under the goſpel, who have not at times a perſuaſion of the Being and Perfections of God, a view of the evil nature and dangerous conſequences of ſin, and who

do

do not see the necessity of a spiritual change, and an interest in the great atoning sacrifice; the truths of the gospel are impressed on their hearts by the Spirit of God. By embracing these happy seasons and attending to the divine influences, thay might become good men and sincere christians; so that it is their own fault they are not. While their minds are thus roused and affected, they feel a disrelish for sensual and worldly objects; they cannot enjoy them with any degree of satisfaction; they see that these are not able to afford rest to their minds; they are excited to prayer, that God would correct what is amiss, and justify them freely by his grace through the redemption there is in Christ Jesus.—These awakenings do not prove a change of heart, they are no evidence that we love God or his ways. They sometimes terminate happily, sinners obtain the mercy they seek, and become the children of God by faith in Christ Jesus—and if it is not always the case, it is because they quench the Spirit, grow careless and secure, neglect God, and indulge to a vicious course. Instances of such apostacy we too often see.

It is not without some struggles, that any, especially young persons who have had a good education, lose these impressions of religion. Before conscience is silenced, they strangely hesitate and balance, as if they were at a loss what to do or which way to turn. Sometimes this motive preponderates,

rates, and sometimes that, they halt between two opinions, which is in effect to have no opinion at all. A sense of danger may awaken and alarm us, and put us on enquiring how we may escape it, but it cannot produce love to God or sincere delight in him. Until we love God, we cannot prefer him to every thing else; and until we prefer him to every thing, it is not to be expected we should give up every thing for his sake. 'Tis true, spiritual and eternal things are infinitely more valuable than any thing this world hath to offer, but we do not see their worth and importance, until we have a spiritual taste and relish, or are, as the scripture expresses it, spiritually minded. Besides, the things of the world are present with us, while the motives of religion are fetch'd from those that are future and invisible; and every one knows that objects, which are present strike us more forcibly, than those that are distant; though the latter are of much more worth and importance. If these future objects sometimes appear real, so as to put us on seeking them, yet it is difficult to maintain a sense of their reality, or to keep them constantly in view. And if they are real, yet their futurity is a circumstance which prevents our attending to them as we ought. As they are future, we are ready to imagine we shall have time enough to think of them, and we will take some more convenient season for it. We shall not feel the evil threatned, or partake of the good promised, till this life is ended; we

may

may therefore purfue the world at prefent, and after fome time provide for futurity.

It is impoffible that men fhould rufh voluntarily into ruin: as much as we are attached to the pleafures of fenfe, we fhould not indulge to them, if we were perfuaded that this indulgence would certainly be followed with remedilefs deftruction, and had a clear view of that deftruction before us. One reafon therefore why men are divided between God and the world, is that they have fome fenfe of the danger of fin, but not deep enough to conquer their inclinations to, nor to deter them from the practice of it.

Another reafon is, that they hope by attending one duty, to atone for their neglect of another; and by avoiding fome fins, to make up for the practice of many others. They are taught that God is not ftrict to mark iniquity, that he is gracious and merciful, flow to anger and of great kindnefs, and they flatter themfelves that he will overlook many failings in perfons who do fo much. If they are not quite fo righteous, fo benevolent, fo circumfpect as they ought to be, yet they attend ordinances, and have a great zeal for godlinefs. Or if they neglect the duties of piety, yet they wrong no one, they are fober and temperate, they do many kind offices to their neighbours, and give alms of all they poffefs. This is a fcheme finely adapted to the corruptions of the human heart, according to which, every one may keep his own iniquity. Thus men divide their hearts between God and mammon, and vainly attempt to serve them both, in opposition to the voice of reason and scripture, which plainly teach, that we cannot serve two masters, and that no one whose heart is thus divided hath any measure of sincerity in his pretences to religion.—If I do not love God above the world and every thing in it, I do not love him at all. If I am not willing to give up all for the sake of Christ, I am not his disciple. The blessed God deserves the highest regard, he requires the whole heart, and if any object share our affection and esteem with him, or is allowed a place in our hearts in opposition to him, it shews, that we have no true religion, whatever we profess. But I would not anticipate what belongs to another head.   Let us,

In the second place consider the instability of conduct which is the natural consequence of a divided state of mind.

Where there is a settled principle of action, whether it be good or bad, the course of life will be correspondent. The man who hath his heart set on this world, and who chuses to enjoy the pleasures of sin, keeps this point in view, and steadily pursues that which is the object of his choice. He endeavors to suppress the dictates of conscience, and to
overcome

overcome the fears and objections which arise in his mind. He is uniform; he is earnest to reach the mark he aims at.—On the other hand, one who hath a supreme love to God, and sincerely devoted himself to his service, hath a stedfast permanent principle, that influences all his conduct. He considers himself as always in the presence of God, and when tempted to sin, cries out with the holy Patriarch, " how shall I do this great wickedness and sin against God!" This principle of divine love is also a powerful stimulus to right practice, and gently constrains to holy obedience. A christian's highest ambition is to be like Him who is the greatest and the best of Beings. His most earnest desire is to serve and glorify Him who hath laid him under the strongest obligations. His most raised expectations are of enjoying Him, who is the inexhaustible source of all good. These hopes are strengthened by the experience he hath of the pleasure which attends the practice of holiness in this life.—This pleasure, though greatly interrupted, and mingled with a thousand doubts and fears, doth yet far exceed all the pleasures of sin, and sometimes arises to joy unspeakable and full of glory. All this delight a christian considers as only a small prelibation of that fulness of joy, which the gospel allows him to hope for through Jesus Christ.—You cannot wonder that one who is possessed of such principles, who believes the truth of religion, and hath such joyful expectations, is fixed and determined in his course of action; that he is in the language

of

of the apoſtle, " ſtedfaſt, immoveable, always a-bounding in the work of the Lord."

But a man whoſe mind is perpetually fluctuating between God and the world, and cannot determine which to prefer, will always be wavering and unſteady in his practice; he will turn this way or that according to the motive which happens at the time to be predominant. " Unſtable as water, he cannot excell." His character, like his conduct, is dubious and uncertain, you cannot well pronounce him a man of the world, and certainly he is not a chriſtian. Chriſt will not own him to be a diſciple, and he is miſtaken if he thinks favourably of himſelf. As the apoſtle ſpeaks of thoſe who are deſtitute of charity, one of ſuch a fickle inconſtant mind is *nothing*; he is nothing in the ſight of God; he hath no real worth and excellency; he is truly odious, and juſtly contemptible; and in ſuch a divided ſtate of mind he can do nothing to any purpoſe. He cannot give himſelf an unbounded latitude in vice, becauſe he retains ſome belief of the being and perfections of God, and fears to diſpleaſe and offend him. He hath ſo much ſenſe of religion, that he is at times very ſerious and thoughtful, wiſhes he could be a chriſtian, is willing to do ſome things which God requires, and reſolves to repent and reform; but when he meets his vain companions, hath a ſudden proſpect of great gain, or of gratifying ſome favorite inclination, the temptation

tion is too strong, he is led away and enticed. Sometimes he is watchful and circumspect, devout and regular, and seems to be a man of piety and virtue; at other times, the world engrosses his heart, and he is overwhelmed in the cares and pleasures of it. One day, he sees the importance of religion, and determines to make it the great business of life; another, he is forgetful of God, and behaves as if there was no life after this. At one time you see him professing a zeal for God, and making a shew of sanctity; at another indulging himself in practices directly contrary to all the rules of the gospel of Christ.

Such an inconsistency of conduct is not always owing to a formed design to impose on the world. These religious appearances are not absolute hypocrisy and deceit. These men often think themselves better than they are, and intend to be what they profess. But their hearts deceive them, because they have no acquaintance with the transforming energy of divine truth—they have no settled principle of action to govern them, and to oppose to the temptations with which they are assaulted, and so are easily overcome. Their hearts are not " right with God", and therefore they are " not stedfast in his covenant".

III. Let us now in the third place consider the folly and danger of such a temper and conduct as I have described. If

If there was no other confideration than the anxiety and uneafinefs which a fickle irrefolute temper neceffarily produces ; methinks this fhould determine and fettle us. The double-minded man is " like the troubled fea, which cannot reft, whofe waters caft up mire and dirt." Or as it is expreffed in the context, " He that wavereth is like a wave of the fea, driven with the wind and toffed." " Thofe imperfect and undetermined impreffions of religion which he feels, ferve rather to perplex and torment, than guide and fecure him." The fenfe he has of divine things will not fuffer him to be eafy and at reft in a vicious courfe; but is not fufficient to produce that peace and quietnefs which is the genuine effect of true religion. He is ever finning and repenting, refolving and breaking his good refolutions. A man thus torn and diftracted muft doubtlefs be very miferable. He enjoys no comfort here, he can have no rational profpect of happinefs hereafter. For whatever fhew fuch men make of religion, they are ftrangers to God and the fervants of fin. " Let not that man" fays the apoftle, " think that he fhall receive any thing of the Lord."

In matters perfectly indifferent, a man may chufe this or that, or he may hefitate and prefer neither, and yet be fafe. But this is not the cafe in matters of religion ; here is no fuch thing as neutrality. God requires the heart, he demands our time, our talents,

talents, and he will admit of no competitor; the nature of the thing admits of none. God is our rightful Lord and Sovereign, there is a neceſſary relation between him and us; from whence reſults an unavoidable obligation upon us to love, obey and ſerve him. He neceſſarily requires us to be holy as he is holy. Now every one is holy, or he is not. He loves God, or he doth not. There is no medium. The holineſs of the beſt is not perfect; in our preſent imperfect ſtate, who is there that doeth good and ſinneth not? But when the mind is determined for God, and we ſincerely aim at a conformity to his nature and will, without any limitation or exception, we are holy according to the gracious tenor of the goſpel of Chriſt.

This holineſs doth not conſiſt merely in an abſtinence from groſs ſin, or an external or partial obedience to the commands of Chriſt. It is an inward principle. It ſuppoſes that we have a ſupreme regard to the Lord our Maker. That we love the work as well as the reward. That our obedience is free and unconſtrained, and that we can chearfully obey all his commandments. All who have not this inward principle of holineſs are the "ſervants of corruption." Some are more abject ſlaves than others, but all are more or leſs in ſubjection. It is not our having good thoughts now and then, nor our purpoſing that we will ſome time or another become the ſervants of God; nor our reſolving on the preſent time,

and

and doing some things that are right and fit in consequence of such resolutions, that will prove us to be holy ; unless we determine to change every bad habit, to leave every wicked practice, and to make the will of God our only rule. It is not the laying a restraint on our lusts for a time, or being almost persuaded to be christians, that will constitute us heirs of the promises. So much as to hesitate in so plain and important a case shews the prevalency of our corruptions, and that sin hath dominion over us. "Their heart is divided ; now shall they be found faulty".* Such as these will have no advantage of their temporary resolutions and partial reformations. They will be accounted and treated as children of disobedience. Would an earthly prince look upon a rebel subject, with approbation ? Would he receive him into favor, reward and honor him, because he had some thoughts of returning to his duty, which he never put in execution ? Or because he hesitated a great while and never came to a conclusion ? Would not his irresolution in a cause where his duty was so plain, be an additional affront ; and aggravate rather than extenuate his guilt ?

Irresolution produces delay, and delays in this case are exceeding dangerous, because this is the only time of our probation, and this time may be very short. Nothing is more uncertain than the life

* Hos. 10. 2.

life of man. We know not what a day, what an hour, what a moment may bring forth; as death leaves us judgment will find us, which will determine our state forever. There is no time after this life, to correct any mistakes we have made during our continuance here. It is therefore of infinite consequence that we die well. Every time we put off this important concern, we do, for ought we know, consign ourselves to everlasting destruction; because if we die, during this delay, this will be the certain consequence. It will not avail, that we always designed to set about this great work, this only shews that we were convinced of it's necessity; and of consequence, that in delaying, we have acted against the light of our own minds. If we neglect the present time, we know not that we shall have any other. We ought not therefore to hesitate a moment, but to set about the work of repentance immediately; we should make haste, and make no delay, to keep the commandments of God. If there was any doubt what was our duty, or what was our interest, our conduct might admit of some excuse. But in so great, so necessary a work, upon which an eternity depends, irresolution is a crime; it is a crime which carries it's own punishment with it, in that disquietude it necessarily occasions, and which exposes to greater misery than we can now conceive of.

I am to conclude with a serious exhortation to all, to give their hearts to God wholly and without any reserve. And here I observe in the first place,—Religion is not a fiction. You have sufficient evidence of the great truths on which it is founded. An heathen poet once said, Fear first made Gods: and others have represented religion as the contrivance of some cunning politician. There is no less folly than impiety in these wild assertions. The being of God is capable of demonstration. " The invisible things of God are clearly seen, being understood by the things that are made, even his eternal power and Godhead," and he who can believe, that all things came into such a state as we find them in, by mere chance, or without counsel and design, is prepared to deny first principles, and to hold both sides of a contradiction.

If there is a God, if he is such a holy wise and good Being, as he is represented to be, he cannot be an unconcerned spectator of the conduct of moral agents. He must will their conformity to himself, and his own holy nature. He must be displeased with those who oppose his will by acting contrary to it. He must be pleased with those who love, serve and obey him. He must be disposed to punish the one, and reward the other. I own, upon the principles of what is called natural religion, we cannot determine that God will reward a creature who hath deviated from the path of duty, as it is evident all the children of Adam, capable

of

of moral action, have done. Here, revelation comes to our help. We are told, how God may be just, and yet justify the sinner who believes in Jesus.—I go on therefore to say,

The revelation we have of God and of his will is the truth. We run no hazard in trusting to it, and in venturing the salvation of our souls upon it. The evidence of this revelation rests on the perfections of God. It would be no way consistent with the natural notions we have of God, to suffer such things to be done in favor of a false religion, as makes the assent of an honest and enquiring mind reasonable, if not necessary. The christian religion is from God. All the doctrines and precepts of it are divine. The more we examine them, the more do we see of the wisdom and goodness of God in them. We are not called to follow cunningly devised fables. The gospel delivers the words of truth and soberness. We are required to believe nothing, but what we see reason to believe; and to do nothing, but what it is right and fit we should do. "He hath shewed thee, O man, what is good; and what doth the Lord thy God require of thee, but to do justly, and to love mercy, and to walk humbly with thy God?" God requires of us to believe in his Son; to repent of our sins; to be holy in all manner of conversation. For our excitement, he promises the most glorious rewards to him who believes, repents, and obeys the gospel;

and

and threatens the most amazing punishments to the wicked and ungodly. In the one, we see his infinite grace; in the other, we behold his awful justice; and in both, we see how wisely the sanctions of his gospel are calculated to produce obedience to it. Men, under the government of their lusts, are apt to form objections against the degree of the punishment threatned; and they sometimes almost persuade themselves, that God will not execute his threatnings. We easily believe what we wish may be true. But how little effect would any punishment short of what is threatned have upon men, when even these threatnings are in so many instances ineffectual?

If there is a future state, if we are probationers for that state, and must be miserable or happy, according to our behavior in this state of trial, religion is a most serious business, and we ought diligently to attend to the arguments and motives which the gospel presents. God allows us to examine the nature and evidences of that which is proposed to us for our belief and practice; to weigh all that can be said on both sides, and to act agreably to what appears to us to be right and fit. We are directed to prove all things. If upon inquiry, you find christianity to be true, as if you examine with any measure of seriousness, you undoubtedly will, you cannot but own, it is reasonable you should form your faith and practice by it.

If

If religion is a reasonable service, why do you halt between two opinions ? Why do you not with seriousness and diligence engage in it ? If it be not, gratify your lusts without controul, walk in the ways of thine heart, and in the sight of thine eyes. We are willing to join issue with you here; let it all turn on this point. This is not because we look upon it as a matter of indifference how you determine, we think it far otherwise : but because we are persuaded the religion of Christ will bear examining; the more carefully and seriously it is look'd into, the more it will approve itself to the reason of man.

Is it not reasonable, that you should serve the God who made you ? Is it not reasonable, that you should consecrate all the powers of your souls to him who gave you these powers ? who hath sent his Son to redeem you, from that state of sin and guilt into which you were sunk ? and who hath so greatly distinguished you by committing to you the oracles of God ? Is it not reasonable, you should be accountable for the talents with which you are entrusted ? Ought you not often to think of the account you are to give to him ? Are not the sanctions with which the law of God is guarded worthy your attention ? Is it not fit, your fears should be alarmed with the threatning of utter destruction from the presence of the Lord ? and your hopes raised by the prospect of a glorious immortality ?
Ought

Ought you not to be sollicitous to avoid the one, and attain to the other? I am persuaded you must answer each of these inquiries in the affirmative. Why then are you at all irresolute? Why do you waver and hesitate what is to be done? Why do you fluctuate this way and that, as if you were in doubt which way to turn? It is not, my brethren, because you are at any uncertainty what is your duty, or what is your interest. It is because your lusts are too prevalent, and you are governed by sense, and not by reason. Your mind and conscience condemn you. There is not one of you, who doth not in his sober hours wish he could act otherwise. There is not one of you, unless he is hardened through the deceitfulness of sin, who doth not determine to alter his course of life before he dies. Some of you are perhaps almost persuaded, but you cannot find resolution enough to bid adieu to your lusts, to resign yourselves wholly to Christ, and to live as the gospel obliges you to live. And so you are continually fluctuating between God and the devil; and undetermined whether to chuse life or death. Was it a much less danger, was you in hazard of losing only your temporal life, or any valuable interest in this world, he must be destitute of christian benevolence, who should not immediately give the alarm. You will not wonder then, that your friends, that your ministers, cry aloud, when they see you in danger of losing your souls. Compassion to your souls, yea compassion to their

own;

own, obliges them to do all they can, to save you from impending ruin.

You allow what we call upon you to do, is necessary to be done. And if so, what time so good as the present? It must be done one time or another; all the time you delay, you make the work so much the more difficult. One reason you find it so hard now, is because you have defer'd it so long; and is not the difficulty likely to increase, the longer you defer it?—But, I beseech you, consider, are you sure of having any other opportunity? Most certainly you are not. And will you delay a work which is necessary to be done, and which you may have no other opportunity of doing?—If you die in your sins, you are undone for ever. Possibly, this is the only time you may have to repent. And surely the possibility of this, shews the folly of making any delay; you run a dreadful venture, every moment you neglect this important interest. Be earnest with God to grant you the influences of his Spirit, to sanctify and change you. You have spent a great deal of time in vanity and folly, your thoughts have been imploy'd in contrivances to gratify your appetites and passions. You have been enquiring how you should be rich and great in this world. Thus you have been dead, while you have lived, dead to all rational purposes of living. Tis time to awake out of sleep. You have a great deal of work to do, and
very

very difficult work.—For though the ways of religion are juftly ftiled ways of pleafantnefs and all her paths peace, yet it has its difficulties. Chrift's yoke is eafy, but it is a yoke, it is a reftraint, which will occafion many ftruggles and conflicts. The entrance on the fervice of Chrift is attended with peculiar difficulties, efpecially to thofe who have indulged vicious habits, and been children of difobedience. Oh! therefore lofe no time, be no longer unftable and wavering, confent to no parley; but ftrive to enter into the ftrait gate, and to walk in the narrow way which leadeth unto life. Your obtaining an intereft in the favor of God depends on his mercy and grace; you have reafon to hope from the goodnefs of his nature, from the merits of Chrift, and from the gracious declarations of the gofpel, that if you feek you fhall find; but if you will not hear, if you will go on to treafure up wrath againft the day of wrath, you muft perifh, there is no help.

In particular, let me befeech you, my young friends, to begin with God. Devote your fprightly powers and the vigor of youth to his fervice. This will be an unfpeakable advantage to you if you die young, and will afford you great comfort if you live to be old. On all accounts the prefent is the beft time you can have to enter on a religious courfe; you are now moft fufceptible of good impreffions; you will have lefs interruption from the cares

cares of the world, and your early piety will be peculiarly acceptable to God. Whereas, if you indulge to vice, while you are young, you will gradually lose your tenderness of mind, and God may be provoked to take his Holy Spirit from you. Be persuaded then no longer to hesitate, but give your hearts to God now, while it is an accepted time and a day of salvation.

As to those who are advanced in years, and have grown old in sin, I fear, I greatly fear, all exhortations will be lost on them.—If your minds had not been blinded by the God of this world; and you had not contracted a great degree of hardness and stupidity, you had not stood it out to this day, against the warnings and exhortations with which God hath favoured you—Your case is exceeding dangerous, it may not be desperate. But surely you have no time to deliberate, whether you will comply with the calls of God or not. If you defer your repentance now, in all probability you defer it forever. Submit to Christ, before it be too late; the young find it difficult to renounce the pleasures of sin, and to make the entire surrender of themselves to God; you, who have confirmed habits of sin, may expect still greater opposition. But the more difficult the work, so much the greater reason is there for earnestness, activity and diligence.

To conclude, Let us all make religion our bufiness. Indifference and inftability, in an affair of such importance, are greatly criminal, and will juftly render us contemptible in the fight of God and man.—It is worthy all our attention and it requires it—it is no eafy matter to govern our lufts and paffions, our affections and appetites; to live above this prefent evil world, while we live in it, and have fo much to do with it.—Let us then be watchful and circumfpect; and confcious of our weaknefs, and liablenefs to be led aftray, let us be much in prayer to God for his all-conquering grace. We are weak in ourfelves, but we can do all things through Chrift which ftrengthneth us.

SERMON

SERMON II.

The Excellency of the human Soul.

GENESIS II. 7.

And man became a living soul.

IN the beginning God created the heavens and the earth. He spake and it was done, he commanded and it stood fast. "God said, let there be light, and there was light."—But the creation of man is introduced in a manner peculiarly adapted to awaken our attention. "And God said, let us make man after our image." This manner of expression was designed to intimate, not, that God took any time to deliberate on this part of his work; not, that He had occasion for the assistance of any other being; but only the superiority of man to the inanimate and animal creation, of which an account had been given before. "The Lord God formed man of the

dust

dust of the ground, and breathed into his nostrils the breath of life, and man became a living soul." These words evidently teach us, that man is constituted of two distinct parts, a body and a soul; and point out the gross composition of the one, and the pure spiritual nature of the other. These substances, so essentially different, are by the power of God wonderfully united.

The body only is visible, and is admirably fitted to answer the end for which it is designed. It much excells the bodies which are given to the other creatures of God on this earth. We are, to use the words of the inspired psalmist, " fearfully and wonderfully made." The perfection of parts in our bodies, their symmetry and proportion, their coalescence and agreement, render them both comely and convenient. But still the body is but a beautiful piece of clay; " there is a spirit in man," which communicates life and motion, " and the inspiration of the Almighty hath given him understanding." " The body without the spirit is dead." —This spirit or soul is every where in scripture represented as superior to the body; as something excellent in it's kind, and highly to be valued. Agreably, my design at this time is,

First, To discourse of the excellency of the human soul. And then,

Secondly,

Secondly, To make those practical remarks, to which the subject naturally leads us.

First, I am to discourse of the excellency of the human soul.

By the excellency of the soul, I intend it's original superiority to the other creatures of God in this lower world, or to the body with which it is united. For, in its present state, even the contemplation of our souls will lead to many humbling considerations. " Nothing," as one observes, " is so great, nothing so worthy admiration as man, when we consider him only in one point of light : Nothing appears so low, so worthy pity and contempt, when we consider him in another. —If we look with attention on those marvellous faculties, with which the Creator hath endued us ; we may, with some appearance of reason, assume an air of grandeur, and account ourselves among the most perfect and happy creatures : But when we place ourselves in another situation, and cast our eyes on our weaknesses, our foibles and follies, nothing can appear more despicable than ourselves ; nothing more humbling than for us to know that we are human creatures."

We are called at present to view the bright side of the subject, to consider the excellency of the human soul ; we cannot do this, without observing
many

many of those humiliating circumstances, which ought to be ever before us.

In order to evidence the excellency of the soul of man, let us consider it's nature—it's powers—it's capacity of happiness—the eternal duration for which it is designed—to which I may add, the great things God hath done to make it happy.

1. We begin with the nature of that soul or spirit there is in man.

My design is not to enter on any nice and philosophical inquiry, concerning the difference there is in substances, or in what this difference consists. The most learned sage is as ignorant in these points, as an illiterate peasant: After his most laboured disquisitions, he only darkens counsel by words without knowledge, and to which he scarce fixes any ideas; or if he hath ideas himself, he doth not communicate any to others.

How much are we at a loss, when we contemplate this essential part of ourselves! We can rather say what it is not, than what it is. It is something distinct from the body, though closely united to it; and may be separated from it. We call it a spiritual immaterial substance; by which we intend, that it is not the object of our senses, as the body is; it

hath

hath no length, breadth or thickneſs.—It animates the body, and is the ſource of all vital action. While it continues united to the tabernacle of clay, *that* derives a luſtre from it, and is exalted above all the creatures that exiſt on this earth. But when this union is diſſolved, the body is ſoon reduced to putrefaction and rottenneſs, which ſhows that the ſoul is not only different from, but ſuperior to the body. The ſcripture, which is our ſafeſt rule, teaches us to call this ſoul a ſpirit, and that it hath all the properties of a ſpirit. In this reſpect, man partakes of the nature of Angels, thoſe ſuperior Beings, who are ever in the preſence of God, and do his commandments : " Are they not all miniſtring ſpirits ?" Yea more, I ſpeak it with humble reverence, he partakes in a meaſure of the nature of God, the greateſt and the beſt of Beings. " God is a ſpirit." The glorious God, when he created man, ſtamped his own divine image upon him, and gave him ſome impreſs of the Deity. He was a moral agent, capable of acting right, and of intellectual ſpiritual enjoyments. Man was made ſuperior to the creatures around him, not only in his body, which was of a more noble conſtruction than theirs ; but he was eſpecially ſuperior in his ſoul, which was allied to the Creator, and capable of converſing with him. But the beſt idea we can form of the human ſoul, is from the conſideration of it's various properties and qualities. Which leads me,

In

In the second place, To argue the excellency of the soul, from the powers and faculties with which it is endowed.

It hath understanding, will, and affections. It is capable of thought and reflection. It forms ideas, connects them together, and compares them with each other. It judges of fitness and unfitness; it deliberates, chuses and determines. It remembers what hath passed, and approves or disapproves, according as we have acted right or wrong. It can by imagination transport itself into the most distant climes, take into it's view all future ages by a quick succession of ideas, and fetch delight from the most distant periods. It hath desires and hopes to which nothing finite is equal; it forms some just notions of the great God, and hath a capacity of loving him, of rejoicing in his love, and of the eternal enjoyment of him. These faculties of the soul, excellent as they are, are capable of continual enlargement. The very exercise of them tends to enlarge them. The more we think, the more capable we are of thinking, and our knowlege may be increasing to eternity. The other powers of the mind, follow the understanding, and by reason of use, they make proportionate advances. By this exercise of it's powers, the soul would gradually grow wiser and better, in a perpetual progression towards perfection. If indeed, we consider man as sin hath made him, the faculties of the soul are

greatly

greatly weakened and depraved; he sees things as it were in a false mirror, by means of which they appear quite otherwise than they are; good appears evil, and evil good. In consequence of this wrong judgment, the will chuses perversly, and the affections are placed on objects unworthy of them. But I speak of the soul, as it is in itself, and as it came out of the creating hands of God; and blessed be his name, the mediation of Christ makes way for it's restoration to a superior state of light and purity, to that it lost by sin. Man is again by grace made like to God, and capable of being happy with him. Which leads me to observe,

Thirdly, The capacity which the soul of man hath of happiness.

As man is made with such noble powers, so he is capable of a superior degree of happiness. The animal creation can have only animal or sensual pleasures. The mind of man hath a capacity for more rational and sublime enjoyments. He is a reasonable creature, and was designed for pleasures of an intellectual nature. He was formed to contemplate on the nature and perfections of God; to observe the power, wisdom, and goodness, discovered in the works of God, and to act agreably to the notices he should, from time to time, have of what God required of him. This was the law of his nature, and if man had acted agreably to this law, he would

have been happy. The knowlege of God, and a conformity to his nature and will, conſtitute the happineſs of a reaſonable creature. This leads to a ſtate of quiet and reſt which nothing elſe can afford. 'Tis true, while ſoul and body are ſo cloſely connected, the wants of the body neceſſarily affect the mind, and render it uneaſy; the mind therefore cannot but be ſo far pleaſed with ſenſual gratifications, as it is thereby delivered from uneaſineſs. Nor is it ſinful to gratify our ſenſes, provided we keep within reaſonable bounds, and aim at rendering ourſelves hereby, more capable of ſerving God, which was all man would have aimed at, if he had not departed from God.—But theſe ſenſual gratifications are no way ſufficient to give reſt to the human mind; and we ſhall always find ourſelves miſtaken, if we look for happineſs from them. The deſires of our ſouls are infinite; no created good can ſatisfy them. We therefore ſee the men of this world are ever preſſing after ſomething further, they whoſe acquiſitions are greateſt, are reſtleſs and uneaſy, as they are who have nothing. The reaſon is, this world is no way calculated to fill our minds, or to make them eaſy and happy. There is an emptineſs in all worldly enjoyments, when compared with the deſires of our ſouls. "There is," as the wiſe man ſpeaks, "no good in them", no ſolid, ſubſtantial, ſatisfying good. The pſalmiſt was obliged to repair to God as the only ſatisfying portion; " Whom have I in heaven but thee, there is none on earth I deſire beſides thee." Being capable of knowing
God,

God, of contemplating, and imitating, his glorious perfections, the soul finds that happiness which it in vain expects any where else. And how great must this blessedness be! Nothing but the satisfaction of it's desires can yield happiness to any creature; the desires of the soul are vastly large; if these desires are satisfied, the happiness which will be the consequence hereof will be inconceivably great.

How excellent and noble must that spirit be, which is capable of deriving so great happiness from the Deity! Man was made capable of this felicity when he came out of the creating hands of God. He might have secured an unalienable title to it. He forfeited all pretensions to favor by transgressing the law of his Maker. In consequence of the sin of man, the human frame was weakened and disordered: He who was before innocent and happy, became a depraved and guilty creature: He could not think of God without horror, because he could think of him only as an enemy.

Through Christ, provision is made for our admission to a greater degree of happiness, than Adam would have had a title to, according to the constitution he was placed under, even though he had not sinned. God hath taken occasion from the sin of man, to glorify the riches of his mercy and goodness.

Fourthly

Fourthly, Another thing, which tends to give us an exalted idea of the human soul, is the eternal duration for which it is designed.

Philosophers tell us, that the soul of man is a simple, uncompounded substance; that it is in it's nature indivisible, and incorruptible, and hath no tendency to a dissolution: And from it's immateriality, they argue it's natural immortality. Whatever force there may be in this argument, it is too nice and abstruse for every one's capacity, and must leave the most in a state of uncertainty and doubt.—It is a supposition quite as agreable to reason; that every creature depends on God, for it's continuance in being, and capacity of acting. If He then should withdraw his influence, the soul would cease to be. God is the only independent Being; there can be no other.—But though the soul is entirely dependent on God, it is independent on any other. No one else hath power over it, to put it out of existence, or destroy it's activity. "Fear not them," says our Lord," which kill the body, but are not able to kill the soul: But rather fear him which is able to destroy both body and soul in hell."

If this be the true state of the case, that the soul hath such an absolute dependence on God; we cannot with certainty prove it's immortality, in any way, but by his express declarations. Our faith in this doctrine must rest wholly on divine revelation.

If

If God hath declared that the soul shall eternally exist; it is of no importance, whether we can prove by reason and philosophy, the soul to be immortal or not. There is no doubt but God can continue it in existence. The only question then is, what saith the scripture? and this is so clear, that it can admit of no dispute. " Life and immortality are brought to light by the gospel." Says the apostle Paul, " As in Adam all die, so in Christ shall all be made alive." * This is spoken of as the great promise of the gospel, "This is the promise he hath promised us, even eternal life." † This blessed hope of a glorious immortality is set before the righteous for their quickening and encouragement. But a future state of existence is not confined to them. All, both good and bad, are represented in our Saviour's description of the last judgment, as appearing before the Son of man; and as a conclusion of the whole it is said, " These shall go away into everlasting punishment, but the righteous into life eternal." ‡ The truth is, by the mediation of Christ, mankind are again put on their probation, and their future state will be determined according to the things done in the body—all will be raised, both good and bad; but the one " to everlasting life," the other " to shame and everlasting contempt."

And hence it is, if I may so speak, that there is such a contest between heaven and hell, God and the

* 1 Cor. 15. 22.   † 1 John 2. 25.   ‡ Mat. 25. 46.

the Devil, about the foul of man. The great God, in his infinite goodness and grace, hath consulted our eternal well-being, and uses a variety of means to effect it.—On the other hand, Satan is unwearied in his attempts to ruin us. Surely it must be a prize of some worth and value, which thus engages the attention of both worlds. This will appear more fully if we consider,

Fifthly, The great things God hath done to make our spirits happy.

He not only made man with a capacity of happiness at first; but he placed him under such circumstances, as would be likely to secure it. He set before him such arguments and motives, as were adapted to influence a reasonable creature to that obedience, upon which his happiness was made to depend. And when man had ungratefully broken through all the obligations he was under, and had rebelled against his Maker; God did not inflict upon him that punishment which he justly deserved; He conceived thoughts of mercy; and contrived that wonderful scheme for his redemption, which is the admiration of Angels. He sent his own Son in our nature, to suffer and to die, that he might reconcile a guilty world to himself, and purchase eternal salvation for us. He sent his holy Spirit, to create us in Christ Jesus to good works, and make us meet for the inheritance of the saints in light. He hath favoured us with a revelation of his mind and will, which is able to make us wife unto falvation, through faith which is in Chrift Jefus. He fends his minifters, who are to exert all their fkill and ability, to perfuade us to accept his offered grace. He condefcends to befeech us to be reconciled to God—He hath inftituted ordinances to carry on this great defign. He hath fet before us promifes and threatnings, to operate on our hopes and fears, thofe leading paffions in human nature. —It is not eafy to conceive, how God could have done more than he hath done to make us happy, unlefs he had taken away the freedom of our wills, and compelled us to that, which he defigned fhould be our own choice. Can any one think God would have done all this, if the foul of man had not been exceeding precious?

It is this—it is the foul—which gives us a dignity in the creation of God, and makes us in any meafure confiderable—Not that we have any great matter to boaft, or to be proud of; we have, 'tis true, a place among the creatures that are called rational; but we are, perhaps, the loweft that come under that character; we know fomething, but how little, in comparifon with what we do not know! —When we compare ourfelves with the Angels, and confider the wifdom and greatnefs of thofe excellent creatures, which we may gather from the account given of them in fcripture, how vaftly inferior

are

are we to them! We were made like, but not equal to them. But how do we sink into nothing, when we compare ourselves with the glorious God, who is infinite in those perfections, of which he hath communicated but a small degree to us!

These humbling considerations, would have been suitable for man in his original state of knowlege, innocence, and happiness; much more now he hath so greatly debased and dishonored himself by sin; so as to be far inferior to what he originally was. We were made but little lower than the Angels; but little lower in the rank of beings, and in our capacities and endowments. But by sin, we have lost our nearness to the Angels, and are become like the beasts which perish.—We have no reason then to think highly of ourselves: But yet we ought to set a great value on our own souls.—'Tis the immortal soul makes us what we are, creatures capable of rational pursuits, and everlasting happiness; capable of knowing God, of partaking of his likeness, and enjoying that good which flows from him. Whatever rank we bear in the creation of God, how mean soever we are in the estimation of superior Beings, yet our souls are to us of infinite worth. They are ourselves—they are all in our make and constitution, that is of any value; and they are made for eternity. It is therefore of infinite consequence to us, that we secure the well being of our souls; because, if they are gone, all is gone as to us. If our souls are unhappy, we are unhappy, for

the

the foul is the man. I therefore repeat what I juſt obſerved, that to us, our fouls are of infinite value. They would be ſo, if they were much meaner than they are—and however low man is, when compared with the infinite God, or with the Angels, or even with what he himſelf once was, or was deſigned to be; yet God hath put a dignity upon human nature, by what he hath done for our advantage; by the pains he hath taken, and the coſt he hath been at, ſpeaking of him after the manner of men, to make us happy and bleſſed.

IMPROVEMENT.

Firſt, We are led to reflect with gratitude on the goodneſs of God, who hath given us theſe ſpirits, and endowed them with ſuch powers and faculties as they are poſſeſſed of.

God is our Creator; He is the Former of our bodies, and the Father of our ſpirits; he not only animated the body which was before only duſt; but the ſoul he united to it, was capable of reaſon and tho't, of underſtanding and willing, of loving and enjoying. "There is a ſpirit in man, and the inſpiration of the Almighty giveth them underſtanding." Whatever advantage we have in our make and conſtitution, if in any thing we excel the other creatures (and moſt certainly, we have more wiſdom than the beaſts of the field, and more underſtanding than the fowles of heaven) it is God who maketh us to differ, and we have nothing but what we have received from him. He gave us our being, and he gave us such a being as we have. When therefore we take a view of ourselves, consider the nature and capacity of our spirits, the happiness we are fitted for, and the great things God hath done that we might possess it; how can we forbear crying out with the devout psalmist, " bless the Lord O my soul and all that is within me, bless his holy name!" Surely, we are under the highest obligations to him, who hath given us such excellent powers. We ought to praise him, who hath made us capable of this delightful work. When God made his creatures, he was at liberty to make them as he pleased—The potter hath not such absolute power over the clay, to make one vessel to honor, and another to dishonor, as God had in making his creatures—The potter must consider the fitness of the clay for the vessel he designs, the nature and the quality of it: but there could be no sort of fitness in the creatures of God, before they had a being. The Angels above, man on earth, and all the inferior creatures, were made what they are, according to the divine pleasure. There could be no reason for the one or the other, out of himself. i. e. there could be no reason, taken from the creature, why this was an Angel, and that a man; why this was a seraph and that a brute—This sovereignty of the Deity, is a strong argument to excite those to gratitude, who have been distinguished in their creation.

Secondly,

Secondly, Though we have spirits capable of such great things, yet let us remember we are not capable of every thing.

Compared with the Angels we are weak, ignorant creatures. Let us think of this, when we are disposed to entertain high tho'ts of ourselves. We have immortal spirits, but they are closely united to tabernacles of clay, which confine them in their operations; and oblige us to live and act, in some measure, like the beasts: Our minds are affected with the wants of the body; our natures call for food, as the animal creation doth ; and we are obliged, at frequent returning periods, to submit to a kind of death, for our relief from the burdens of the day, and to render us fit for the purposes of life. If by our souls, we are akin to heaven, by our bodies we are nearly allied to earth ; these cannot keep pace with the mind ; they clog and hinder it in it's contemplations ; they soon grow weary, and oblige us to desist from close thought and application.

Some there are, that need to be put in mind of this, who have too exalted thoughts of human nature, and the extent of our understanding, as if nothing was beyond it's reach. Our minds, in the present state, cannot be kept on a constant stretch. Nature may be overborne ; and by too intense thinking,

thinking, some have been render'd incapable of all rational agency. The transition is easy from the height of human wisdom, to downright folly and madness.—Age will weaken the mind, if nothing else. Festus discovered his acquaintance with human nature, though in that instance he was grosly mistaken, when he supposed that Paul's much learning had made him mad. Possibly there is but little danger in this respect, because there are but few close thinkers : but surely, 'tis a humbling thought, that the human mind is so limited and circumscribed.

Thirdly, Let none presume to find fault with their Maker, that they are not made more excellent than they are.

There are some who are never satisfied ; instead of being thankful that they were made superior to the brutes, they are ready to murmur that they were not made equal to the Angels. They enquire, why they are united to these earthly and mortal bodies, and have so much weakness and infirmity attending them. To such as these, the rebuke of the apostle may be fitly applied, " shall the thing formed say to him that formed it, why hast thou made me thus ? Hath not the potter power over the clay, to make one vessel to honor and another to dishonor?" "Might not he who was at liberty to give thee being or not, give thee such a being as he thought fit ? Hath

Hath he endowed thee with noble and excellent powers, and made thee capable of exalted happinefs, and wilt thou find fault, that thou art not made better or happier? Can any thing be more infolent and ungrateful?—Befides, much of that weaknefs thou complaineft of, is not to be afcribed to God our Creator. Man had, in his original make, knowlege and ftrength enough, to afford him a good degree of felicity, and to preferve him free from pain and uneafinefs—It is fin that makes us fuch weak imperfect creatures as we find we are. Let us not then charge upon him, that which is owing to the folly and ingratitude of man. Further, and which ought for ever to filence every hard thought of God, he hath made provifion in Chrift, for our recovery from that ftate of imperfection and fin, to which we are reduced. So that if we be not wanting to ourfelves, we fhall be like the Angels, which kept their firft ftate. We fhall refemble them, in their entire conformity to the will of God, and the happinefs which naturally flows from it.—The way to attain this bleffednefs, is not to find fault with the nature God hath given us, which is the moft unreafonable thing in the world; but diligently to improve thofe excellent means with which we are favored, of growing better and happier.

Fourthly, Since God hath given us living fouls, and endowed us with reafon and underftanding;

we

we are under the higheſt obligation, to uſe our reaſon, and to act reaſonably.

We ought not to reſign our reaſon to others; whatever opinion we may have of their ſuperior abilities. We are capable of thinking and acting for ourſelves, and God expects we exerciſe the powers he hath given us. We ought, indeed, to uſe the help of others; we ſhould modeſtly attend to the inſtructions of thoſe who are ſuperior to ourſelves, and receive what light we can from them; but we are to think and judge for ourſelves—No man is infallible; and if by implicit faith in others, however wiſe and good, we think and act wrong, we ſhall be juſtly accountable for what we do amiſs; becauſe we have not uſed that capacity which God hath given us of coming at truth.

But, if it is a fault not to uſe our reaſon, it is more criminal to contradict it, as we do whenever we are guilty of ſin. How fit and right is it, that we ſhould devote thoſe powers to God, for which we are indebted to him! There is no reaſoning, that more ſenſibly ſtrikes the mind with conviction, than that of the Pſalmiſt, " Serve the Lord with gladneſs: come before his preſence with ſinging; know ye that the Lord he is God, it is he that hath made us, and not we ourſelves: We are his people, and the ſheep of his paſture." It is a moſt evident truth, that he who hath made us, hath a right

right to our submission and obedience. He hath a title to us, and to all our capacities and talents, which cannot be alienated. Whatever he requires of us becomes our indispensable duty. The infinite rectitude of his nature makes it impossible, he should command any thing unfit or unreasonable; and whatever he commands becomes fit and right, from the relation we stand in to him, as he is our Creator and we are his creatures.—To present ourselves to him, a living sacrifice; to make the surrender of our whole souls to him; and to imploy all our powers and faculties, as he directs and requires, is our most reasonable service. If we have capacities above other creatures; what more fit, than to imploy these capacities, to the honor of him who hath made us to differ? This argument gathers strength; when we consider, that God hath not only given us souls, endowed with such noble powers; but that he upholds our souls in life, and daily continues to us our reason and understanding.

How ungrateful and sinful are they, who, instead of devoting themselves wholly to him, serve those lusts and passions, which are opposite to his nature and will!—Who, instead of making it the great business of life to honor God, which is the great end of their being, continually affront and dishonor him!—How much better had it been for such as these, if they had been among the inferior creatures of God, had never been favoured with reason and understanding;

understanding; yea, unless they repent, it had been better for them, never to have had a being. For most surely, God will have honor from them, if not in an active, yet in a passive way. He will glorify himself in the destruction of those, who will not glorify him by their holiness and obedience.

Let us therefore improve our talents, so that the great end for which they were given to us, may be answered. It is true, the reason of man is so disturbed by the apostacy, that it is not of itself sufficient, even where it hath the help of revelation, to conduct us to true happiness; nor can we by the efforts of reason alone, overcome our passions and appetites, which, in the present state, are impetuous and irregular. But, blessed be God, the gospel directs us where we may obtain all necessary help: and assures us, that whatever God commands, may be performed, by the assistance of the holy Spirit, who is given to men for this very purpose. The goodness of God, in affording such almighty aids, lays us under the strongest bonds to make use of them, and to act that rational and wise part, which he requires of us.

Fifthly, We ought to consider others, as of the same nature with ourselves, and to treat them as brethren.

It is the common privilege of mankind, that they are endowed with a soul or spirit. They are

reasonable

reasonable creatures. This is the glory of man. It is his reason, which distinguishes him from the lower creation. This gift of heaven is confined to no station, no circumstances in life. A consideration which should keep us from despising, or abusing our fellow men. Perhaps, they are not so rich or great as we are, according to the common estimation of greatness. Perhaps, they are poor, and in an inferior situation. But they have souls as well as we—rational and immortal souls: And probably, have as large a share of understanding. For if we were greater than we are, or in a higher station; it would not prove, that we are superior to our neighbours in mental accomplishments. "Great men are not always wise, neither do the aged understand judgment." Or if we excel some, yet may we not find others who exceed us much more? We should not like they should despise, ill-treat or abuse us. Why then should we deal in this manner with others?—Besides, if we are superior to our brethren, we have the more to be accountable for: And they, with their few talents, by their better improvement of them, may be placed above us, with our many.— The greater capacity any one hath, the more ready should he be, to help and support those who have less.

We are all children of the same Father; one God hath created us; and he hath, in the essential part of our constitution, fashioned our souls alike. We ought

ought, therefore, to treat one another as brethren. This we may do, and yet a suitable distinction be preserved.—The meanest slave hath a soul as good by nature as your's, and possibly by grace it is better. A dark complection may cover a fair and beautiful mind. Every soul is beautiful, that resembles the moral character of the blessed God, who is the standard of perfection.—Masters would do well to consider this; probably, if they did, some would see reason to alter their conduct to their servants. Most certainly, they who have any sense of religion, would endeavor to their utmost, to promote the happiness of those, whom providence hath placed under their care.

Sixthly, Have we spirits so excellent in themselves, and capable of so great happiness, how unworthy of us are those pursuits, in which men are too generally employed!

If we look abroad in the world, we shall find them most strangely immersed in sinful pleasures; or pursuing after worldly enjoyments, with as much eagerness, as though these things could yield them happiness. Yea, is it at all necessary, that we should look abroad? shall we not find too much of this temper in ourselves? How worldly! how sensual are we! But have we not reason to be ashamed of such a low groveling temper? Are we capable of noble and sublime pleasures, even of enjoying God the

the supreme good, and shall we content ourselves with delights, which we enjoy in common with the brutes? Are we made for eternity, and shall we pursue a happiness, which, will inevitably fail us, in a very little time? But in truth, your expectations of happiness from this world are empty and vain. You hew to yourselves cisterns, broken cisterns, that can hold no water, in the neglect of the inexhaustible fountain of living waters!—Besides, we must soon leave the world and all things in it: The rich man died as well as Lazarus the beggar. What relief—what satisfaction—can it afford in another world, to think we were rich & great in this! It is a humbling reflection, that we have been so long unworthily employ'd. Let us not repeat our folly; but let us lay up treasure in heaven; which will afford enjoyment, substantial in it's nature, and permanent in it's duration.

Seventhly, How much reason is there, to lament the apostacy of man; which hath debased our nature, and degraded us among the creatures of God!

You have heard how excellent a creature man is—It is his soul or spirit which distinguishes him. He hath powers capable of noble employments, and exalted happiness—But alas! this spirit finds no delight in things spiritual; this rational being acts

acts directly contrary to reason. Instead of governing his passions and appetites, he allows them to govern him. Worldly objects court his affections, and he suffers himself to be enticed by them. The soul cleaves to the dust, and is excessively fond of this world. It prefers earthly things to God, and to those divine pleasures, which it might derive from this all perfect Being.—Certainly, there is something amiss—Things are not with us as they ought to be—These capacities were given to us for more noble ends. Can this be the creature who was made in the image of God; and placed at the head of this lower world?—Yes, verily it is—But oh how changed from what he originally was!—He hath lost his innocence—He is become a sinner—Satan hath set up his throne in the soul; and the powers of the human mind are too much subjected to this usurper—The understanding is dark, and reason is often perverted. The will chuses sensual delights, in preference to those intellectual pleasures, for which man was designed. The consequence of such a wrong choice must be fatal. A creature, capable of thought and consciousness, who acts contrary to the law of his nature, cannot be happy; his own reflections must make him miserable.

It may well affect us with grief and sorrow, when we consider things calmly and seriously, that man is thus fallen from God: That sin hath been introduced

troduced into the world ; which hath had such fatal effects on the human constitution.—Why God hath permitted sin to be in his system ; and whence arises the connection, between the sin of Adam, and those evils which are the consequence of it, are questions, not so easily answered, as some vainly imagine. The facts are certain ; that sin is in the world ; and that the first sin of the first man, was the occasion of all the sorrow and trouble which his posterity are subjected to. This is perfectly agreable to scripture ; and there is no way of accounting for the introduction of evil, either moral or penal, which is attended with less difficulty than this.

We have reason to think, this apostacy would not have been permitted, if God had not determined to glorify the riches of his grace, by sending his Son, to introduce a new dispensation ; under which, the salvation of man is made a possible thing ; his time of probation is renewed ; and he becomes a candidate for a glorious immortality. We cannot have so great reason, to lament the apostacy of men ; as we have to rejoice, in the report of the gospel of the blessed God.

Eighthly, Let us often think of the excellency and worth of our souls.

God hath put a great honor upon them, in making them after his image. He dignified them by
sending

sending his Son to redeem them from sin, and all it's fatal consequences; and by using such a variety of means, to make them happy and blessed forever. By this he hath shown, that in his sight, they are of great price. Shall we then despise and neglect them? We,—to whom they are of such vast importance? It becomes us, to contemplate the dignity of our natures, not in order to feed our pride, or to give us exalted thoughts of ourselves; but to put us on a due improvement of the powers, with which God hath distinguished us. We ought to consider, how much depends on our acting right; the inconceivable happiness or misery, which awaits us in another state. The salvation of our souls is the one thing needful. It is the only thing, about which we have any reason to be very sollicitous; we ought to pursue this in the first place, and with an earnestness proportionate to it's infinite importance.

Finally, How great will be the misery of those who lose their souls!

This is by no means an impossible supposition: It will be the case with some; it will be the case with us, if we do not accept Christ in his whole mediatorial character. Notwithstanding all he hath done, to promote the happiness of men; they may by their impiety and disobedience, miss all the advantage of his mediation, they may lose their souls. This doth not intend a deprivation of existence;

iftence; the foul may be loft, in the fenfe of fcripture, though it's being is continued. It may exift, without enjoying any degree of happinefs. It may be in fuch a ftate, as that it's exiftence may be no favor. Yea, it may be reduced to fuch a degree of mifery, as that to be put out of being, would be a kindnefs, and annihilation a privilege. In fuch a cafe, the foul would be in a worfe ftate, than if it was abfolutely loft, in a literal fenfe. No temporal evil can be compared with this. No temporal good can make amends for it. " What is a man profited, if he gain the whole world, and lofe his own foul ? Or what fhall a man give in exchange for his foul?"

The infelicity of a creature, who hath only an exiftence in mifery continued to it, will always bear fome proportion to it's capacity of happinefs. The beafts, who are adapted for a lower degree of pleafure, can have only a lower degree of pain. The Angels, who by their original conftitution, have a capacity for nobler and higher enjoyments, are capable of more intenfe forrow and uneafinefs. Man is between both; he is not capacitated for fo great a degree of happinefs or mifery, as the Angels are; but, as compared with the inferior creatures of God, he is capable of exalted happinefs; fo he is of an anfwerable degree of mifery—of uneafinefs and pain, in proportion as his faculties are, in themfelves, noble and excellent. There will, indeed, be a great difference in the final ftate of bad

bad men; according to the degree of their criminality. But the gospel pronounces a sentence of condemnation on all, who die in impenitence and unbelief. As it opens a glorious state of immortality to the righteous; so, it reveals the most amazing punishment to the wicked and ungodly. Nor can they have the least room to expect any new exercise of divine mercy. There will be no other plan laid for the relief of those, who reject and despise that only method, which the wisdom of God hath appointed, " There remaineth no more sacrifice for sin, but a fearful looking for of judgment."

As we would avoid so awful a doom; Let us make our application to the Redeemer and Saviour of men, in the exercise of faith and love. Let us trust to his merits, and obey his precepts.— This is what God expects from all who enjoy the gospel; and with the greatest reason, Christ is worthy our highest regard; whether we consider what he is in himself, or what he hath done for the children of men. Let us not be so infatuated, as to prefer the things of time and sense, to this excellent Saviour, in whom, it hath pleased the Father that all fulness should dwell. But let us commit our souls into his hands, who is able to keep that which we commit unto him against that day— that great and important day, when he will come to be glorified in his saints, and to be admired in all them that believe!

SERMON

SERMON III.

Jesus Christ the only Source of Rest and Happiness.

JOHN VI. 68.

Then Simon Peter answered him, Lord, to whom shall we go? Thou hast the words of eternal life.

IN the preceding part of this chapter, our Lord had declared himself to be the bread of life.—Many were displeased at the mysterious, and figurative manner, in which he saw fit to discourse to them.

Far from condescending to their unreasonable cavils, and perverse humours; he went on to rebuke

buke them for their unteachable difpofition; and at the fame time, teftified the happy effect of his doctrine, upon thofe who were in a proper temper to receive the truth. "The words that I fpeak unto you, they are fpirit, and they are life." i. e. What I have faid, is abfurd and unprofitable, if you underftand me in a literal fenfe; but if you receive the doctrine I deliver, in it's true fpiritual fenfe, it will be of unfpeakable advantage; it will begin, and carry on, that divine life in your fouls, which will terminate in eternal glory and happinefs. "But there are fome of you, that believe not;" although I have given fuch convincing evidence, of my divine miffion, and exalted character. On this account it is, that "I faid unto you, that no man can come unto me, except it were given him of my Father." Nothing but almighty power, can remove prejudices fo deeply rooted, or bring men to fubmit to the gofpel I preach, who are fo entirely oppofite to the nature and defign of my kingdom. "From that time many of his difciples went back, and walked no more with him." They had been influenced to follow him, only by fecular views; but they now found, that there was no room for expectations of this kind; Jefus had openly difclaimed a temporal kingdom, and gave no encouragement of great things in this world. Befides, they preceived, that he was perfectly acquainted with the infincerity of their hearts; and could not be impofed on by their pretences of regard and fubmiffion; they therefore

laid.

laid aside the mask; cast off their specious shew, and appeared in their true character.

Upon this defection, Jesus took occasion to try the faith of the twelve apostles, "then said Jesus unto the twelve, will ye also go away?" To this enquiry, Peter answered, in the name of the rest, "Lord to whom shall we go? Thou hast the words of eternal life." A noble confession! made, just when our Lord seemed to be left almost alone, and was deserted by those crowds, which used to attend upon him. The words express the sense the apostles had, of the insufficiency of every scheme of happiness, which the mind of man could devise.—Their hearty acquiescence, in the admirable plan which divine wisdom had formed—and their firm belief, that this was most wisely adapted, to afford that rest, to the minds of men, which they would in vain pursue, in any other way.

The disciples of Christ acted a most wise and rational part. The dispensation of Moses had always pointed to a Saviour "who was to come," and introduce a more perfect scheme of religion. When Christ came, they found that he exactly answered the predictions of their ancient prophets: that he taught a religion, perfectly adapted to the state of human nature, and calculated to make men wiser and better. At the same time, he opened to them, the most glorious prospects after this life; when they

they would drop the weaknesses and follies of the present state; and be admitted to the highest felicity, their natures were capable of. God also bore witness to his illustrious character, and divine mission, "by signs and wonders, and with divers miracles." What could this world offer, to induce them to renounce such an excellent system of truth; or to part with such glorious prospects? What other scheme of religion could propose so great advantages, or had equal attestations? It is an unspeakable mercy to us, that we are favored with the christian revelation—It is the greatest folly to neglect and despise it.

"To whom shall we go? Thou hast the words of eternal life."

What I intend, in discoursing on these words, is to show the justness of the sentiments expressed, or implied in them. In order to this,

I shall, First, Set before you, the insufficiency of every scheme of happiness which man can propose; while he neglects Jesus Christ, and the method of salvation, which God hath constituted by him.

Secondly, I shall consider, how wisely the gospel dispensation is calculated, to afford rest and quiet to the mind of man.

First,

First, I am to set before you, the insufficiency of every scheme of happiness, in the neglect of Jesus Christ, and that method of salvation which God hath constituted through him.

" To whom shall we go?" Where have we any, the least prospect, of finding rest? Shall we seek it from the things of this world? How few are capable of attaining great things here!—Of the multitudes, who make the acquisition of wealth, the great object of their wishes and pursuits; it is but here and there one that succeeds, and reaches the mark he aims at. They lay fine schemes, and are full of vast projections; they labour and toil, night and day, to raise an estate. But their schemes prove abortive; their projections evaporate; and they meet with continual crosses and disappointments. It is well, if they arrive at a mediocrity, and do not sink into poverty and distress.—How many are the slaves of ambition! They aspire to places of power and dignity; are fond of high titles, and would gladly govern a whole community.—It is easy to perceive, that but a small part of these can attain their end; every one cannot be chief; and the most would better consult their reputation, if they were content to move in a lower sphere.—If we fail of wealth, we cannot live in pomp; roll in luxury; or indulge to pleasure; unless we call it pleasure to be as sordid as the beasts, and to be continually intoxicated with strong drink; and, I

am

am sorry to say it, the poorest among us, can easily find means to procure this kind of happiness.

But be it so, that we can attain every worldly enjoyment we wish for; riches, honor, and the means of sensual delights; perhaps, a sickly carcase incapacitates us, from taking that pleasure in them, we vainly expected; perhaps, some friend, or relative, whom we loved, is in distress; or they whom we have obliged, are wicked and ungrateful; and make the basest returns for our acts of kindness and affection.—This imbitters all our pleasure; and prevents our taking comfort in our otherwise agreable situation.

But if we suppose nothing of this; yet every state hath it's particular cares, anxieties, troubles, and disappointments; so that the most prosperous man is far from being happy. There is a void in his soul, which this world cannot fill, he wants to change the scene, and to contrive some new enjoyment; notwithstanding all his acquisitions he is discontented and uneasy; and possibly, at a greater distance from true rest and quiet of mind, than when he began his pursuit.

Besides, whatever worldly good he obtains; or however capable he is of enjoying it; yet, amidst all, he knows he must die, and enter into the world of spirits, where these things cannot follow him, or yield him any satisfaction, if they could. What

an

an awful, what a gloomy reflection is this, to one, who hath confulted only, how he might eat, drink, and be merry! Who hath been forgetful of God; and hath taken no care, to improve his time and talents, to the honor of his Creator and Lord! who hath been dead while he lived; dead—to all purpofes of living! Confcious of guilt—and confcious he muft be of guilt, if he hath any confcioufnefs, any reflection at all; he cannot think of God without fear; he cannot look into the other world, without amazement; he trembles at the thought, of appearing before a holy, juft, an almighty Deity, who hath been witnefs of all his impiety; and who, he may reafonably conclude, will demand an account of the talents committed to him—of the deeds done in the body.

This is the ftate of men, who feek a portion only in this life. They will lie down in forrow, and confufion will cover them. "In the midft of laughter," fays the wife king Solomon, "the heart is forrowful, and the end of that mirth is heavinefs." It is not alway with perfons, as they appear. A jovial countenance is not a certain indication of an eafy mind; and men often run to the pleafures of fenfe, only to forget their forrows; and to get rid of the horror they feel within.

But if the world cannot give peace, where elfe fhall we look? What religion, befides the chriftian, an, can afford any rational expectation, of ease and quiet?—Shall we go to the Jews? Their religion, it is true, came from God; but it was only a schoolmaster to lead us to Christ. The law and the prophets, they testify of him. The more we study them, the more we shall see of Christ in them. And, it was chiefly, as it had a reference to him, the great Mediator, that the religion of the Jews, ever afforded rest to its votaries.

Shall we repair for rest to the religion of nature? The religion of nature—What is it?—Where shall we find a compleat system of this fine scheme, which some men cry up with so much ostentation; and on which they bestow such high encomiums. How uncertain are some of its first principles, if we take away the aids it hath received from revelation! Where shall we find its attestations? How flat and jejune are many of the precepts of the best heathen philosophers!—How very different from each other are pagan writers in their schemes of religion!—What a mixture of error and absurdity!— Where is the authority to enforce their systems on the consciences of men?—Besides, What door of hope, doth the religion of nature open to the sinner? What doth it contain, to quiet the conscience of one, oppressed with guilt? Doth it instruct us that God is good? Doth it not also teach us that he is just?—If his mercy give us some ground of hope, will not his infinite rectitude make us afraid? In what a maze of uncertainty are we left!—And

what

what a gloom is scattered around us! Especially, if we neglect a scheme of religion, that hath pretensions at least to divine authority; and which, the most obstinate deist must own, hath much to be said in its favor; which, if true, cannot be despised with innocency; nor rejected with impunity. It not only promises the greatest blessings, to those who cordially embrace it; but denounces the most amazing destruction, to the unbelieving, impenitent, and disobedient. " He that believeth shall be saved; he that believeth not shall be damned."——

Having endeavoured to shew, the insufficiency of every other plan, Let us now consider,

In the second place, How wisely the gospel dispensation is adapted to give ease and rest to the mind of man; and to conduct him to that happiness, which he vainly pursues in any other way.

" To whom shall we go? Thou hast the words of eternal life."

Christ was a Teacher sent from heaven. He had the fullest attestations to his divine mission; and the religion he introduced, was worthy an infinitely wise and good Being.—The christian revelation helps us to form right and becoming sentiments of the Deity. It makes it certain, that God can pardon sinful man, in a perfect consist-

K   tency

tency with his own absolute rectitude. It contains the most kind and gracious declarations to fallen man. It teaches us our duty, and what are the necessary means, in order to obtain the perfection and happiness of our reasonable natures. "Come unto me," says our Lord, "all ye that labor and are heavy laden, and I will give you rest." †—That rest, which they in vain sought any where else, was to be obtained from Jesus Christ. "The words that I speak they are spirit, and they are life." The words, even of our Lord himself, did not necessarily produce their genuine effect. Many who heard Christ, did not believe on him. Some, who had profess'd a regard to him, and attended on his ministry, openly deserted his cause, and walked no more with him: They were not made, either wiser or better, by hearing him, who spake as never man spake: They returned, "with the dog to his vomit," and with "the sow that was washed, to her wallowing in the mire." But, under the influence of the Spirit of God, the preaching of Christ had the most blessed, the most salutary effects. His hearers became spiritual and holy, the children of God, and partakers of the divine nature.—They were begotten by the word of truth; and introduced into a new, a spiritual life. Christ gave them rest—not, by opening to them worldly treasures—not, by raising them to exalted stations—not, by leading them to the pleasures of sense—No, but, by

con-

† Matthew 11. 28.

convincing them, that their happiness did not depend on these things; by taking off their affections from worldly objects; and by leading them to God, the only source of true felicity. The Christian revelation gives no assurance of riches and grandeur in this world; but, it teaches us to despise earthly things; to be contented with the situation, in which providence hath placed us. Where it hath it's proper influence, it spiritualizes the affections, it makes us heavenly-minded, it disposes us to converse with God, and to lead lives of universal holiness and obedience, which is the only probable way to have peace in our own minds.

It is the gospel, and that only, which answers that great and interesting enquiry, What shall we do to be saved? This reveals to us, that God is reconciling the world unto himself by Jesus Christ.—When we view this great, this holy, this just Being, in the face of Jesus Christ, or as he manifests himself in the gospel; how amiable! how excellent doth he appear! Conscious of guilt, trembling for fear, we behold an almighty Saviour, who came into our world, upon the most benevolent design; who not only, while he lived, taught the most heavenly doctrine, and set a bright example of the most perfect virtue, but died to atone for the sin of man, and by his blood to cleanse us from all unrighteousness. " He died for us, the just for the unjust, that he might bring us to God." The

death

death of so glorious a person, being by God himself substituted, instead of the death of the offender, answered all the purposes, that could have been answered by our punishment. God hath, by this wise constitution, displayed the infinite rectitude of his nature, even when he exercised his mercy to the sinner. * " Whom God hath set forth to be a propitiation, thro' faith in his blood, to declare his righteousness for the remission of sins that are past, through the forbearance of God, to declare at this time, his righteousness : That he might be just, and the justifier of him which believeth in Jesus."

It is to depreciate the merits of Christ, and to despise the mercy of God, only to entertain a doubt, whether Christ is able to save ; or whether God is ready, on account of his merits, to pardon the believing, returning sinner. It is to disbelieve the most express declarations, and the most ample assurances, of him who is truth itself. Doth the scripture so plainly, so repeatedly declare, " He that believeth shall be saved ?" Doth our Lord invite sinners, all without exception, to come to him for life and blessedness ? and shall we harbour one distrustful thought ?—Knowing, that we are believers in Christ, we may be satisfied, not, that God will forgive us, but that he hath forgiven us. " There is no condemnation to them that are in Christ Jesus." †—" Who shall lay any thing to the

* Romans 3. 25, 26.   † Romans 8. 1.

the charge of God's elect? It is God that juftifieth, Who is he that condemneth? It is Chrift that died, yea, rather, that is rifen again, who is even at the right hand of God, who alfo maketh interceffion for us." †

What a glorious door of hope, doth the gofpel open to the believer in Chrift!—That God, who was once his enemy, is now his friend—That juftice, which once demanded the punifhment of the guilty finner, now pleads for his deliverance from condemnation.—We, who, if judged by ftrict law, have no righteoufnefs, are confider'd as righteous—are juftified, on account of Chrift's righteoufnefs; God " hath made him to be fin for us, who knew no fin; that we might be made the righteoufnefs of God in him." Chrift endured amazing fufferings, on account, or by means, of our fins; we partake of the moft important bleffings, on account of his righteoufnefs.

And what an encouragement is this gracious conftitution to a chriftian! What an excitement to univerfal holinefs! Till we have a view of God, in and by Jefus Chrift, he appears a confuming fire, awful and terrible, there is no certainty, that he will take any favourable notice of our fervices, or accept our obedience. No wonder then, a finner—opprefs'd with a fenfe of guilt—deftitute of hope—hath no thought of returning to him. But, when

† Rom. 8. 33. 34.

when the glorious God appears seated on a throne of grace; proclaiming deliverance to the captive; inviting the backslider to return; promising every valuable and important blessing, to those who accept his invitation, and come to him through Jesus Christ; how great the encouragement, which the sinner may take from hence, to repent and turn to God! With what entire confidence may he trust to the assurances of the word, that God will graciously accept his imperfect works of righteousness, which are by Jesus Christ to the praise and glory of God! What an argument is this, to devote ourselves to this most kind and benevolent Being! "Ye are not your own; for ye are bought with a price: Therefore glorify God in your body, and in your spirit, which are God's." How constraining a motive to one, who hath a just sense of the love and goodness of God, manifested by his Son Jesus Christ!—We may talk of the beauty of virtue; of moral fitness; of the reason and nature of things; of the tendency of holiness, to promote our health; our ease; our reputation in the world; and, it must be owned, they are all arguments of great weight; but a clear view, an affecting sense of the sufferings of Jesus Christ, and a due consideration of the end and design of these sufferings, are arguments, which will weigh more, with a true christian, than all the rest—A sense of the torments to which sin exposes us, may make us afraid of sinning, but it is the goodness of God, that leadeth to repentance—That goodness which is illustriously

dis-

displayed in the christian revelation. This powerful motive, makes every other consideration appear light, and unimportant. This, duly impress'd on the heart, will engage us, to run with chearfulness the race set before us; to run and not be weary; to walk and not faint. He, who hath much forgiven, and who hath a just sense of the obligation, will love much. He who loves God much, will evidence this love by keeping all his commandments; and in keeping the commandments of God, a christian will always find great reward. An inward principle of religion, will quiet his passions, regulate his affections, and fill his soul with a calm, a joy, which a stranger intermeddleth not with. The greater progress he makes in the divine life, so much the more reason he hath to be satisfied, that he is born of the Spirit.—The more he hath of the temper of a disciple of Christ, so much the more certain it is, that he is his disciple—this he accounts his highest honor; his greatest happiness.— The more certain he is, that he is one of Christ's disciples, so much the greater comfort doth he derive, from the great and precious promises of the gospel, that God will take him under his guidance, his care, and his protection; that he will make all things work together for his good; that he will be his Friend, his Father, his Portion.

The promises do not include an exemption from death. The christian knows that he must die. There is no discharge in that war.—In

this

this respect, there is one event to the righteous, and to the wicked. But faith scatters the horrors of the grave. The gospel reveals a resurrection of the dead. "As in Adam all die, so in Christ shall all be made alive." St. Peter says, "Thou hast the words of eternal life." And the apostle John tells us, "This is the promise, he hath promised us, even eternal life." This eternal life, we are to enjoy; not, in this weak imperfect state; not, in this vain and sinful world, where we are surrounded with cares, sorrows and temptations: but, in heaven; where the wicked cease from troubling, and the weary are at rest; where sin and sorrow are no more; where we shall see Christ, our Saviour and Lord; and enjoy God, without interruption, without intermission; where only we can know, how much God hath done for us, and how much good he hath laid up in store for them that love him. What can disturb one, who hath such views, and such prospects! With what contempt may he look down on the joys and sorrows, the frowns and flatteries of a vain world! None of these things move him; nor doth he account his life dear, so he may finish well, and enter into the joy of his Lord. How did the apostles and primitive saints, triumph over the king of terrors, when he put on the most gloomy form! They rejoiced, that they were counted worthy to suffer for Christ; and chearfully resigned up every thing they held dear in this world, even life itself, for his sake. Such was their

regard

regard for their master; such was the blessed influence of the religion they professed. Death is so far from being a terror to a christian, who is possessed of the assurance of hope, that he esteems it a friendly messenger, sent to release him from this prison, to which he is at present confined—a harbinger of the glory which God hath promised and prepared. When by faith he takes a view of the heavenly Canaan, and looks forward to that rest which remains for the people of God, he would not live always in this uncomfortable world; he can hardly content himself in this vale of tears; and cries out with joy and gratitude—Come Lord Jesus, come quickly. He thinks with holy transport of that blessed time, when this mortal will put on immortality; and this corruptible will put on incorruption; and death will be swallowed up in victory: When Christ who is our life shall appear, and we shall appear with him in glory: When we shall be admitted to to the beatific vision of God, in whose presence is fulness of joy, and at whose right hand are pleasures for evermore.

These are great things for a sinful worm to look for. But a christian doth not allow himself to stagger through unbelief. He doth not object his own unworthiness, his exceeding sinfulness, his aggravated guilt. He remembers that he hath the word and promise of the true and faithful God: " Hath he said and shall he not do it? Or hath he

L spoken,

spoken, and shall he not make it good ?"—Under all his fears and doubts, he repairs to that Saviour, who hath the words of eternal life, and hath taught us the way to a blessed immortality. With intire confidence, he ventures his soul upon the truth of christianity; he relies upon the merits of the Redeemer; and daily commits himself to him, being persuaded, that he is able to keep the sacred depositum, and will present him faultless before God, and his Father, with exceeding joy.

IMPROVEMENT.

First, We learn from what hath been said, the wisdom of the true christian.

With what sincere pity, and tender emotions, did the disciples who still adhered to Christ, look upon all those who left their Master, and relinquish'd their expectations from him, possibly for ever! Just so may you, who have an inward acquaintance with christianity, look upon all those who reject Christ, and neglect his great salvation. Perhaps, they are rich and prosperous; perhaps, you are poor and despised: But they are the enemies of God, and exposed to his eternal wrath; whereas he hath called and chosen you, and made you heirs of eternal blessedness. Would you change states with them? Most certainly you would not. You cannot be a christian, and repent of your choice. You

cannot

cannot but know, that you act the moft rational and wife part. You cannot but look on them as fools and madmen, who eat, drink and are merry, while hanging over the pit of eternal deftruction—Why then do you envy them their good things, which will laft but a little while, and will terminate in remedilefs perdition? Why are you difcontented with your lot? What! though you meet with difficulties and trials; thefe are defigned for your benefit; they are but for a feafon, and will be followed with endlefs happinefs and joy. When you confider your character and your profpects, it ought deeply to humble you, that your lives are in no degree anfwerable. You walk too much by fight; you live too little by faith. Your hearts are unreafonably attached to earthly things, though you are citizens of Zion, the Jerufalem that is above.

Secondly, How great obligations are you under to thankfulnefs, who are made heirs of eternal l●!

Inftead of looking on the men of the world with any fort of envy, you ought to adore and praife God, who hath made you to differ from them. It is not owing to your own fuperior reafon, that you are better then others; Divine grace hath made you what you are. But for this, you had been like

thofe

those around you, who chuse a portion in this life, in preference to that glorious state of immortality which the gospel reveals : You would, like them, spend your money for that which is not bread, and your labor for that which profiteth not. When you taste the pleasures of religion, when you contemplate the happiness of the future state—Think of the goodness of God in sending his own Son to die for you.—Meditate on the love of Christ, in submitting to be a man of sorrows ; in giving himself an offering, and a sacrifice to God ; in becoming obedient unto death, even the death of the cross. —Think for whose sakes he endured these amazing sufferings ; it was for us, sinners—Think of the end he had in view ; it was, that the salvation of man might be accomplished, in a consistency with the perfections of the Deity. He died, that you might live through him.

Can they be thought to have a just sense of this infinite love, who neglect an ordinance which Christ hath himself enjoined, as an expression of regard to him ; and which is peculiarly adapted to beget and increase our affection to him ? They, who continue in this neglect, notwithstanding all the arguments that are used with them, with as little concern, as if it were a matter of indifference, whether Christ is obeyed, or not ? May not the words of the text be applied to them—"Will ye also go away?" Whither can you go with so much advantage, as to this

holy

holy ordinance? Is not your neglect of it, the reason that you are so dead in all the offices of religion? And that you do not walk more circumspectly, and more uniformly, in your christian course? Indeed, a bare attendance on ordinances, is not enough to constitute you christians; you must have respect to him, who hath the words of eternal life, or you will reap but little advantage from your observance of the institutions of religion. If you do not partake of the bread of life which came down from heaven, you can receive no spiritual nourishment.

Let those who profess the religion of Christ, be careful to evidence their sincerity to the world, by an answerable conversation. Since you do not expect happiness from earthly things, why do you discover such an earthly temper? Why are you so deeply affected with the joys or troubles of life? Recollect, that this world is not your home, and that you have expectations which the world cannot disappoint. "Seek the things that are above, where Christ sitteth at the right hand of God." Cast your cares and burthens on the Lord, and he will sustain you. We are all quickly to go hence, we are to leave the present evil world, we are to go to our Father's house—There we shall be at rest. Let us contemplate that happy time, when that Jesus, who hath favoured us with the words of eternal life, and the means of attaining it, will give us eternal
life

life itfelf. Oh! the joy of that bleffed day, when our great Redeemer will defcend from heaven, with a fhout, with the voice of the Arch-angel, and with the trump of God; and will invite us to the bleffednefs he hath purchafed, in that tranfporting language; "Come ye bleffed of my Father, inherit the kingdom prepared for you, from the foundation of the world?" Oh! the bleffednefs of that ftate, when we fhall be free from fin, which ought to be our greateft burthen; and fhall know, even as we are known. "Having a promife of fuch reft, let us not feem to come fhort of it through unbelief."

Let finners in Zion, tremble at the thought of that eternal feparation, which will be made in the great day, between the righteous and the wicked; and of thofe inconceivable torments to which they will be configned, who fhall be found at the left hand of the Judge. Let them forfake thofe lying vanities which now delude them, and caft themfelves upon the mercy of God through Jefus Chrift. Your fins are many; your guilt is great; but Chrift is able to fave to the uttermoft, all them that come to God through him,

SERMON

SERMON IV.

The Dominion of an omnipotent Deity a Reason for Joy and Praise.

REVELATION XIX. 6.

Alleluia : *for the Lord God omnipotent reigneth.*

IN the preceeding chapter, we have a prediction of the overthrow of myſtical Babylon, the ſeat of the beaſt, by which is intended the deſtruction of *Rome* papal, or the fall of the man of ſin, whoſe kingdom was founded by human policy and power, and hath been ſupported by every kind of unrighteous deceit. An Angel is repreſented as proclaiming aloud, " Babylon the great is fallen, is fallen."—From the

the description we have in this prophecy, it seems, as if *Rome* like ancient *Babylon*, was to be reduced to a heap of ruins, never to be rebuilt, but to remain desolate and uninhabited. Her destruction was to be sudden, entire, and perpetual.

When this persecuting power was thus totally destroyed, the heavenly church is introduced, with united voices, singing an anthem of praise to God, for his righteous vengeance on the cruel oppressors of his people; and for his faithfulness, in supporting, protecting, and delivering his persecuted saints. "After these things, I heard," says the apostle John, "a great voice of much people in heaven, saying, Alleluia, salvation, and glory, and honor, and power, unto the Lord, our God. For true and righteous are his judgments, for he hath judged the great whore, which did corrupt the earth with her fornications, and hath avenged the blood of his servants at her hand. And again, they said, Alleluia; and her smoke rose up for ever and ever. And the four and twenty elders, and the four *living creatures*, fell down and worshipped God, that sat on the throne, saying, Amen, Alleluia." When this hymn of praise was ended, there came forth an order from the throne, or seat of the divine presence, to the saints on earth, to join in these heavenly acclamations of praise. " And a voice came out of the throne, saying, praise our God, all ye that fear him, both small and great."—" A voice from the throne,"

throne," says Mr. Lowman, " is from the glory, or
" the oracle ; this shews the great authority and
" solemnity, with which this order was published.
" The praise of God, to which this oracle directs,
" seems somewhat different from that of the fore-
" going hymn ; that hymn was to celebrate the
" praise of God, principally on account of his faith-
" fulness and justice, in the punishment of a per-
" secuting power, which had long oppress'd the
" faithful servants of Christ. But this, as appears
" by the following hymn, in obedience to the di-
" rection of the oracle, is principally to praise God,
" for the happy and glorious state of the church,
" consequent upon this punishment of their ene-
" mies ; that happy and glorious state of the
" church, suppose, wherein it is said to live and
" reign with Christ a thousand years, and which is
" more largely described in the following chapter.
" For which great goodness of God, all good men
" are prepared, by this solemn thanksgiving, to
" express their hearty and grateful acknowledge-
" ments." The word was no sooner given to
praise God, than it was instantly obeyed. " And
I heard as it were the voice of a great multitude,
and as the voice of many waters, and as the voice
of mighty thunderings, Alleluia ; for the Lord God
omnipotent reigneth. Let us be glad and rejoice,
and give honor to him, for the marriage of the
Lamb is come, and his wife hath made herself
ready." The exact period, when these prophecies
will be accomplished, is not mentioned ; at least

not so clearly, as that we are able, certainly to determine when it will be. They who have pretended to ascertain it, have only published their own mistakes. But there is enough known of the infinitely perfect Jehovah, to satisfy us that he will be faithful to his promises, and that the cause of truth and righteousness will finally prevail against all opposition; a reasonable foundation this for rest, for gratitude, for praise.—It is a reason for joy and thankfulness, that there is a prospect of such a time—The reason will be stronger when the time actually comes—Then, when his enemies shall be subdued under him, the Lord will triumph gloriously.

We are not to suppose, that the blessed God is, at other times, only a spectator of the things that take place in the world. His direction and government of events are limited to no particular season; he always sets at helm, and superintends universal nature. This consideration may well quiet our minds, and affords a reason for peace comfort and joy, when things look most dark: The call to gratitude and to praise is still more evident, when this glorious Being appears for the help of his people, and grants them salvation. " The word Alleluia or Hallelujah, is a most lively and comprehensive expression of praise, often used, and translated, *Praise ye the Lord*, in the Psalms, the five last of which, with several others, begin and end, as this heavenly hymn doth, with that word."

What

What I propose in this discourse, is,

First, To consider the title by which the great God is described in the text—" The Lord God omnipotent."

Secondly, To speak of his universal dominion and government.

Thirdly, To shew, that this consideration is a reasonable foundation for joy and praise.

First, I am to consider the title by which the great God is described in the text—" The Lord God omnipotent."

By the omnipotence of God, we understand a capacity or ability of doing whatsoever he pleases. An arbitrary power, in the imperfect sons of men, we justly abhor; but in God, we connect with it the idea of infinite reason and goodness. The will of God is always determined by his perfect wisdom, and is entirely consistent with absolute perfection. Whatever God wills is wise and good, holy and just. It is not enough to say, his will is not inconsistent with these attributes, there is the exercise of these attributes in all he wills, in all he does. To say, therefore, that God doth according to his will or pleasure, is to say, that he doth what is right and fit, that which is dictated by his wisdom, and which becomes an all-

all-perfect Being. In this sense we are to understand that expression, "Thou hast made all things, and for thy pleasure they are and were created."

The power of God is infinite; it extends to all things possible, to all things that are consistent with the perfection of his nature. It doth not extend to impossibilities; it would be absurd to say, God could do a thing and not do it at the same time. To do a thing wrong and unfit, would be an imperfection; and therefore to suppose such a capacity in God, is not to honor him, but to make him in our thoughts, altogether such an one as ourselves.

That God is omnipotent, no one will be disposed to deny, who considers what great things he hath done. What can be beyond the reach of his power, who formed this stupendous universe? and spake innumerable worlds into being? He who hath communicated such amazing powers and abilities to his creatures, who hath constituted causes sufficient to produce such great effects, must have all power in himself. If it may not be said that infinite power is displayed in the works of God, because they are finite; yet we rationally conclude, that the being who produced them is infinite in power. To fix limits to his power, who hath done so much, is to the last degree unreasonable. To make objections against his omnipotence, because he hath not done all he could do, is evidently absurd;

surd: It is to say he is not omnipotent, because he hath still a power of acting. It certainly implies nothing absurd or contradictory, to ascribe this attribute to God: Whereas it contradicts all our notions of a Deity, to suppose any thing too hard, or too great, for him to do. If he is not infinite in power, he is not infinite in any perfection. His other attributes can extend no further than his power. Consequently, he is not God, he is not a Being of infinite perfection. If we deny the Deity any one attribute, we involve ourselves in all the difficulties and absurdities of atheism. Therefore, the scripture, which was designed to give us just notions of God, ascribes to him every perfection, and in an infinite degree. Particularly, it teaches us, that " power belongeth unto God." ¶ " In thine hand," says the devout king Jehoshaphat, " is there not power and might, so that none is able to withstand thee?" * " I know," says holy Job, " that thou canst do every thing."† In another place, speaking of God, he says, ‡ " He is wise in heart, and mighty in strength, who hath hardened himself against him, & hath prospered? Which removeth the mountains, and they know not: which overturneth them in his anger. Which shaketh the earth out of her place, and the pillars thereof tremble. Which commandeth the sun, and it riseth not: and sealeth up the stars. Behold, he taketh away, who can hinder him? Who will say unto him, what doest thou?" In the New Testament, we find an Angel saying,
" With

¶ Psa. 62. 11. * 2 Chron. 20. 6. † Job 42. 2. ‡ 9. 4.

" With God nothing shall be impossible." * And our Lord says, " With men it is impossible, but not with God, for with God all things are possible." †

I am, in the second place, to show that this glorious Being, who is the Lord God omnipotent, hath the government of the world in his hands. " The Lord God omnipotent reigneth."

The power of God is not a mere capacity of nature, which he suffers to lie idle and useless. It is continually in exercise, and ever hath been. It discovers very narrow and contracted sentiments, to confine the creating power of God to this earth, or system, or to what we know and are acquainted with: One can scarce imagine, that there were not creatures before man, upon whom God might exercise his infinite perfections. It is much more reasonable to suppose, that the Almighty hath been, through eternity, producing worlds, and creatures to inhabit them. The word heaven, as used in scripture, may sometimes include in it the infinite expanse, all above or besides this earth; it may contain a large and wide creation; and all these things his hands have made; his word spake them into being. " I have made the earth, and created man upon it. I, even my hands have stretched out the heavens, and all their hosts have I commanded."

The

* Luke 1: 34. † Mark 10. 27.

The same omnipotent Creator, which brought the world out of nothing, gave the different parts of the creation, their various natures and laws, their situation and motion, as he saw fit. And having made them, he exercises his power, his goodness, his wisdom, in preserving, directing, and governing them. The providence of God extends as far as the creation. Whatever he hath brought into being, depends upon him for its continuance in being; its having existence one moment, doth not make its existence necessary the next; its former existence is not the cause of its existing afterwards; it continues in being, not because it hath existed, but because this is the will of the Creator. And if the will of God determines the continuance of a thing created, he must also determine the state and circumstances in which it shall continue: It must be under such laws and regulations, or have such powers and capacities as he sees fit to give it. There can be no accident with respect to him, no change or alteration unknown to, or unforeseen by him; because he always hath, in one grand view, all events, past, present and to come. Nothing comes to pass without his influence and appointment.

There is, indeed, a difference between creatures that are moral agents, and those that are not. The latter have no capacity of acting; and move only as they are put in motion by some external agent. The former have an internal power of acting, and are

are capable of chusing, willing, and determining. A creature devoid of such a power, cannot have a moral capacity, nor be under any moral obligation. "A being who cannot act at all, most certainly cannot act well or ill, virtuously or viciously." It is evident, that too many of those creatures whom God made with a capacity of acting right, have deviated from the path of duty, and been guilty of moral evil. To ascribe the wickedness of his creatures, to the all-perfect Deity, is impiety: We ought not to entertain the tho't, that he made them wicked at first; or, that they became wicked afterwards by his impulsive influence. The apostle James will not allow it to be said, that God tempts men to sin, much less can he compel them to be sinful. "Let no man say when he is tempted, I am tempted of God; for God cannot be tempted with evil, neither tempteth he any man." ¶

God is not the author of sin; he doth not make men sinful; though, for wise and holy ends, he permits sin to be in the world, continues the existence of the wicked and ungodly, and their powers of action. He affords them means of coming to the knowledge of their duty; he is ready to grant them all necessary assistance to right practice; when he sees fit, he lays his restraints on the lusts and corruptions of men; and always over-rules their evil conduct to some valuable end. As he hath an entire view of all that will be, of the actions of

¶ James 1. 13.

of free agents, as well as all other events, so he hath laid his plan accordingly. " It is true," saith Mr. *Wollaston*, " this amounts to a prodigious scheme, in which all things to come are as it were comprehended under one view, estimated, and laid together: But when," says he, " I consider what a mass of wonders the universe is in other regards; what a Being God is, incomprehensibly great and perfect; that he cannot be ignorant of any thing, no not of the future wants and deportments of particular men; and that all things, which derive from him as the first cause, must do this so as to be consistent with one another, and in such a manner, as to make one compact system, befitting so great an author: I say, when I consider this, I cannot deny such an adjustment of things to be within his power." The all-wise God hath not excluded sin from his system; but he hath so calculated things, as that the sins of men shall not break in upon the order of his scheme, but shall rather be subservient to his designs.

We may sometimes, though not always, see wise and good ends, in things that at first look dark.— For instance, if the cause of virtue seem to be oppressed, and almost overwhelmed; men, who have very imperfect views, may think it is because God hath no regard to what passeth here; or, which is worse, that there is no distinction between good and evil, virtue and vice: But God may design to correct those whom he loves, for the defect of their love to him, for their conformity to the world, and fondness for the pleasures and enjoyments of it: He may design to purge out their dross, and to prepare them for another and eternal state.—Do the wicked triumph? some may think, it would not be thus, if the world were governed by a holy, a just, a wise Being: But God may suffer them to rise high, that their fall may be more conspicuous, and that he may display his power and justice in their destruction. That he will do this, sooner or later, is clear from the declarations of his word: If these predictions are not fulfilled in this world, they will be fulfilled in another. A future state will set all to rights: God may then discover his approbation of moral rectitude, and his infinite displeasure at sin, by rewarding the righteous, and punishing the wicked, according to their works. However particular events may seem to look otherwise, yet the scripture evidently teaches us, that God hath the good of his church always in view. It doth not prove the contrary, that things have a dark aspect to us, who are but weak short-sighted mortals. Those very things, which we think are dark and threatning, may be designed in favour, and may issue in the greatest good. If we lay together what we are taught in the several parts of scripture; it seems, as if every great event, which hath any connection with the church of God, was to verify some prediction, or to fulfil some promise. And as all is to issue in the prosperity of the church, and in the

triumph

triumph of virtue and goodness; so, it is probable, all things that come to pass are made to conspire to this end. A Being of infinite wisdom and almighty power can make things to terminate, quite differently from our views and expectations, and even from their own natural tendency; the event may be very different from, yea contrary to, what would have taken place without his particular interposition. And though we do not, at present, see any thing which looks like such a happy winding up of things, as we are taught to expect; yet, there have been, from time to time, illustrious displays of divine power and goodness. The God of heaven hath often interposed for the relief of his people, when they have been in low and difficult circumstances; he hath protected them in their greatest dangers; he hath scattered the clouds that seemed ready to break over their heads; he hath granted them salvation, when, according to their view of things, there was least reason to expect it; or he hath afforded success to their undertakings, even beyond their hopes. Thus, he hath preserved to himself a church in the world, notwithstanding the attempts of earth and hell to destroy it. He hath delivered it, when its enemies seemed ready to swallow it up. And, at particular times, his cause hath flourished and triumphed; religion hath prevailed; and its enemies have been made to hide their heads.

These

These great events both scripture and reason teach us to ascribe to the power of God. "Whatsoever," saith the devout psalmist, "the Lord pleaseth, that doth he in heaven and in earth, and in all deep places. ¶ "He doth according to his will in the army of heaven, and amongst the inhabitants of the earth; and none can stay his hand." † "There are many devices in a man's heart, nevertheless the counsel of the Lord, that shall stand." ‡ Our Saviour teaches us that the providence of God extends to the most minute events; "Are not two sparrows sold for a farthing, and one of them shall not fall to the ground without your Father." § Surely then, he doth not neglect human affairs; he directs and governs those important events, which affect communities, kingdoms, and countries. If he attends to the circumstances of individuals, so as to number the very hairs of their heads; we may with reason suppose, that he is Governor among the nations, and ruleth to the ends of the earth.

We sometimes say, that things come about in the course of nature; "but the course of nature, separate from the agency of God, is no cause, or nothing. If there are laws, by which natural causes act, and things succeed one another in a regular uniform manner, and with but little variation; and

¶ Ps. 135. 6.   † Dan. 4. 35.   ‡ Prov. 19. 21.   § Mat. 10. 29.

and in general the conſtitution of things is preſerved;" theſe laws are nothing elſe than the will of him, who is the Author of nature. If He ſhould ceaſe to will the connection between cauſes and effects, the connection would immediately ceaſe. I cannot, therefore, well underſtand what they mean, who deny the divine ſuperintendency; and ſuppoſe a certain eſtabliſhed order, or courſe of things, according to which they muſt come to paſs. A mere law, or order, ſeparate from the will and power of God, cannot exiſt; and if they mean the will and power of God, governing all events, they own the thing we contend for—that God governs the world.

Before I diſmiſs this head of the divine government, I would add, that God governs the world by Jeſus Chriſt. "All power is given to me," ſays our Lord, "in heaven and in earth. † And the apoſtle, ſpeaking of the glory of Chriſt, ſays, "God —hath put all things under his feet, and gave him to be Head over all things to the church." ‡ Some have ſuppoſed, that the Son of God is intended by the "Lord God omnipotent" in the text; as he is elſewhere called "the mighty God." Whether this be ſo or not, it is certain, as Mediator, the kingdoms of Providence and of Grace are committed to him; "the government is upon his ſhoulder." His adminiſtration will continue, till he hath ſubdued

† Matthew 28. 18.   ‡ Epheſians 1. 22.

dued all things under him; "and then shall the Son also himself be subject unto him that put all things under him, that God may be all in all." §

I proceed now to the third general head, viz. This consideration, that the great God governs the world, is a reasonable foundation for joy and praise. " Alleluia, for the Lord God omnipotent reigneth."

It is an everlasting source of comfort, that the government of the world is in the hands of a Being of infinite wisdom and goodness—of one, who doth not afflict willingly, nor grieve the children of men—of one, who knows how to bring light out of darkness, joy out of sorrow, order out of confusion—of one, who can over-rule even the passions and corruptions of men to his glory—of one, who hath promised, to make all things work together for good to them that love him; and that the cause of truth and righteousness shall finally prevail against all opposition.

It is a reason for holy joy and praise, that this wise and good Being, who hath promised so much to his people, is able to do what his goodness inclines him to do; and to accomplish all that he hath promised. " None can stay his hand, or say unto him, what doest thou?" * " Behold the nations

§ 1 Cor. 15. 28. * Daniel 4. 35.

tions are as a drop of a bucket, and are counted as the small dust of the balance; behold, he taketh up the isles as a very little thing. All nations before him are as nothing, and they are counted to him less than nothing, and vanity." § With what serenity and patience, may that man possess his soul, who can view all things under the direction, controul, and government, of an infinite Being, who always intends the good of his creatures; who knows wherein their happiness consists; and whose power can effect what his goodness designs. It is impossible he should do any thing amiss. He necessarily doth that which is best to be done. It no ways becomes us creatures of yesterday, to find fault with any thing God does; or to entertain doubts and suspicions, whether that world which he governs, will be well governed. It is contrary to all the rules of reason and religion, to suffer ourselves to sink into despair, or a restless anxiety, because things do not turn out according to our expectations and desires; or because we meet with things that are for the present, not joyous but grievous. It is because men have not just sentiments of God, and proper notions of his government, that they do not always acquiesce in the disposals of his Providence; or else, it is because we are too much attached to this world, and not enough conversant with another.

If we consider our situation here only, or chiefly, things may have a very unpromising aspect; but when

§ Isaiah 40. 15. 17.

when we confider our connection with another ftate, thofe things which feem to be againft us, may have a quite contrary tendency—they may be calculated to wean us from a world we are too fond of ; to purify our fouls ; and to prepare us for that ftate of perfection, to which God purpofes to raife us ; and in this view they are moft merciful difpenfations ; not to be deprecated as evils, but rejoiced in as benefits. We ought always to account that to be good, which tends to our advantage upon the whole; we may not therefore repine at temporal calamities and afflictions, becaufe we may eafily conceive, that in the conclufion of things, it may turn out beft that we have met with them.

Efpecially, may the man of religion and virtue rejoice in the confideration of the divine government. Confcious of an upright heart, knowing that he hath committed his foul into the hands of the Redeemer and Saviour of men, he can look upon God as reconciled to him through Jefus Chrift ; he can furvey the promifes with inward delight and fatisfaction, affured that they will be fulfilled in him ; he can caft his care upon the Lord who careth for him ; he looks on the afflictions he meets with, as the tender corrections of a Father, and not the punifhment of an angry Judge. Secure of the divine protection, he is unmoved, tho' befet with threatning dangers, and furrounded with evils, which a righteous God fees fit to bring on an

ungodly

ungodly world. By faith he looks beyond the grave, takes a view of the promised land, and rejoices in the prospect of a blessed immortality.

But if a christian finds reason to rejoice in the divine government, when his outward circumstances are dark and perplexed; or when God writes bitter things against him; surely, there is room for the exercise of joy and praise, when he is surrounded with blessings; when his situation in this world is easy and pleasant, and goodness and mercy continually follow him.

All the good things which a christian enjoys, he considers as conferred on him by God, he meditates on them with gratitude, and his devout soul breaks forth in ascriptions of praise to him who hath made him to differ from others. Since God governs the world, we ought to eye his hand in all the good we experience, whether as members of society or as individuals; we ought to rejoice in his government, to maintain a constant sense of his goodness, and to give unto him the glory due to his name. This hath been the practice of the saints in all ages. We have a bright example of gratitude in the royal psalmist, his mouth is always full of the praises of God; he never seems so much in his element, as when he speaks of the goodness of God, and his loving-kindness to the children of men. "I will sing of the mercies of the Lord forever; I will make known his faithfulness to all generations."

nerations." There is no duty more reasonable in itself; more delightful to those who practice it; and which more becomes those, whom he hath made capable of this heavenly employment. "Praise is comely for the upright." They have the most to be thankful for, they are the most capable of performing this excellent duty, and therefore they are under the strongest obligations to attend it. Good men ought to praise God for common or extraordinary mercies; for private or publick, for temporal or spiritual blessings; for the dispensations of providence that are opposite to their desires and inclinations, as well as for those that are agreable to them. In every situation their pious minds may find reason to speak well of his name. Whatever their outward condition is, the Lord is their portion; they are the children of God; and heirs of glory.

I shall now lead you to some reflections suitable to the subject we have been upon.

In the first place, How great and glorious does the blessed God appear in the character of "the Lord God omnipotent!" We gaze at a distance on earthly monarchs; we account them great, because they are surrounded with attendants, who wait their nod, and stand ready to fulfil their commands. But how little, how contemptible do they appear, when compared with the infinite God!
Their

Their power reaches over some small part of this lower world; the power of God extends not to a part, but to the whole of this globe; it reaches throughout universal nature; it is not limited by the creation; infinite space lies open to omnipotence. Whatever he wills, he is able to do. None can control, none can resist his power.—How great! how awful is this almighty Lord! With how much reason doth the guilty sinner tremble before this glorious Being, who is justly incensed at his crimes; who is able to crush him into nothing in a moment; or if he continues his existence, can render it compleatly miserable! You fear a man that shall die, and the son of man that shall be made as grass; and dost thou forget the Lord, thy Maker, that hath stretched forth the heavens, and laid the foundations of the earth? The most that man can do, the greatest evil all the men on earth can possibly inflict, is, to take away your life; they can kill the body, after that there is no more that they can do, but God is able to destroy both body and soul in hell, wherefore, says our Lord, "I say unto you, fear him." It is a comfort, that while we contemplate the almighty power of God; we can think of his power, as guided by consummate wisdom, and tempered with boundless goodness. These attributes render this great and terrible Being, an object of esteem and love. He is peculiarly amiable in the view which the gospel gives us of him, reconciling the world to himself by Jesus Christ. Interested in the merits of the Redeemer, we may think of the omnipotence of God, with sacred delight and joy, knowing that it will be imployed for our protection and advantage; and that we shall be kept, by the mighty power of God, through faith unto salvation.

Secondly, Doth the Lord God omnipotent reign? we learn, why the enemies of his church have not been able to prevail against it. It hath not been for want of those who have had malice sufficient, that the church of Christ hath not been overwhelmed and destroyed. But he that sitteth in the heavens, and beholdeth all the children of men, hath restrained their wrath, and confounded their cruel designs. Under the protection of heaven, this little flock hath been preserved, though surrounded by ravening wolves, and roaring lions. The word of God hath sometimes grown mightily and prevailed. The power of those who have opposed Christ and his cause, hath not been equal to their will, or christianity had long ago been exterminated. Our Lord Jesus Christ, having all power in his hands, conducts all things for the good of his church. None can proceed further than he permits them. He hath been the hope of his Israel; he hath not suffered his cause to sink; and he hath promised, that the gates of hell shall not prevail against it. His church will continue, his cause will triumph, his saints will be joyful in glory; and all opposing powers will be confounded.

Thirdly,

Thirdly, The confideration of his univerfal dominion, fhould lead us to make our grateful acknowledgments to the great Governor of the world, when things go well with us. Have we enjoyed many comforts in this life? Have we been preferved when in danger? Have events, whether of a public or private nature, turned out favorably? And fometimes beyond, or contrary to our hopes? We muft not think a chance hath happened to us; but fhould rejoice in the Lord, and give glory to his name. Whatever means we have ufed, however probable they were, yet the divine bleffing hath made them effectual. You often fee that the moft probable means fail, while thofe that are moft unpromifing are crowned with fuccefs; this teaches us, that there is no neceffary connection between the means and the end; and that all fecond caufes are in the hand of the great firft caufe. Let us then religioufly acknowledge the providence of God in every favorable event. Let us abundantly utter the memory of his great goodnefs, and fing of his righteoufnefs. The goodnefs of God ought more deeply to affect us, becaufe we are infinitely unworthy of the leaft mercy. Every favor ought to lead our thoughts to Jefus Chrift, that great, that unfpeakable, that comprehenfive gift, through whom every other good flows to us.

Fourthly, Since the government of the world is in fo good hands, we ought quietly to fubmit, when things are ordered contrary to our defires and expectations. Whatever evils we meet with, we are sure that as sinners we deserve them. The least we can do is to be silent; Job went further; deprived of every thing, he says, "the Lord gave, the Lord hath taken away, blessed be the name of the Lord." It is no unreasonable thing to rejoice in affliction; when we consider that all is ordered by a Being of infinite wisdom and goodness, we justly conclude that what he doth is wise and good. Tho' we meet with trials that are hard to bear, yet if we are good men, we have reason to think, that it is best we should meet with them. They are in covenant love, and are designed to make us partakers of the divine holiness, and to prepare us for a better state. "The Lord God is a sun and shield: the Lord will give grace and glory: no good thing will he withhold from them that walk uprightly."

Fifthly, Doth the Lord God omnipotent reign, let us not be anxious about futurity, but let us commit all our concerns to him—To be distressed about what is to come, argues a distrust of divine providence. It is certain, a restless anxiety cannot possibly be of any advantage. It will not alter the course of things, and it greatly unfits us for what we have to go through. It is indeed fit and right, to take a prudent care of our outward affairs, and to attend the duties of our station; but all beyond this—is wrong, it is sinful. Commit your works unto him, who hath the supreme disposal of all things. In all thy ways acknowledge him, and he

will

will direct thy paths. Undertake nothing without consulting him; and in prosecuting your lawful undertakings have his glory in view; and remember, that success, even in the common affairs and business of life, depends entirely on his over-ruling providence. Having committed your case to him, in serious fervent prayer, leave yourselves with him; submit to his all-wise direction and disposal; saying, the Lord do that which seemeth him good. Having done this, in patience possess your souls; you are secure under the protection of him, who hath all nature at his command. I pretend not to promise you exemption from outward trials. God may see them necessary to bring you to glory; in which case, you are to place them under the head of mercies. Every thing is in mercy which tends to promote your spiritual good, your eternal welfare. These will be your sentiments, another day, whatever you think now.

If you are, and continue enemies to God by wicked works; it is a tho't full of terror, that the Lord God omnipotent reigneth; that he whom you have offended by your sins is possessed of almighty power, and is able in such a variety of ways to punish and destroy you. "The Lord reigneth, let the people tremble." The evils of this life are but a faint emblem of that amazing misery which awaits the sinner in another state. It ought therefore to be your first and chief concern, to commit your soul into the hands of him, who is a-

ble

ble to keep that which you have committed to him against that day. Your great desire should be, that you may become true christians, that you may have a title to the promises, and may be heirs of glory. To be indifferent here, and to be anxious about any temporal interest, is most unworthy stupidity. " Seek first the kingdom of God, and his righteousness, and all these things shall be added unto you." You are to seek *first* the kingdom of God and his righteousness, this supposes you are not to neglect other things. We have such connections with this world, and such necessary attachments to it, that we cannot but be affected with our situation here, whether it be prosperous or adverse. Religion is so far from forbidding this, that it rather injoins it. It obliges us to praise God for mercies, and to be humbled under afflictions; to acknowledge our dependance upon him; and to commit our affairs to him. This hath been the practice of God's people in all ages, a practice which hath been attended with happy success.

May God, by the dispensations of his providence, prepare us for that glorious place of rest, where we shall be free from those troubles and anxieties, which render this world so uncomfortable; where we shall have continual tokens of his love, and eternally solace ourselves in the enjoyment of the CHIEF GOOD! Amen.

SERMON

SERMON V.

Charity more excellent than Faith or Hope.

---

1 COR. XIII. 13.

And now abideth faith, hope, charity, these three ; but the greatest of these is charity.

IN the preceding verses the apostle Paul speaks of Charity in the highest terms. It far exceeded the gifts of the Holy Ghost, upon which the Corinthians valued themselves, and of which they were so ostentatious. " I shew unto you a more excellent way." This way was to pursue and cultivate that divine love, without which the most shining

ing gifts, and the higheſt pretences to religion and a virtuous character, would be of no advantage.

In our text he makes a compariſon between charity or love, and the graces of faith and hope, and gives the preference to love. "Now abideth faith, hope, and charity, theſe three; but the greateſt of theſe is charity."

My deſign is to illuſtrate this paſſage of ſcripture under theſe three heads,

Firſt, I ſhall particularly conſider the graces ſpecified in my text.

Secondly, I ſhall enquire in what ſenſe they are ſaid to abide.

Thirdly, I ſhall ſhow that charity excells both the other, or is the greateſt of the three.

Firſt, I am to conſider the graces mentioned in the text, faith, hope, and charity, theſe three.

The firſt is Faith, a grace that is peculiarly celebrated in the New-Teſtament. "By faith the elders obtained a good report." Faith in general is an aſſent to, or perſuaſion of a truth propoſed to us, upon the authority and teſtimony of him who declares it. It relates to things that are not preſent;

sent, or which are not the objects of our senses. It supposes that we have credible evidence of their existence, and therefore believe them to be. The evidence on which faith rests is not always equally clear and certain, and therefore faith is not always equally firm. When we believe upon the testimony of men, we consider them as fallible, and therefore the faith which is built upon it will not rise to so high a degree, as when we believe upon the testimony of the God of truth.—The apostle plainly points out a very great difference between divine and human faith. †. " For this cause also, thank we God without ceasing, because when ye received the word of God which ye heard of us, ye received it not as the word of men ; but, as it is in truth, the word of God, which effectually worketh also in you that believe." An assent is due to the word of men ; but our assent to the testimony of God should be answerable to his unquestionable veracity.

This divine faith, of which our text leads us to speak, is an internal conviction of the truth of religion ; and particularly of the scripture which is given by inspiration of God. The first principle of all religion and of all faith is the existence of a Deity. This great and fundamental truth, we cannot, indeed, be said to believe on the testimony of God in his word, because we must believe his existence before we can receive a revelation from him. We

† 1 Thess. 2. 13.

We understand there is a God by the things that are made. But when we are satisfied that a revelation is from God, it is rational to believe whatever he therein declares concerning himself. As he perfectly knows himself, so he is capable of giving his creatures more just conceptions of his nature, than they can possibly form by the exertions of their own reason. We have in the sacred scriptures, a clearer view of the nature, the character, the perfections of God, than men have ever attained, or than they are capable of attaining in any other way. The apostle says, " He that cometh to God must believe that he is, and that he is a rewarder of them that diligently seek him." The utmost length the light of nature can go, if it can go so far, is, that God will reward a creature who hath never deviated from the law of his nature, or from that constitution under which he was placed by his Creator. It affords no assurance that he will pardon a sinner, or accept of any duty performed by him : Man therefore having sinned hath little encouragement to repentance and obedience. Mere reason cannot remove his apprehensions of punishment, or give him any reasonable hope of good. All the expectation he can justly have of any reward, is founded on the manifestation God hath been pleased to make of himself in the gospel. He hath in this gracious dispensation proclaimed his name, " the Lord, the Lord God, merciful and gracious, forgiving iniquity, transgression and sin." The faith, therefore, which

which hath respect to God in the character of a rewarder of them that diligently seek him, is founded, so far as it hath any foundation at all, in divine revelation.

Christian faith is a belief of the truth of the religion of Jesus Christ, or an assent to the testimony which God hath given of his Son, who hath now in the end of the world appeared, to put away sin by the sacrifice of himself. The doctrine of a Mediator dispels the clouds which surrounded the Deity, and discouraged our access to him; it throws a light on the divine character, and raises the sinner to the most glorious hopes. In the exercise of faith, the christian receives Jesus as a Teacher come from God to bear witness unto the truth, and to give his life a ransom for all. He yields a firm assent to the history which the New-Testament gives of his spotless life, his miraculous works, his meritorious death, his triumphant resurrection, and glorious ascension into heaven, where he is exalted at God's right hand, to give repentance unto Israel and forgiveness of sins. He carries his views beyond this world, and looks for a blessed state of immortality. "Faith," as we are told by the writer to the Hebrews, " is the substance of things hoped for, and the evidence of things not seen." It gives as it were a present existence to things hoped for, and is persuaded of their truth and reality, though they are invisible and

and future. This affent of the mind is not of the fame kind with that which we yield to things feen, but it is as real, and according to the nature of the evidence on which is founded, it is as firm. It refts upon the fecurity of the divine promife, that the bleffings promifed will certainly be granted.

You obferve, that I am fpeaking, as I fuppofe the apoftle doth in our text, of faith in a large fenfe, and not of faith as it juftifies a guilty finner. Juftifying faith immediately refpects Jefus Chrift, this faith refpects all divine truth, the whole revelation of God. It includes juftifying faith, but it comprehends a great deal more than is directly implied in that. I mention this to prevent miftakes, though I am not certain there is fo much reafon for the diftinction as hath been fuppofed.

The fcripture doth not commonly denominate every cold and feeble affent to divine truth, faith. It certainly doth not, when it fpeaks of it in terms of the higheft approbation, and makes fuch great promifes to the believer. We read of believing "with the heart." † Faith confiders what God hath revealed, not only as true, but as of the greateft importance, and calculated to promote the moral perfection and happinefs of mankind, and therefore receives it with approbation and affection. When the apoftle fays " Faith is the evidence of things not

† Rom. 10. 10. Acts 8. 37.

not feen," the word he ufes, as critics have often obferved, is exceeding ftrong and emphatical, it fignifies a clear conviction, an evident demonftration,—" fuch a kind of reafon and argument, as both convinces the underftanding, and engages a man to act according to that conviction." Faith gives divine truths a prefent fubfiftence, fo that we tafte of their goodnefs, and experience their power influencing our whole temper and conduct. For this reafon it is, that divines have generally taken confent into their notion of faith; though this is not any part of faith in a ftrict fenfe, but rather an effect of it. The evangelift feems to lead us into this way of defcribing faith, when he fpeaks of receiving Chrift and believing in him as one and the fame thing. ¶ "To as many as received him, to them gave he power to become the fons of God, even to as many as believe on his name."

Faith then in a gofpel fenfe implies, that we receive Chrift, and that we receive him in his whole character; that we fubmit to his authority, confent to follow his example, and rely upon him to conduct us to a ftate of eternal happinefs. Many expreffions in the New-Teftament feem to intimate that faith is not an act of the underftanding only, but of the will; therefore it is commanded as a duty, " This is his commandment, that we believe on the name of his Son Jefus Chrift." And unbelief is
spoken

¶ John 1, 12.

spoken of as a sin, "He shall reprove the world of sin, because they believe not in me." Faith is a holy disposition, a love of the truth, a principle of virtue and piety, it produces universal obedience, and influences those who are possessed of it to yield themselves up to Christ, to be for him, for him entirely, and without any reserve.—It is no way material whether you take this conformity of heart to the truths you believe into your notion of faith. Most certainly, where there is not this conformity, your faith is vain, dead, and unprofitable.—Such a divine operative principle as this, hath a divine author, it is a grace of the Holy Spirit. "To you," saith the apostle, "it is given to believe."—This gracious habit, powerful as it is wherever it subsists, may be greatly strengthened. Our Lord teaches his apostles to pray, "Lord encrease our faith."

Secondly, The next grace which our text leads us to consider is, Hope.

Hope is, in general, a reasonable expectation of such things as we desire; or, the satisfaction which the mind takes in the prospect of them.—We call it an expectation, to distinguish it from simple desire. We may desire, may wish for many things, which we cannot hope to obtain.—It is an expectation of something good, this distinguishes it from fear,

fear, which is an affection of mind opposite to hope.—We speak of it as a reasonable expectation; men sometimes look for great good, when their expectation is only an airy flight of imagination; or, is built on a foundation that is false and deceitful. If this may be called hope; yet it is not that hope which is placed with faith and charity, which is encouraged by the God of truth, and is a grace of the Spirit. This blessed Spirit cannot be the author of delusion; the views he presents to our minds are agreable to truth; the desires he excites are after a real good; the hopes he inspires have a sure foundation. This hope of the christian is founded on the promise of God; and may reasonably extend as far as the promise, but all he expects beyond this, is vague and uncertain. God is faithful who hath promised, who also will do it; but he is under no obligation to bestow any good which he hath not promised, or to gratify any expectations which he hath not given reason for. Good men sometimes desire to be distinguished in the world; to be in a situation of grandeur and opulence. I shall not undertake to determine how far such desires are lawful; but when a christian entertains hopes of temporal blessings, however desirable they may be in themselves, or whatever encouragement he may take from some general expressions of scripture, he may find himself disappointed, and his hopes frustrated. We have no warrant from scripture, to expect this or that particular
worldly

worldly emolument or distinction, which we, perhaps through ignorance or corruption, desire or wish for; but we have sufficient reason to hope for those temporal blessings which God shall see to be for his glory and our good, without being able exactly to determine what those blessings are; because God hath promised that "all things shall work together for good to them that love him, to them that are called according to his purpose."

The christian's hope being, as we just observed, founded on the promise of God, is conversant about things that are unseen and future. What we now enjoy, we can with no propriety be said to expect. We may hope for the continuance of a good which is now present, because the continuance is a future thing; but so far as it is present, we do not hope for it. "Hope that is seen," says the apostle, "is not hope; for what a man seeth, why doth he yet hope for?" ‡ And therefore christians are spoken of as looking "not at the things which are seen, but at the things which are not seen." The great object of their hope is the perfection of their nature and of their happiness in a future world. "This is the promise that he hath promised us, even eternal life."

This promise of an eternal state of blessedness, includes in it whatever is necessary to fit us for that state,

‡ Romans 8. 24.

ftate. It contains all the particular promifes of fpiritual bleffings which we find in the facred fcriptures, of light to preferve us from error, of ftrength to mortify fin, of power to refift and overcome temptation, of affiftance to practice the duties which God requires, of growth in grace, and perfeverance in a ftate of holinefs. Having fuch great and precious promifes, a chriftian may reafonably hope for the bleffings promifed; even for all that grace which is neceffary to prepare him for glory. But it is fuppofed, that he himfelf is alfo active and diligent. It is in the ufe of our endeavors, while we attend on the means of improvement, that God communicates his divine influence. If we fo hope in the promifes of God, as to think that there remains nothing for us to do, but that we may fit at eafe, and fhall have the aids of the Spirit of God, whether we feek them or not, we abufe the doctrine of grace, and difhonour the gofpel of Chrift. The promifes of fpiritual bleffings always fuppofe that we are in fome fit temper to receive them; that our graces do not lie dormant in the foul, but are in fome degree of exercife. They are made to fome virtue, fome habit, fome activity in us; "They that wait on the Lord fhall renew their ftrength; they fhall mount up with wings as eagles, they fhall run and not be weary, they fhall walk and not faint." The doctrine of divine influence in forming our minds to virtue and holinefs, is fo far from making our endeavours ufelefs, that the

apoftle

apostle makes use of it as an incentive to diligence. * " Work out your own salvation with fear and trembling, for it is God that worketh in you both to will and to do of his good pleasure." And then only can we conclude our hope is a grace of the Spirit, and built on the promises, when it is accompanied with the most vigorous endeavors to be what God hath promised to make us. " He that hath this hope, purifieth himself as he is pure."

It affords unspeakable relief, to a soul that is purified in any measure from sin, that after this life, where he hath been called to so many conflicts, tossed in so many storms, and distressed with so many weaknesses, he shall enter on a state of perfect rest, holiness, and happiness; and that his happiness will be as durable, as it is great. When the christian hath the witness in himself, that he is an heir of heaven, he may in some degree partake of the happiness of that blessed place, and rejoice in hope of glory. He may have some prelibation of the joys of a future state, from a persuasion of their reality, and a well-grounded hope of his interest in the Redeemer, and in the promises of God through him.

It is not every one who professes to hope for heaven, that hath a title to it. Some have only " an uncertain fluctuating expectation of that which may be

* Philippians 2. 12.

be, or may not be."—Others are deceived in the foundation of their hope—There is the hope of the hypocrite which is as the spider's web, and will fail him when he hath most need of support. That hope which is the effect of divine influence on our souls will never make us ashamed. It arises from our perceiving in us the temper of heaven; and it tends to make us meet for the inheritance of the saints in light. It gives a new force to every spring of action, and powerfully urges us to press towards the mark for the prize of the high calling of God in Christ Jesus. This " hope we have as an anchor to the soul both sure and stedfast, and which entereth into that within the vail. Whither the forerunner is for us entered, even Jesus made an High-Priest for ever."

I have now attempted to give some just notion of christian hope.—It agrees with faith in this, that the object of it is unseen; but they are very distinct graces.—They differ in their objects; it is true every thing that is an object of hope is also an object of faith; but we believe many things which we do not hope for.—Faith respects things that are past as well as those that are future: Hope only those that are to come. " Through faith" says the apostle, " we understand that the worlds were framed by the word of God ." But the creation of the world is a thing we do not hope

hope for.—Faith takes into its view both good and evil: Hope only things that are good.—Faith is conversant about the threatnings as well as the promises: Hope only about the promises.—Faith and hope are also different acts of the mind, where the object about which they are conversant is the same.—Faith is a persuasion, that what God hath promised, he will certainly accomplish: Hope lays hold of the good that is in the promise, and in a sort anticipates the enjoyment of it.—Faith is an assurance that God is true: Hope is the satisfaction which the mind hath in the prospect of the happiness which is promised.—Immensely great is the blessedness which God hath provided for the children of men, and which is opened to us in the gospel of Christ. This blessedness is future, we cannot at present be admitted to it; now faith gives it a subsistence in the mind, and hope in some degree enjoys it; it is a kind of fore-taste of the happiness of heaven.—The influence which so great blessedness ought in reason to have on men, is very much abated by its absence and distance, how clear soever the promise. These graces in some measure supply this defect, and in proportion to their strength and activity, they will have the most happy effect; they will render us superior to every worldly consideration, and cause us to be holy in all manner of conversation.—Faith is the foundation; hope is the superstructure; and if the foundation be well laid, as it is when Christ and the promises

are

are the basis, we cannot raise our hopes too high; we cannot look, we cannot hope, we cannot wish for more, than God will in his appointed season bestow. Let us image to ourselves, the greatest good the human mind is capable of conceiving: Let us daily enlarge our views and desires, the blessedness promised will far exceed our highest conceptions and largest desires. " Eye hath not seen, nor ear heard, neither have entered into the heart of man, the things which God hath prepared for them that love him."

The last grace mentioned in our text is Charity, or Love.

Now love is in general a benevolent propensity or affection of the mind, proceeding from an apprehension of some excellency in the object, or some advantage which we receive from it. When this inclination is directed towards God, it is called love to God. When it is directed towards man, it is called love to man, or as it is expressed in the New-Testament, 'love to our neighbour, love to one another. Supreme love of God, and the sincere love of man, are shed abroad in the heart by the Holy Ghost; " the fruit of the Spirit is love." Mankind are too prone to be " lovers of their own selves " in a bad sense, to be meanly and sordidly selfish. How perfect soever God is in himself, however good he

hath

hath been to man, yet " the carnal mind is enmity against God." And with respect to man, " the spirit that is in us lusteth to envy." There may indeed be some kind of affection towards God, and a tender regard towards some of the human race, where there is no principle of religion : But that ardent, uniform, universal love, which christianity ever recommends, is an emanation from him who is love and the fountain of love.

Some suppose that by love or charity in our text, the apostle intends only love to men ; this is undoubtedly the subject of which he had been treating in the preceding context, and to which it is likely he had a particular reference in this place. But when he speaks of charity at large, and as a divine grace, it seems reasonable to conclude we are to take in every thing that is an object of it ; and especially love to God, which is the foundation of all virtuous love.

This love of God supposes just apprehensions of his nature and perfections. A man may feel some emotions of soul towards God, some affection of heart, when he thinks of him as the Former and Preserver of the universe, or when he surveys the beauties of the creation, and with what wonderful art all things are ordered for the convenience and comfort of man. His affection may rise higher, when

when he is acquainted with the hiftory of redemption; when he is told how God hath pitied fallen man, and fent his Son to be a propitiation for him. A lively defcription of thefe things may melt his foul into tendernefs and fome kind of love. The great God, when fet before him in this engaging light, may appear amiable. He may be forry he hath offended fo good a Being, and may refolve for the future to pay a proper regard to him. But all this time, he hath only a partial view of him, his contemplations are confined to the expreffions of the divine goodnefs. When afterwards the Deity is reprefented in the glories of his holinefs, his rectitude, his power, however thefe perfections are foftened by goodnefs; his heart rifes againft the Being poffeffed of them, this is not the God he had been imaging to himfelf, his affection ceafes, his defires vanifh. Whatever God is, whatever he does, muft be taken into view, as far as we are capable, when we form our conceptions of him. If we love God, we muft love his whole character. We muft love him as a holy, a juft, a powerful, as well as a good Being. 'Tis true, we cannot form too high ideas of his goodnefs, " God is love." But this is not his whole character, he is poffeffed of other perfections, which are as effential to him as goodnefs. And if we do not take thefe into our idea of him, the Being we conceive of is not God, whatever we afcribe to him. 'Tis only an imaginary

nary being, and our love is also imaginary: there is no such object as we pretend to love.

You will not understand me as if we were not to love God for his goodness, this is a part of his character, and a part of it which is truly amiable. It is by no means to be excluded, but we are not to confine our thoughts to this, if we do, we do not love God, whatever emotions we feel, whatever affection we pretend. In like manner, if our love of God proceed only from a belief of his love to us, it is not that divine grace which the scripture speaks of in so high terms. Some men, when they think of the instances of divine goodness to them, how God hath fed and clothed, protected and preserved them, especially if they imagine he hath set his love upon them, and made them heirs of the promises, are wonderfully moved with a sense of the distinction which is made between them and others, and their affections are engaged to him who hath done such great things for them. And this they call love to God, whereas it is only self-love, or natural gratitude.

I am far from thinking that self-love is a vicious principle, or that it is the design of religion to eradicate all regard to our own happiness. On the contrary, we are bound to love ourselves, and to do what we can to promote our own good, especially

specially our eternal felicity. The fault of the most is, that they neglect the care of their souls, and are too forgetful of that state into which they are hastening. The design of religion is not to destroy, but to regulate and sanctify our love of ourselves. Much less would I speak contemptuously of gratitude to God for his goodness to us. Nothing is more base than ingratitude: it is odious when we are guilty of it to men; it is much more criminal when it terminates on the blessed God. You can scarce fix a worse character on any one than to say he is an ungrateful man. When rightly exercised, gratitude is a virtuous principle, and a strong evidence of a good heart. But when we think of nothing in God, but his goodness to us, and are so employed in contemplating our own excellencies, as to forget, or to take but a slight notice of the infinitely superior excellencies that are to be found in him, it proves, not that we love God, but that we love ourselves. Now though self-love under proper regulations is not criminal, but right and fit, yet it doth not follow because we love ourselves that we certainly love God; if it doth, every one may be said to love God, for " no man ever yet hated his own flesh". Self-love is a natural principle, and if we advance no higher than nature, however it is improved, we have no reason to think we are born from above. A true christian admires and esteems all the divine excellencies, and can derive comfort and pleasure from the most awful at-

tributes

tributes of the Deity. He loves God for his holiness as well as his goodness. He doth not argue that God is an amiable Being merely because he hath determined to make him happy; for if he sees no other excellency in the divine nature, whenever he doubts of his own good state, he must doubt of the divine perfection. Whereas a sincere christian discerns an infinite excellency in God, however he may deal with him. He loves God, though he is not certain that his love proceeds from grace, and so cannot determine whether he is an object of divine love, whether he is in a state of favor with God or not.

Love unites the mind to the object beloved; you see the men of the world eager in their pursuit of worldly enjoyments, their souls cleave to them, they follow hard after them, they are unwearied in their endeavors to obtain them, in this way they shew their affection to them. So the christian thirsts for God, for the living God; his soul tends upward; he looks for rest from him, and from him only; he rejoices that God is what he is, he doth not wish him to be any thing else; he sees him to be an all-perfect Being; he desires to be united to and to enjoy him; this is all the happiness he expects; this is all the happiness he wishes for; he loves God above all; he delights in him as the chief good; he loves him on account of his own infinite excellency, and on account of his goodness to the children

dren of men; he defires nothing befides him; nothing in comparifon with him; nothing but what is confiftent with a fupreme affection to this greateft and beft of Beings.

This love of God is an exercife of the mind, but it is not a merely filent contemplative affection, it fets every fpring in motion, it leads to fubftantial acts of piety and obedience, it influences to all thofe practical expreffions of love which we are capable of. "This is the love of God that ye keep his commandments."

Where there is true love to God, it produces as its genuine effect, love to mankind. The view of his perfect goodnefs and moral rectitude gradually changes the foul into a likenefs to God. If we love a holy, righteous, good Being, we certainly love thofe qualities which form his character, and if we love thefe qualities, we fhall endeavor to form ourfelves by them, and to conduct agreably to them. Where there is a fupreme love of God, there will be an hatred of an oppofite character, and we cannot cherifh difpofitions in ourfelves which tend to form a character to which we have a fincere averfion. One who takes his notions of God from the gofpel, and hath an affection for him as he is reprefented there, cannot indulge to envy and wrath, malice and revenge. The amazing philanthrophy lanthropy of God will soften all his paffions, and influence to benevolence, kindnefs and love. A fenfe of the divine goodnefs in fending his Son to fave man, in providing fo great happinefs for thofe who deferved no favor at his hands, cannot fail to convince us of the excellency of goodnefs and charity even to the moft unworthy ; and muft have a moft wonderful efficacy to produce in us love to our brethren. " Hath God fo loved us, and fhall not we love one another,"—how conclufive the argument!—how forcible the motive!—What chriftian can refift it? In vain doth any one pretend to be fwallowed up in God, or to have a fupreme regard to him, who fails in this moft natural expreffion of love, which God alfo hath made the teft and evidence of it. " If any man fay, I love God, and hateth his brother, he is a liar. For he that loveth not his brother whom he hath feen, how fhall he love God whom he hath not feen."

The gofpel directs chriftians to exhibit a fpirit of love and benevolence to the whole human race; our bleffed Mafter defigned that every one within its reach fhould feel the happy effects of his religion; that they, who would not embrace it themfelves, might partake of the goodnefs of thofe who did.—Such is the genius of the gofpel—fuch are the generous fentiments it tends to infpire. That our Saviour had thefe large views when he recommended love to his difciples, is evident from his

parable

parable of the good Samaritan, which was designed as an illustration of the command, "Thou shalt love thy neighbour as thyself." This command plainly supposes that a degree of self-love is fit and right, otherwise we should be cautioned to oppose and suppress it, and not to make it the rule and standard of our love to others. Indeed if self-love is always criminal, and we are to endeavor wholly to eradicate it, it seems hard to account for the promises and threatnings of the word of God, those powerful addresses to our hopes and fears, which are entirely useless principles in religion if we are to be divested of all love to ourselves. Pretences to an absolute disinterestedness are idle and imaginary, if no worse. It is what God never designed, what he hath not instituted any means to effect. We must be made new creatures in a physical as well as a moral sense, before we can attain to it.— But there is no need of using arguments to satisfy men that they may be lovers of themselves; they know it full well; too many are so confined to themselves as to forget their brethren, and to sacrifice every thing to what they imagine to be their interest. The great difficulty is to persuade them to love any besides themselves; to love their neighbours as themselves. *As,* when used by our Saviour in this precept, is a note of similitude and not of equality Men will always have some special regard to themselves, but we are to love our neighbour sincerely and without any dissimulation;—our love to him should bear some proportion to our self-love—we ought to prefer his greater interest to our less, his spiritual to our temporal.

This love to our neighbour consists in a sincere benevolence towards mankind, and in a disposition to express our regard in all the ways we are capable of and have opportunity for. It implies a desire of their best good, and all suitable endeavors to promote it, a universally kind temper and affectionate carriage towards them. A general account of this virtue, and the manner in which it is expressed, we have in the preceding context; " Charity suffereth long and is kind; charity envieth not; charity vaunteth not itself; is not puffed up; doth not behave itself unseemly; seeketh not her own; is not easily provoked; thinketh no evil; rejoiceth not in iniquity; but rejoiceth in the truth; beareth all things; believeth all things; hopeth all things; endureth all things." This is the description which the apostle gives of charity; and what an amiable! what an excellent grace is it! What a paradise would this world be, if it universally prevailed! as the want of it makes it a place of uneasiness and vexation. This description is so full and and copious, that we need add nothing to it. Whoever answers the representation which is here set before us, hath all that love which the gospel requires. If he hath that command of his passions; that meekness and patience; that benevolence, good nature,

and

and condescension; that candor, generosity, and disinterestedness, which are here recommended. If he is free from envy and pride, is disposed to entertain the most favorable thoughts of his neighbour, can rejoice in his good, and never ceases in his endeavors to promote it; surely he cannot fail in those expressions of esteem and regard to all about him, which they have any right to expect, but will be ready to every act of kindness and office of love, according to their respective characters and circumstances. He will love his neighbour as himself, and carefully attend every social duty.

This charity is always to be exercised with prudence and wisdom. Though it "believeth all things" and "hopeth all things," yet this is only where there is reason to believe and hope. Charity is not blind, nor doth it connive at wickedness. "It rejoiceth not in iniquity," but the charitable man to his sorrow is witness of a great deal, and it is his endeavor according to his station, capacity, and opportunity, to reclaim the vicious, to reduce the erroneous, to confirm the wavering, as well as to support the afflicted, and relieve the indigent.

This christian love, I have said, extends to all mankind, but it is not exercised alike to all. Tho' all men have something valuable in them, something we ought to esteem and love; yet some have much more desirable qualities than others. Some are wicked and ungodly, others resemble God in holiness;

holiness; these latter are to be preferred in our offices of love: "The saints," says the psalmist, "the excellent in the earth, in whom is all my delight." There are also social instincts implanted in us by the Author of nature, to which he designed we should attend, and which are necessary to keep the world in tolerable order; such is the mutual affection between parents and children; between those of the same family, the same community, and the like. These instincts of nature christianity doth not condemn; it rather encourages and strengthens them. But though it is reasonable we should first take care of our own, our own relations and friends; yet it is selfish and mean to confine our regard to them. If christian charity begins at home, it doth not end there; it is generous and diffusive; wherever there is an object, the charitable man esteems himself bound to exercise his love. This law of charity our Saviour calls "a new commandment." Not that love was a new duty: it is a fundamental law of nature, and the spirit of every dispensation of God to mankind. But the noble sense in which our Lord explained it was new to the Jews. It was literally a new commandment as He proposed it, "A new commandment I give unto you, that ye love one another as I have loved you." It was urged from a new motive, and enforced by a new example, the example of Christ, which ought to be most cogent with those who profess themselves his disciples.

SERMON

SERMON VI.

Charity more excellent than Faith or Hope.

1 COR. XIII. 13.

And now abideth faith, hope, charity, these three; but the greatest of these is charity.

I Endeavoured in the last discourse to give some account of the graces mentioned in the text.

I am now, according to the method proposed, to inquire in what sense these graces are said to abide.

Faith, hope, and charity are particularly mentioned, because they are very much at the foundation of all moral rectitude. All other virtues of the christian life are connected with and included in these. For instance,

I. "Faith is necessary to the very being of religion or virtue. "Without faith," says the apostle, "it is impossible to please God; for he that cometh to God must believe that he is, and that he is the rewarder of them that diligently seek him." What room for piety, unless we believe there is a God, an all-perfect Being, to whom we may address our devotions, and yield our homage? How can there be virtue without a sense of our obligation to the supreme Lord—a law without a law-giver? How can we imitate God, unless we form just notions of his perfections? The heathen had their "Gods many, and Lords many;" but the deities they feigned to themselves, were impure, unjust, and cruel: And who could think they would be displeased with vices in their votaries, which they practised themselves? Some, among those who have been favoured with revelation, have entertained false, absurd, and even wicked sentiments of God—their practice hath been correspondent, ridiculous, absurd and wicked. We shall always form our notions of right and wrong according to the ideas we have of God. That will appear to us right and fit which we think agreable to the nature and will of the Deity whom we adore; and the contrary

will

will appear evil. That we might not fall into any mistake, God hath in his written word revealed to us what he is, and what he requires of us. This is a distinguishing favor, " he hath not dealt so with" every " nation ; and as for his judgments they have not known them."

The scripture teaches, that God is a Being of all possible perfection, that he is holy, just and good ; that he is acquainted with every part of our moral conduct, that he hateth all the workers of iniquity, and that he is armed with omnipotence to punish them. What can have a greater tendency to deter men from sin, and to excite them to the practice of universal holiness, than a firm belief, an impressive sense, of these great and important truths? A persuasion, that we are always in the presence of this infinite Being, who gave us all our talents, and to whom we are accountable for our improvement of them, must have a most powerful influence on a rational mind ; it must make us afraid of displeasing him, and earnestly desirous of approving ourselves to him. It may perhaps admit of dispute, whether the will of man is always determined by the greatest apparent good ; or, which comes to the same thing, by the last dictate of the understanding. But however this point is decided, it must be granted by all, that there may be motives strong enough to produce their genuine effect.

It

It is scarce supposable, that a being possessed of a principle of self-preservation should rush voluntarily on his own destruction; or that he should not chuse to be happy rather than to be miserable. The reason why men who profess to believe the great truths of religion do not act agreably, is because their assent to them is feeble and uncertain. If a man was admitted to behold the glory of heaven, and actually saw the misery of the damned, he would certainly endeavor to avoid the one and to obtain the other. This would undoubtedly be the effect, so long as there was any hope, that his endeavors would be crowned with success.

But what shall the sinner do? Having broken the law of God, he becomes an object of justice, and can find no way of escaping the righteous judgment of God. His faith in God abstractly considered cannot assure him relief. But in this extremity faith views Jesus Christ; it views him as set forth to be a propitiation, and contemplates the Deity according to the amiable representation we have of him in the gospel. Encouraged by the assurances of the word, a sinner returns to God with his whole heart, and believing there is mercy with him, he engages in the work of repentance and universal obedience. Take away the views which the gospel gives us of the blessed God, and the belief of a future state, what have we to raise us above

bove this world? What encouragement to oppose our lusts? What excitement to virtue? If men die like the brutes, it would not be so absurd in any to say, let us eat and drink for to-morrow we die. But when we consider ourselves as entering into an eternal state, an eternity of happiness or misery according to the things done in the body, what a powerful incentive is it to a life of piety and holiness!

It was their belief of a blessed immortality that supported the ancient patriarchs under their respective trials, and animated them to such exalted piety and holy fortitude, as procured a most honorable testimony from God, and rendered them illustrious examples to the saints in all ages. "These all died in faith," they received and entertained the promises of a future life, and the glorious prospect carried them triumphant through the dark valley. But however strong and eminent their faith was, the dispensation of Jesus Christ gives us much clearer and fuller evidence of future life and immortality, than the saints had under the Old-Testament. So some understand the apostle, when he says "life & immortality are brought to light by the gospel."¶ He doth not intend, that there was no evidence for the doctrine of immortality before the coming of Christ, but that the gospel removed the doubts and

¶ 2 Timothy 1. 10.

and uncertainties in which this truth had been involved: it more plainly afserted, and more clearly revealed this fundamental article: and therefore the arguments used by our Saviour and his apostles for a life of purity and holiness, are not so frequently taken from the present state, as they were under the former dispensations; but we are directly pointed to another world, and taught to look not at the things which are seen, which are temporal, but at the things which are not seen, which are eternal. Under the influence of these great and precious promises, believers cleanse themselves from all filthiness of flesh and spirit, and perfect holiness in the fear of God; they despise earthly things; they pursue something higher—something better; with Moses they esteem the reproach of Christ greater riches than the treasures of Egypt, for they have a respect to the recompence of reward— " This is the victory that overcometh the world, even your faith." But our faith being imperfect, the victory we obtain by means of it is imperfect also; in proportion as we increase in this grace, we shall rise superior to earthly things, we shall be heavenly in our conversation.

II. As Faith so also Hope hath very great influence on our moral temper. Says the wise man, " hope deferred makes the heart sick." What then must be the case, where there is no hope at all? What but death and destruction? " If thou
Lord,"

Lord," says the psalmist, "shouldst mark iniquities, O Lord, who shall stand ? But there is forgiveness with thee, that thou mayest be feared:" Plainly intimating that the only foundation of religious fear, is the thought that there is forgiveness with God. When a man hath no hope of the mercy of God, and the mind is sunk into a state of dejection and despair, there will be little or no spirit or strength to resist temptation, the unhappy wretch will rather abandon himself to vice, and gratify his lusts without controll. There have been such awful instances of the fatal effects of this unhappy state of mind, as should make us very cautious how we yield to it. To think our case desperate is the most effectual way to make it so.

On the other hand, when we view the blessed God in the light in which the gospel places him, when we represent him to ourselves as ready to receive and embrace the penitent returning sinner, and to treat him with the tenderness and love of a father ; when with faith and confidence we survey the great and comprehensive blessings which he allows and encourages us to hope for ; how animating the consideration ! And what a tendency hath it to put us on seeking those holy dispositions, which are necessary to qualify us for the blessedness he invites us to partake of ! When we not only firmly believe the promises, but by a lively hope enjoy beforehand the blessedness promised, it is

scarce

scarce possible but we should press forward to that perfection, which is the end of our faith and the great object of our hope.

Besides, as the christian's hope, when it is a grace of the spirit, is not a merely uncertain fluctuating expectation of the good contained in the promises, but contains some degree of confidence that we have a title to this good, so it naturally produces a deep sense of obligation to him who hath so greatly distinguished us, and raised us to such glorious hopes. And a just sense of our obligations to the blessed God, will powerfully constrain us to love, serve and obey him.

Some indeed will tell us, that a persuasion of our good state tends to make us indolent and careless. But if such ingratitude is agreable to the constitution of human nature, it is human nature depraved and vitiated, and not corrected and sanctified by the Spirit of God. When any are renewed by divine grace, their minds are in some good measure in a right state; their views are rectified; they reason justly, and conduct with propriety. To such as these, the experience they have had of the goodness of God, and the happiness he hath provided for them, affords an almost irresistable argument in favor of universal purity. The only reason any one can have to think he hath a title to the rewards of heaven,

heaven, is his finding in himself those marks and characters to which the promise is made; the more visible these marks are, so much the higher do his hopes rise. The exercise of grace is the proper scripture evidence that we are in a state of grace. When therefore a christian doth not feel the power of religion in his soul, when he becomes slothful and inactive in the work of the Lord, he can have but little reason to think he is a child of God, or an heir of glory—His hopes necessarily vanish—and he must be destitute of that peace comfort and joy, which the promises of the gospel tend to inspire: If he attain to the blessedness of heaven at last, which he cannot be sure of, he will have a lower seat there, than he would have had, if he had maintained a close walk with God, and had lived in the uniform practice of holiness and virtue. If these are not motives to the noblest improvements and highest attainments in the divine life, I know not what are. An assured christian is most likely to be a growing christian, he will naturally aim at further degrees of increase and proficiency. No one who is not satisfied of his interest in the promises can feel the force of the apostle's argument, with which he concludes his fine discourse on the resurrection—" Therefore, my beloved brethren, be ye stedfast, unmovable, always abounding in the work of the Lord, forasmuch as ye know that your labour is not in vain in the Lord." †

It

† 1 Corinthians 15. 58.

It appears by what hath been said, that faith and hope are very much at the foundation of religion and virtue. They greatly tend to promote the chriſtian temper.

III. This is not leſs true of charity, the other grace mentioned in the text. This is the chriſtian temper itſelf; it is that to which faith and hope were deſigned to bring us. Where love is, there is every grace.

A ſupreme love of God being implanted in the ſoul, all other virtues ſpring from it. A chriſtian finds himſelf attracted to him as his centre. He knows no happineſs where God is not to be enjoyed. He thinks every thing evil which ſeparates him from this infinite good. He follows after him in all the ways of his appointment. He maintains a conſtant intercourſe with him in the retired exerciſes of devotion. He prizes the ordinances of the goſpel, and viſits with ſacred pleaſure the place where he hath recorded his name, and where his honor dwelleth. His duty is his delight; and to glorify his Father in heaven his higheſt gratification. Animated by this divine principle, he reſiſts every temptation, he abſtains from every evil practice, he walks with holy circumſpection, and aims at a perfect conformity to him who is the ſtandard of perfection.

If

If we love God, we shall love Jesus Christ. We shall love him as there is in him a perfect resemblance of his heavenly Father, " being the brightness of his glory, and the express image of his person." We shall love him, as he hath effected a reconciliation between God and man; and laid a happy foundation for our becoming the objects of divine love and complacency; as through him, we have a delightful prospect of attaining a conformity to the moral character of the Deity, and to a state of compleat blessedness in the everlasting enjoyment of him.

If we consider love in its reference to mankind, that universal benevolence, which the gospel so warmly inculcates and so earnestly recommends, will always lead to the practice of every social virtue. It will keep us from every thing that would be injurious to our brethren; it will prompt to the most tender and affectionate carriage. Whatever duty we owe to our neighbour, in every station and relation; whatever God requires us to do for our fellow men, or they can reasonably desire from us, is all contained in the law of love. " For he that loveth another, hath fulfilled the law. For this, thou shalt not commit adultery, thou shalt not kill, thou shalt not steal, thou shalt not bear false witness, thou shalt not covet; and if there be any other commandment, it is briefly comprehended in this saying, namely, thou shalt love thy neighbour as thyself.

self. Love worketh no ill to his neighbour: Therefore love is the fulfilling of the law." Whenever our neighbour hath occasion for our help, or we see an opportunity of serving him, if we have sincere affection to him, we shall immediately embrace it. We shall not willingly harbour ill thoughts of him, or form designs against him; much less shall we say or do any thing to his prejudice.

Thus I have shown how all other graces or duties are connected with or included in those specified in our text. They are the springs of all religion: If these should cease, all religious motion and activity would also cease; but if these graces are in us and abound, the happy effect will be, we shall be neither barren nor unfruitful in the work of the Lord. There is no branch of holiness, which is not one way or another grafted on these cardinal virtues.

But we are to inquire not only why these graces are selected, but why they are said to abide. It is probable this is said to shew how much these graces excelled those extraordinary gifts, of which he had been speaking in the preceding chapter, and which were the occasion of such fierce contentions in the Corinthian church. Miraculous gifts were very useful in the first days of christianity to rouse mankind to attention; the gift of tongues was peculiarly necessary, to enable the professors of the gospel to

converse

converse with those who were not acquainted with their native language. But useful as they were, they did not convey any excellence to those who were possessed of them, nor were they always accompanied with inward purity. They were designed only for the present exigency, and were to be withdrawn when christianity was established in the world, and the sacred canon was compleat. "Whether there be prophesies, they shall fail; whether there be tongues, they shall cease; whether there be knowledge, it shall vanish away." But the case was very different with respect to the sanctifying graces of the Spirit: These gave men a real worth and excellency, and were to continue in all ages of the church. "Now abideth faith, hope and charity," those three eminent graces which are necessary for the support of true religion. If these should fail, christianity would be at an end; God would have no church in the world. These virtues constitute the christian character, and are the standing marks of a disciple of Jesus Christ. The least degree of true piety and holiness is to be preferred to the highest gifts. It was to be preferred to the extraordinary and miraculous gifts which were dispensed at the first promulgation of the gospel; and there is a parity of reason, or rather, the reason is stronger, that true virtue or goodness should be higher in our esteem, than the most eminent gifts any one can arrive at in these days. Although therefore we may covet earnestly the best

gifts

gifts that are now attainable, yet the gospel shews us a more excellent way; namely, to cultivate a spirit of love, to seek a nearer resemblance of the divine nature, and to secure a title to everlasting glory and happiness.

When the graces or virtues specified in our text are said to abide, it intends that they abide in every true christian. It is not enough that they are to be found in the church, or in some particular members of it, as was the case with the extraordinary gifts of the Spirit; they must be in every one who professes subjection to the gospel, they are essential to a disciple of Jesus Christ. He who hath not these graces, whatever he hath else, is nothing; he hath no excellency in the sight of a holy God, and he hath no foundation for peace and comfort in his own mind. But if he is possessed of faith, hope and charity, though he is destitute of every other accomplishment, he is in some measure what he ought to be; he is happy in the favor and love of God; and may rejoice with joy unspeakable and full of glory.

These excellent graces must not only be in us at some particular time, but they must abide. If we please ourselves with the thought, that having once exercised the grace of faith, or of hope, or charity, we are now in a safe state, and that there remaineth no more for us to do, it shows that we
are

are quite unacquainted with the nature of these excellent graces, and know not what true religion is. They are not so much particular acts of the mind, as gracious habits, and abiding principles of action, which must accompany the christian through the whole of life. If he should lose his faith, he would lose his religion, he could have no notion of duty, nor any sense of obligation.—A christian deprived of hope is weak as other men, he hath nothing to support him under the difficulties and trials of life, or to encourage him in the pursuit of glory, honor, and immortality.—Love is the very essence of christianity. There is not a greater contradiction in nature than a christian without love: You may as well suppose a man without a soul, or a rational mind without ideas. It is so necessary, that if a disciple of Christ should become destitute of love, he would, in effect, be in the same state he was in before he was a disciple. He would not be a christian, whatever he had been, or might now profess. The promise of God, that christians shall inherit eternal life, includes a promise to secure them from losing those gracious dispositions which are necessary qualifications for it. Nor may we content ourselves with any supposed habit of faith, hope, and love; we should keep them in continual exercise, and in this way they will continually grow and increase, till we arrive at the fulness of the stature of perfect men in Christ Jesus.

It is generally supposed, that when the apostle says, "Now abideth faith, hope and charity," he intends, that faith and hope are to cease with this life, whereas charity never faileth. This is not said, and some interpret the words quite otherwise. They consider them as connected with the preceding verse. "For now we see through a glass darkly; but then face to face: Now I know in part; but then shall I know even as also I am known. And now abideth faith, hope, and charity, these three; but the greatest of these is charity." i. e. says Mr. Lock, "Now we see but by reflection, the dim, and as it were enigmatical, representation of things; but then, when we shall be got into a state of perfection in the other world, we shall see things directly, and as they are in themselves, as a man sees another when they are face to face. Now I have but a superficial, partial knowledge of things, but then I shall have an intuitive, comprehensive knowledge of them; as I myself am known, and lie open to the view of superior seraphic Beings, not by the obscure and imperfect way of deductions and reasoning. But then even in that state, faith, hope and charity will remain; but the greatest of these is charity." 'Tis most certain, that many things will be the objects of faith to the saints, when they arrive at a state of perfection in heaven, as well as while they continue on earth. For instance, they must believe things that are past, and which will not then be the objects of their sight: They must
believe

believe the promife of God, that their happinefs fhall not ceafe, but fhall continue and increafe thro' eternity. They muft hope for the good that is to come, for the enlargement of their capacities, and the everlafting fatisfaction of all their defires.—" There will," fays Dr. Guyfe, " ever be a firm perfuafion of the truth of all that God fhall make known in that ftate, and an entire truft and confidence in him, for the endlefs perpetuity of all poffible bleffednefs ; and feparate fpirits there will, doubtlefs, live in an affured hope and expectation of the refurrection of the body, together with all the glory, which will attend that final manifeftation of the fons of God." In this view of things, faith and hope will remain, as well as charity, to eternity. But faith and hope will be very different from what they are now, and will anfwer very different ends, fo that it is by no means certain, that the common interpretation is not a juft one, as I may more particularly fhow hereafter.

I fhall leave the confideration of the other propofition to fome future opportunity—And fhall conclude at prefent with one or two reflections.

In the firft place, May it not ferve for a great leffon of humiliation, to confider how fmall a degree we have of thofe excellent graces, which are of fo much importance in the chriftian life ? Is it not owing to a defect here, that we have fo little of the fpirit of religion, and are fo negligent in the practice of it ? That a cold indifference and unworthy

worthy sloth prevail in a cause that calls for all our zeal and activity? That so many prefer the things of time to those of eternity? The mean enjoyments of sense, to those rational and divine pleasures which the gospel opens to our view? These are often the sorrowful complaints of good men when they reflect on the state of things in general; and which I fear we have all particular reason to make, when we reflect on ourselves. Were we sensible of our sinfulness, indigence, and guilt—did we entertain just conceptions of the goodness of God, and the kind provision he hath made in the gospel for our relief, certainly we should immediately repair to Christ the kind Saviour of men for relief and safety, we should submit to him, and rely upon him, in all those characters and offices which he sustains for the benefit of the children of men—Had we a powerful conviction of the great truths of religion, and did we maintain a constant pleasing sense of the perfections of God, we should not be so easily moved with every temptation, we should aim at being imitators of God as dear children, we should watch over our thoughts, our words, our actions—Had we a joyful well-grounded hope of that blessed immortality which the gospel promises, we should not be so anxious about earthly things; we should not find it so difficult to endure the trials and sufferings of the present state; we should be contented with the distributions of Providence, and resigned to the will of the all-wise disposer; we should commit

ourselves

ourselves into his hands, and be willing he should take his own way to conduct us to glory—Did the love of God reign in our hearts, we should chearfully obey all his commandments, our duty would be our delight, and it would be our meat and drink to do the will of our Father in heaven. When we have a peculiar affection to our fellow-men, we can go through any thing to serve them. We think we can never do enough for our children and friends. Oh! with what alacrity should we practise the most difficult duties, if we had that sincere, that ardent, that supreme love which he so infinitely deserves, and so justly requires from us—Finally, were we possessed of that universal undissembled benevolence to our brethren, which is the peculiar character of a disciple of Christ, should we not carefully suppress every angry, every envious, every unkind thought which begins to rise within us ? Should we not do good to all within our reach ? and especially to the friends and disciples of Jesus Christ ?—Happy the man who hath not reason to condemn himself in any of these instances, he may justly rejoice in God, and be persuaded that all is, and will be well with him.—But have not we reason rather to rejoice, that God is not strict to mark our imperfections, and that there is a way, in which we who so often offend, and always come short of those attainments we ought to make, may find pardon and acceptance? Doth it not become us to receive, with humble gratitude, the blessed report of the gospel; and to

rely

rely on the merits of him whom God hath exhibited as a propitiation?

Secondly, Of how great importance is it to be possessed of those graces which are at the foundation of all religion and virtue! We are concerned to have the character of christians, it becomes us to be more sollicitous to have those principles, without which we shall be only as " sounding brass and a tinkling cymbal." Faith, hope and charity, are necessary both to our safety and comfort. They are all graces of the Spirit of God. It is true, the arguments in favor of divine truth, ought to be sufficient to gain the assent of a rational being, and to produce a correspondent practice: But we are naturally inattentive to the truths of religion, and do not feel their importance, till they have such a present subsistence in our minds, as can be the effect only of divine influence. It should therefore be our earnest and constant prayer, that the God of hope would fill us with all joy and peace in believing, that we may abound in hope thro' the power of the Holy Ghost; and that he would shed abroad his love in our hearts. This will make the present world, instead of a vale of tears, a place of rest and happiness. This will cause us to glory in tribulation, to triumph in death, will be a foretaste of heaven, and an earnest of our admission there.

SERMON

SERMON VII.

Charity more excellent than Faith or Hope.

1 COR. XIII. 13.

And now abideth faith, hope, charity, these three ; but the greatest of these is charity.

IN speaking to these words I proposed, First, To consider the graces here particularly specified.

Secondly, To enquire in what sense they are said to abide.

Thirdly, To show that Charity excells both the others, or is the greatest of the three.

It

It is the last of these that now comes under consideration, viz.

To show that Charity excells Faith and Hope, or is the greatest of the three.

This is by no means said to put a slight on these other graces; or to set them in a diminutive point of light. They are placed, you see, in the highest class—these three are the most eminent of all the virtues which adorn the christian. But love is the most excellent of all—It is greater than faith, that necessary and important grace, of which the New-Testament speaks so highly, and to which it ascribes such great things—It is greater than hope, that pleasant and comfortable grace, which affords the mind such vast satisfaction, which is so necessary to support us under the trials, and to quicken us to the duties of the christian life. So the apostle tells us, "the greatest of these is charity."

Faith and hope are great and important graces, but charity is still greater. What makes this a little surprizing, to some who look but a little way, is, that they have a very superficial and contracted view of charity. They consider it as a virtue, which leads us to think well of our neighbour, and now and then to do him an act of kindness. Whereas these are only some of the smaller branches of charity.

charity. They may proceed from the principles of nature. Charity is a divine grace implanted in the soul; which extends as far as there are any suitable objects. It hath respect to every thing that is amiable, and to nothing else. It is true, they who are possessed of this grace often find their affections drawn out to objects that are in themselves mean, base, and unworthy their love: But this is because good men have a great mixture of sin and imperfection while in this life. So far as love is a grace of the Spirit, it implies that we have just views of things, and are suitably affected towards them. God who is the greatest and best of beings is the first object of esteem and affection, and our love is placed upon others, in proportion as they resemble him, and we are connected with them. Of consequence we shall love Jesus Christ above all things in heaven or in earth, as there is in him the brightest resemblance of the Deity. This divine love unites the heart to the whole human race; it includes a sincere affection to mankind, and a disposition to promote their good. It wishes well to all; it esteems those who are worthy of esteem; it hath delight in those who have any thing delightful in them; and expresses itself in such ways as it sees reason and hath opportunity for. It is not a single act, much less doth it consist in external actions. It is a gracious habit—a divine affection—a benevolent propensity—which is exercised whenever an object presents, towards God supremely, towards man universally.

verfally, towards both fincerely. Our Saviour speaks of it as the fum of all religion. " Thou shalt love the Lord thy God with all thy heart, and with all thy foul, and with all thy mind; this is the firft and great commandment—and the fecond is like unto it, Thou fhalt love thy neighbour as thy felf. On thefe two commandments hang all the law and the prophets."† Love comprehends the whole of the religion taught, and the duty required, in the law and the prophets. It is the root from which all that is good proceeds. We perform no duty aright where there is not love. No wonder, when we confider charity in this large fenfe, that the apoftle fpeaks of it in fuch high terms, as greater than either faith or hope—It is more perfective of human nature—It is the end to which the other graces were defigned to bring us—It remains when they in a good meafure ceafe and fail.

Firft, Love is moft perfective of human nature. It renders us moft like to God in dignity and happinefs. Faith and hope, neceffary as they are for us, do not in themfelves affimilate us at all to the Deity. There is no room for either of thefe, or for any thing like them in the all-perfect Being—Faith is credit given to fomething which we know not of ourfelves, upon the authority of another; what a perfon knows, he cannot with propriety be faid to believe. But " who hath directed the fpirit of the Lord, or being his counfellor hath taught him?
With

† Matt. 22. 37, 38, 39, 40.

With whom took he counsel, and who instructed him, and taught him in the path of judgment, and taught him knowlege, and shewed to him the way of understanding ?"† The great God takes all things past present and future into one comprehensive view, all actual and all possible existence. Universal truth is open before him—This glorious Being enjoys perfect unmixed felicity. He cannot be greater, better, or happier than he is, because he is essentially as great, as good, and as happy as he can possibly be. And as he is what he is by necessity of nature, so he is invariably the same. He hath nothing therefore to hope or to fear—Both faith and hope imply some imperfection. Faith supposes that the subject of it hath not a perfect view of things, that he needs the testimony of some other to convince him of a truth proposed.—Hope supposes there is some good we do not enjoy, and which we expect to attain—The essential knowlege and happiness of God takes away all possibility of the existence of these graces in him—But love is a glorious perfection of the Deity.

What but love or goodness could move the great First Cause to produce the creatures which he hath formed? He could have no other motive than to exercise the infinite benevolence of his nature, and that propensity there is in him to do good. As all his intelligent creatures were formed with a capacity of happiness, so happiness was provided for them

† Isa. 40. 13, 14.

suited

suited to their capacity. The goodness of God was particularly displayed in the formation of man, it was visible in the structure of his body, but more in the nature of the human soul, in his capacity of enjoyment, and in the good designed for him. When man had fallen from God, the goodness of God was still apparent, yea, the misery of man afforded occasion for the display of his infinite grace. It was this, which brought the Son of God from heaven, clothed him with human flesh, and caused his bloody sacrifice. This is the source of all the wonders of redeeming love. " In this was manifested the love of God towards us, because that God sent his only begotten Son into the world, that we might live through him."* Every part of this amazing scheme shows that God is good—that he is love. The appointment of a Saviour to relieve creatures so infinitely unworthy—The person constituted to be the Mediator—The sufferings he underwent to procure our salvation—The blessed state of immortality to which the gospel was designed to raise us.

Love is that perfection which God hath delighted to honor. When Moses made that request, "shew me thy glory;" he answers, "I will make all my goodness pass before thee." ¶ And the apostle not able to express the greatness of divine love, says, " God is love." † It is not said, love is a

perfection

* 1 John 4. 9.   ¶ Exodus 33. 19.   † 1 John 4. 8.

perfection of the divine nature, or God hath great love, but "God is love." Love is his very nature, his essence, he is all love. God is often said in scripture to be wife, to be holy, to be just; but this form of expression is never used concerning any other perfection. He is not said to be holiness, justice, or wisdom, but he is said to be love; as if this property of the divine nature was more intimately essential to it than any other. His supreme delight is in himself, because he is most capable of affording satisfaction to his own infinite mind. And for the same reason, he loves his own image wherever he is pleased to impress it. He loves the angels who resemble him in his moral character. He loves all the children of men; but he loves them with a special distinguishing love, who are renewed in the spirit of their minds, and are holy in any measure as he is holy.

We see a great deal of the goodness of God now, we hope for still higher expressions of it hereafter. When the christian thinks what God hath done, and contemplates on what he hath promised to do, he cries out with astonishment, What manner of love is this! But how little do we know in the present state, in comparison with what we shall know, and taste, and feel, when we shall no longer see through a glass darkly—when we shall arrive at that blessed state of perfection which the gospel

encourages.

encourages us to look and hope for—when there will be no fatherly corrections mingled with the expressions of divine love—when we shall meet with nothing which seems contrary to it—nothing which tends to raise objections in our minds against it—when God will manifest himself and his grace in a way beyond and above our present conceptions.—When we, on the other hand, shall have no mixture of darkness, imperfection, or sin, which as so many clouds intercept our view of the Deity, prevent our forming just conceptions of him, and our discerning goodness, where, but for the weakness of our minds, it would be most clear and evident. Then shall we perceive, without the least intervention of a doubt, that God is good; yea, that he is goodness itself.

From what hath been said, it is evident, that when love reigneth in the soul, there is a resemblance of the blessed God, who is the standard of perfection. The more full we are of love, the more we are like him. This grace creates a resemblance more than any other. Goodness is the peculiar glory of his nature, and to be like God is the greatest glory of our's. Love is a ray from the Father of lights—a beam from the Sun of righteousness—It is an emanation from the Deity, and makes us partakers of the divine nature.

How

How excellent! how glorious! do the holy angels appear, according to the account we have of them in scripture, who are full of love. They have the cleareſt views of the Deity—They are wrapt up in contemplation on the infinite excellency of his nature—They admire, venerate, and adore that Being whom they cannot comprehend—They ſee a glory in all God does—They diſcern a beauty, a harmony, a goodneſs, in all his diſpenſations. And they often expreſs their admiring ſentiments, in devout anthems and lofty alleluia's—They praiſe God for what he is—They give thanks to him for making them capable of enjoying any degree of his infinite happineſs—They bleſs God when they ſee others as happy as themſelves—Yea, when the good of other beings is made to exceed their own.— They know not what it is to envy their ſuperior bleſſedneſs—This is ſo far from diſturbing their peace, that they derive happineſs from the happineſs of others. It increaſes their joy that their fellow-creatures partake of it. We read that when God laid the foundations of the earth, " the morning ſtars ſang together, and all the ſons of God ſhouted for joy."† Thoſe benevolent ſpirits rejoiced, that God was about to communicate more of his goodneſs; and that there were like to be other beings to partake of the happineſs which they felt. So entirely diſintereſted, ſo generouſly diffuſive is their goodneſs! From the ſame amiable temper, they chearfully ſtoop to become miniſtring ſpirits

---

† Job 38. 7

to

to mankind. They run—they fly—in obedience to their almighty Lord; and they delight to be employed in acts of kindness and love. They encamp around us—They keep us in our way—They redeem us from evil—They sincerely rejoice when a sinner repenteth—They excite us to good—They convoy the souls of the blessed to the mansions of rest which are prepared for them—and they delightfully mix in the society, and in the praises of the glorified saints. In the Jerusalem which is above, there are " an innumerable company of angels," as well as " the spirits of just men made perfect."† How pleasingly illustrious! are these blessed spirits, while they are continually employed in acts of love; and without regret do a multitude of kind offices to creatures so much inferior to them! In what view could they appear greater or better, than while they imitate God in this amiable perfection of his nature? We can think of their strength, their knowledge, their wisdom, without any sensible emotion; but when we contemplate on them, not only as wise and powerful, but as good, as made up of goodness, and that all their acts of goodness spring from love to their great Creator and Lord, then we esteem, then we love them. This gives them a real excellency, this constitutes their true glory. And thus glorious, thus excellent shall we be, in proportion as we are possessed of that divine temper, which gives such a lustre to the angelic nature. How

† Heb. 12, 22, 23.

How truly excellent is he, who finds the love of God governing his whole foul, and carrying him above all created good, and at the fame time, defcending " in a regular fubordination from God upon the creature" ! and who always acts agreably to this inward propenfity, this heavenly affection ! Such a temper and fuch a conduct conftitute the true dignity of human nature, and are well fuited to the fuperiority which God hath given us in his creation. Can any thing be more fit and right, than that we fhould have a fupreme love of him, in whom centres every thing that is great, every thing that is good, every thing that is neceffary to abfolute perfection ? This is one of the firft dictates of reafon, the firft duty of a rational creature. The argument holds, that we fhould love all other beings, in proportion as there is any thing lovely in them, or which comes to the fame thing, in proportion as there is in them a refemblance of God. Indeed our love is not to be confined to the virtuous and holy. Thefe, it is true, ought to be firft in our affection ; but if we would be the children of our Father in heaven, our benevolence muft reach to all, the evil as well as the good, the juft as well as the unjuft. The example of this all-perfect Being fhould be a fufficient incentive to this univerfal charity. But there are many other motives. Mankind are all our brethren, children of the fame father ; they partake of the fame nature ; they have all immortal fouls, capable of being for-

ever

ever happy, but in danger of everlasting misery. Our wants, our dangers, our hopes, our fears are in general the same, for we ourselves are also in the body, and we ought to do to them, as we should reasonably expect they would do to us, if we were in their situation and they in our's. A change of circumstances is not uncommon in this mutable state, and we may greatly need their help who now ask relief from us. But our love is most like the love of God, when it proceeds from a principle of pure benevolence, and we have no prospect of advantage, at least of none in this life. Such love, in some degree, human nature is capable through grace of attaining, and the more we possess of this excellent spirit, so much the nearer do we approach towards perfection.

Love adds a lustre to every other quality. Look upon a monarch, who hath arrived at great power, amassed large treasures, and acquired extensive knowledge, but is destitute of goodness, hath no tenderness for those who are under him, no desires to promote their welfare: What is his dignity? it resembles that of the prince of the power of the air, who hath a great capacity and ability, but improves it all to disturb the universe, and to injure the creatures of God. Such an one is an object of abhorrence and not of respect; his exalted station only makes his crimes more conspicuous, and his person more detested. But let a prince to his other

eminent

eminent qualities join that of goodness, a love to mankind, a defire to do them good ; let him improve his power and influence to make others happy, how juftly is he ftiled a benefactor? Every one is charmed with his diffufive benevolence, he reigns in the hearts of his fubjects, and his goodnefs makes fuch impreffions as will never be erafed.

Look on our bleffed Redeemer, who never affumed the honors of this world, who lived a private and defpifed life, but went about doing good, was ever follicitous to ferve the bodies and fave the fouls of men, and after enduring the moft unparalleled fufferings fubmitted to death for us finners ; confider him only while he was " found in fafhion as a man," how much more illuftrious doth he appear, than the great and mighty conquerors, who deftroyed cities, overthrew kingdoms, and waded through torrents of blood, that they might extend their dominions, and encreafe the number of their vaffalls! This honor hath every chriftian, fo far as he is poffeffed of the temper, and imitateth the example of the bleffed Jefus. Every approach to that truly divine love which was perfect in him, raifes his difciples to a proportionable degree of excellency and dignity. It makes them honorable in the eyes of men. Even bad men cannot but value a virtue which is fo beneficial to the world, unlefs by it the good man eclipfes them, where they would be tho't to excel. Men of religion honor them as they refemble semble that glorious Being who is the great object of their affection and esteem. "For a good man some would even dare to die." But, which principally deserves notice, they are honorable in the sight of God, whose approbation is of more worth than would be that of the whole intelligent creation. It is more to be valued in itself, and it hath infinitely more important consequences. He hath graciously connected some degree of pleasure and inward satisfaction with this excellent spirit in this life, and he will gloriously own and reward the charitable man in another world.

They who are possessed of this divine love feel a sacred rest and peace, which the world can neither give nor take away. When their love is fixed immediately on God, the mind ever finds enough to yield the most exquisite pleasure, the most ravishing delight. It finds itself lost in pleasing contemplation on the divine excellencies, they are so transcendent—so infinite. The more we think of God, the more deserving he appears to be of our love, till at length creature delights vanish, or become too contemptible for our notice. A soul that hath just sentiments of God, and a holy love to him in exercise, cannot be greatly disturbed with the loss or want of these things, because they are not the principal objects of his desire. If he may have God for his portion, he is content, though he have nothing else;
and

and can join, in some degree, with the psalmist, in his holy transport of joy and exultation, ‡ "Whom have I in heaven but thee? and there is none upon earth that I desire besides thee." He would give up riches, honors, friends, every earthly enjoyment, which comes in competition with his God: He esteems them, when compared with this infinite good, nothing, less than nothing, and vanity. Filled with the love of God, he accounts none of his commandments grievous; he performs them with sacred delight and satisfaction; Christ's yoke is easy and his burthen light. He desires perfection in holiness, and he presses after it; he mourns that sin is so prevalent within him; he watches, he strives, he prays against it; and he rejoices in the thought that heaven is an holy place, and that there he shall be perfect, as in love, so in universal holiness.

Such discoveries of God, and such exercises of divine love, are not experiences, which we may, as it were, gaze at and long for in a distant prospect. Many, many, have been thus highly favoured. This carried the martyrs triumphantly thro' their sufferings; they felt that love to God and desire to be with him, which made them take pleasure in those tortures, which shortened the time when they

should

‡ Psalm 73. 28.

should be absent from the body, and present with the Lord. This hath sometimes raised the saints above the things of time and sense, and caused them to live a heavenly life while they remained on earth. They have found the ways of religion to be ways of pleasantness, and all her paths peace. The allurements and temptations of the world have lost their force, and for a time the attempts of Satan have been fruitless and vain. Have we never, in our sacred retirements, found the love of God shed abroad in our souls to such a blessed degree, as that, although we were not taken up, as St. Paul was, to the third heaven, yet we have forgotten that we were inhabitants of this earth, and have been able with thankful admiration to contemplate, " and to know the love of Christ, which passeth knowledge." ? Can you recollect such precious moments? Say, my beloved brethren, did you ever find any earthly pleasures equal to them? any to be compared with them? It is for want of this supreme love to God, or a more ardent exercise of it, that we enjoy so little true happiness, and that we seek it in the enjoyments of this life which are not capable of yielding it. In the language of inspiration, we " have forsaken the fountain of living waters, and hewed out cisterns, broken cisterns, that can hold no water."

When

When this love to God evidences itself in love to men, it is impossible to express the satisfaction which the charitable man enjoys. To feel no envious, no malicious, no angry thoughts towards our neighbour, to lay aside revenge, to return good will for hatred, to wish well to all, to do good to all as we have opportunity, to be able and willing to communicate happiness to our fellow-creatures, to find ourselves engaged in sincere and earnest addresses to heaven, even for those who have injured and abused us, what a divine calm ! what seraphic pleasure must it yield to the mind ! " No similitude drawn from earthly things can adequately represent it. It is itself, not only an emblem of heaven, but the very foretaste of that serenity of soul which is the happiness of just men made perfect." How blessed is the man, who can rejoice in his neighbour's good as in his own ! Such an one, in a sense, partakes of all the good the all-bountiful God bestows : And how is his pleasure encreased, when he is employed to convey any part of it to others ! It is a saying of our divine Master, happily preserved by St. Paul, " it is more blessed to give than to receive." † " The poor receiver," says one, " thinks himself happy, the bountiful giver certainly is so, the latter is the greatest gainer." Charity is it's own reward. It affords unspeakable delight to the mind, and raises our nature to the highest dignity.—It makes us feel, I speak with humble reverence, something of the happiness

† Acts 20. 35. which

which the blessed God enjoys, who is good and doth good. It anticipates the blessedness of heaven. It yields joy which a stranger to this divine grace cannot conceive, and which the charitable man cannot utter. ¶ " Amongst the many refinements upon pleasure, which this polite age hath produced, it is a wonder to me," says an elegant modern writer, " that so few have hit upon this of relieving the poor ; (one principal branch of the grace I am speaking of). Were it possible for one of our fine gentlemen to enter into all the dismal circumstances of want, poverty and distress ; and to consider how far it might be in his power to remove them, he would be content, perhaps, to part with some of his present enjoyments, or rather to exchange them for those of a more exquisite nature. Methinks a man ready to perish for hunger, has hardly so pleasant a relish for his food, as he that gives it him. We ought heartily to pity the covetous, who do not know the pleasure of being charitable."——But I forget myself, and the short limits to which I am confined, while I discourse on this divine subject.

Secondly, Charity is greater than Faith or Hope, as this is the end to which the other graces were designed to bring us. Faith and hope are important

¶ This discourse was delivered at the quarterly charity-meeting in *Boston*.

tant and neceſſary graces, but that which principally renders them of ſo great importance, is, that they tend to produce that divine love, that conformity to God, which is the perfection of human nature. Theſe eminent virtues would have been of far leſs uſe in a ſtate of innocence. After the apoſtacy of man the ſyſtem of religion was greatly changed and adapted to him as a fallen creature. Our views of God, if man had maintained his integrity, would have been much more direct than they are now, ſomething like what they will be in heaven. There would not have been that darkneſs in our minds, which makes a written revelation neceſſary; at leaſt there would have been no room for faith in a Mediator, which is ſo eſſential to the religion of a ſinner. The happineſs we ſhould have had a title to would have been preſent, ſeen, and felt, and therefore would not have been ſo much the object of hope. We ſhould not have had ſo great need of theſe graces to have brought us near to God, and to have excited in us that love and obedience which conſtitute ſo great a part of the happineſs of a reaſonable creature. We now need faith, not only to teach us that God is, but that he is a rewarder of them that diligently ſeek him, a truth for the knowledge of which we are indebted to revelation. We need hope to purify our ſouls, and to move us to thoſe returns of gratitude and obedience, which we ought to make to him, who hath not only done ſuch great things for us, but hath

Y promiſed

promised more than we can now conceive of. If these graces bring us to a conformity to God, and to that divine temper which christianity tends to inspire, they answer the end, there is no farther occasion for them. These graces then are only means to a great and noble end. Necessary as the means are, the end is greater. All our duty to God and man are summed up in this one word Love; but faith and hope are necessary to enkindle the love of God in our souls, and to influence to fervent charity to one another. Faith and hope are the foundation, charity is the superstructure. They are of no worth, unless they operate by love; but where they are productive of this effect, as they always are when they are graces of the Spirit of God, they are of the greatest importance. "You see then," as one justly observes, "how justly charity claims the pre-eminence above faith and hope. For it stands highest in the very order of nature, as far as the crown in the arched roof of the temple, is above the lowest part of the foundation. Faith is instrumental, and hope farther subservient to charity, but charity is perfective of faith and hope. Faith is the beginner, hope the promoter, charity the finisher of virtue. It is the complement of all duty both to God and man; it is the end of the commandment;" it is the fulfilling of the law; it compleats the christian. When love is perfect, the christian is perfect. It is the sum and end of all religion. It was the religion of paradise—It

was

was the religion of Abraham—It was the religion of Moses—It is peculiarly the religion of Jesus Christ—It is the religion of the saints on earth—and it will be the religion of just men made perfect.

This leads us to say,

Thirdly, Charity is greater than faith and hope, as this remains, when they in a great measure cease or fail—This is generally supposed to be the meaning of the text; and the rather, because it is said a little before, " charity never faileth." It was observed in the last discourse that there will be faith and hope even in heaven: But they will be very different from faith and hope as exercised on earth. Our present persuasion of a future state of immortality is founded on our belief of the divine promise; the satisfaction we have in this persuasion arises from the pleasing expectation of the good contained in the promise. But we are while here, very much unacquainted with the nature of heavenly happiness; we are assured it will be exceeding great, but we cannot tell in what particular employments and enjoyments it will consist. " We know not what we shall be."—— When we get to heaven, we shall have a clear preception of that happiness which we can now scarce form any idea of; we shall partake of those exalted pleasures which are the object of our faith and hope. We shall enter into the joy of our Lord.

Lord. We shall still believe and hope for the continuance of the good we enjoy. But the confidence the glorified saints have of this continuance will be little different from knowlege or certainty. What occasion can they have of evidence, of any testimony to the truth of the promises, or any assurance of their entire and eternal accomplishment, when they find these promises gloriously fulfilling, and the life of heaven actually begun? When they no longer view heavenly objects, through, as it were, a dim mirror, but have an intuitive comprehensive discernment of them? When there will be no tempter to vex their minds with suspicions of their own sincerity, nor any moral imperfection to weaken the evidences of their title to the divine favor.

Besides faith and hope will in a great measure cease as to their use. We greatly need these graces in the present state of imperfection and sin. We need faith to give us right notions of God and of his gracious purposes to the children of men—We need hope to carry us through the trials and difficulties of life—We need both to influence us to holy love, to purify our hearts, and to make us meet for heaven. But we shall have no need of the evidence of faith, when we know as we are known; there will be no occasion for the comforts of hope, when there will be nothing to give us uneasiness; we shall not want arguments to prove that God is good, when we are actually admitted
to

to a felicity, large as our desires, and equal to our capacity of enjoying. We shall have no use for those slow and imperfect methods of attaining knowlege and purity, which we ought to improve here, when we shall have such clear and distinct views of God and divine truth, as will immediately transform our souls into an entire correspondence. We shall not need the means when we have attained the end. We may therefore without impropriety say, that faith will be swallowed up in vision, and hope in enjoyment. But then charity will be in perfection. This illustrious virtue will not only promote, but it will be one principal ingredient of our happiness. We shall be able to contemplate on the great First Cause without interruption from the cares and amusements of this present evil world, or the impertinent suggestions of a busy adversary. We shall see his divine perfections in a glorious harmony; and shall behold his infinite wisdom and goodness where we least expected them. And transported with gratitude and holy joy, we shall join the glorious spirits around the throne in singing praises to God and the Lamb. Our love will be pure and intelligent; our gratitude sincere; and our praises without interruption.

Even in the present state, where our knowlege is so imperfect, when we contemplate the works of God with seriousness and attention, especially when we look into the glorious scheme of man's redemption, we meet with such discoveries of the divine

perfections

perfections as surprize and astonish us; but how many new wonders will arise before the glorified mind? We shall then have a more just sense of our own unworthiness, and a clear perception of the blessings which Christ hath purchased for us; we shall be able, according to our measure, to comprehend, what is the breadth, and length, and depth, and height, of redeeming love, and shall know, in a higher sense than we can now conceive of, the love of Christ, which infinitely surpasses the knowlege of the highest seraph. With the deepest humility, we shall prostrate ourselves before the throne of the all-perfect Jehovah, and cast our crowns at his feet. With pleasing admiration, we shall look on our once crucified but now exalted Lord, and think on his stupendous love, who, tho' he was rich, for our sakes became poor, that we through his poverty might be rich. We shall bless the "God and Father of our Lord Jesus Christ, who hath blessed us with all spiritual blessings in heavenly places in Christ." We shall adore that grace, which hath triumphed over our unworthiness, forgiven our iniquities, healed our moral disorders, conducted us through the snares of this evil world, and brought us safe to eternal glory. Having much forgiven we shall love much. As the capacities of our souls will continually expand, our knowlege of God will increase, and we shall be transformed more and more into his image; and the more we see of God, and partake of his goodness, the more elevated will be our expressions of admiration, of love, of joy and praise.

We shall rejoice with our brethren in glory. In heaven we shall feel no angry passions, no murmuring discontent, no secret envy; we shall be free from wrangling controversies, and perverse disputings; the blessed inhabitants will be of one heart and of one mind; they will be united in one noble society; they will mingle their conversation and their praise. They will congratulate one another, and, if need be, help one another. There will indeed be no occasion of charity to relieve the necessitous, or to assist the distressed, in that blissful state, whence all sorrow is everlastingly banished, and where God himself undertakes to supply every want from his own inexhaustible riches. There will be no room to cover one another's faults, where none will think or do amiss; or to exercise candor and tenderness to the ignorant and infirm, where all are arrived to a full maturity in knowlege and purity. "In one word, God is love, and he that dwelleth in love dwelleth in God, and God in him: and where God dwelleth, all is love, and all is lovely, and therefore all will be happy for ever and ever."

What an affecting thought is it that the world is so much a stranger to this excellent spirit! that there is so little charity among the professed disciples of Jesus Christ! But with what an ill grace shall we lament the want of love in others, if we are destitute of it ourselves. It becomes us first to look to our own hearts, and to secure that divine principle which is of so great importance in the christian life, and is so necessary to prepare us for that blessed world where perfect love and good-will reign forever. The love of God is the fountain of all other rational and religious affection. Where this is found, the mind is full of goodness, and will be ready to all acts of kindness and love. Let us pray, that God would grant us clearer views of his own divine excellencies, especially as they are manifested in Christ, that beholding his glory, we may be changed into his likeness, and may imitate his great example by doing good to all. This divine love will make us like God; it will be an evidence that we are his children; it will be a spring of unspeakable delight in this world; it will prepare us for heaven, as it will be a main part of our felicity there.

> " Then constant Faith and holy Hope shall die,
> " One lost in certainty and one in joy:
> " Whilst Thou, more happy Pow'r, fair Charity,
> " Triumphant Sister, greatest of the Three,
> " Thy office, and thy nature still the same,
> " Lasting thy lamp, and unconsum'd thy flame,
> " Shalt still survive———
> " Shalt stand before the Host of Heav'n confest,
> " Forever blessing and forever blest."

1 PETER III. 19, 20.

By which also he went and preached unto the spirits in prison; which sometimes were disobedient, when once the long-suffering of God waited in the days of Noah, while the ark was a preparing, wherein few, that is, eight souls, were saved by water.

"THE goodness of God," says the apostle, "leadeth thee to repentance." This is the genuine tendency of the divine patience and forbearance; and this is sometimes the happy effect: The hearts of sinners touched by a gentle influence from above, are affected with a sense of their ingratitude, receive the impressions of religion, and are made willing and obedient.

This is not always the case. Sometimes, alas! men perversly encourage themselves in wickedness from that goodness of God which ought to have a directly contrary effect: Because God delays to testify against their crimes, they rashly presume that to-morrow will be as this day, and their hearts are more fully set in them to do evil. This was the conduct of the inhabitants of the old world: They were disobedient notwithstanding the wise methods which God took to reclaim them: They abused his patience and long-suffering, till justice ascended the throne, and doomed them to the most amazing destruction—" By which also he went and preached unto the spirits in prison; which sometimes were disobedient, when once the long-suffering of God waited in the days of Noah, while the ark was preparing, wherein few, that is eight souls, were saved by water."—Various have been the interpretation of these words, which some have esteemed one of the most difficult passages in the whole Bible.

What I propose is to shew—Whom we are to understand by " the spirits in prison"—How Christ went by the Spirit and preached to them—Their inattention to the divine admonitions, and misimprovement

provement of the long-suffering of God—The astonishing catastrophe they hereby brought on themselves—While the few who believed and repented were saved.——When I have thus led you to the true meaning of the words, I shall add those practical reflections which naturally arise from the subject.

First, I am to say who are intended by "the spirits in prison."

Some of the ancient fathers supposed, that the apostle intended the souls of the saints confined in some part of Hades, as in a prison, which they called Limbus Patrum; that the soul of our Saviour went, in the space between his death and resurrection, to this place, released them from their confinement, and translated them to heaven. § The church of *Rome* took advantage of this opinion to introduce their favorite doctrine of Purgatory, which hath greatly added to the revenues of the church, and given their priests an unreasonable ascendency over the consciences of men.—The interpretation of our text, which gave occasion to this absurd doctrine, hath no foundation in scripture or reason, and yet there have been protestant writers, of considerable name in the learned world, who have embraced it.

A

---

§ See Dr. Benson's Differtation on this text.

A learned divine ‖ of the last century imagined, "that the disobedient souls mentioned in our text were in hell, not in the lowest regions, but in the more tolerable parts thereof, that Christ in his spirit preached to them, and prepared them by the glad tidings of the gospel, and after carried them to heaven in triumph, as a glorious spoil taken out of the jaws of the devil." But as Dr. Benson justly observes, though "St. Peter hath mentioned our Lord's preaching to the spirits in prison, yet he says not one word of his delivering any from thence, or of his translating them to a state of glory and happiness."

Some have tho't this notion of Christ's preaching to the spirits in prison, in the time between his death and resurrection, countenanced by that article in the creed called the apostles' "He descended into hell." But this creed is falsly ascribed to the apostles. It was not composed till long after their day.—This article of the descent into hell was not at first inserted in it; and it is quite uncertain what was intended by the words at the time they were introduced, so that nothing can be argued from them, with respect to the meaning of our text. And seeing this passage in the creed, as it now stands, is quite dark and unintelligible, and rather leads to erroneous sentiments, than conveys any important truth, it had much better be wholly omitted,

‖ Dr. Henry More. See his works, page 18.

omitted, when we teach our children this summary of christian faith.   To go on,

Calvin, an interpreter one among a thousand, taught, § that by the " spirits in prison" the apostle intended the spirits of good men in a separate state. These spirits, he supposes were happy before the coming of Christ, but a great accession was then to be made to their happiness. They therefore earnestly looked for that great event and the promised salvation, as watchmen look out from a watch-tower. And according to their expectation, the grace of Christ was manifested to them, and they partook of the blessed influences of his Spirit.—This construction of the words seems by no means natural and easy, and in order to support it, we must conclude either that the apostle called those disobedient who were possessed of a principle of holiness, or that in writing he put one case for another, contrary to all the rules of syntax ; † neither of which is easily to be admitted.

The late Lord Barrington supposed, that the Logos had resided in a visible manner at the entrance of paradise, to guard the way to it—that when the world was to be destroyed, this Logos left the place of his residence and went into the ark
—that

§ Vid. Calvin Comment. in Loc.

† Discrepat (fateor) ab hoc sensu græca syntaxis. Calvin.

—that "he preached to those, whom God had shut up in it as a prison and safe custody; who had been disobedient all the time that God waited with patience on the old world; which was while Noah was building the ark; but became obedient, after that the Logos, going into the ark, preached unto them." ¶ But to this it is replied, "It is not evident that Noah's family were disobedient all the while that the ark was preparing—that they were converted in the ark—or that the Logos preached, or so much as resided in the ark—Besides, the ark is no where called a prison, nor is it the usual phraseology of scripture to call living men by the name of spirits, whereas that word is often applied unto the dead."

Mr. Hallett says, "it seems pretty plain, that, before the coming of Christ, death was a state of insensibility. But as our blessed Saviour carried the penitent thief into heaven with him, so he seems to have awakened the souls of all the good men that had died before him from the beginning of the world. In this sense, says he, it seems necessary to understand what the apostle says, 1 Pet. 3. 19. By which spirit (or soul of Christ, when separated from his body) he went and preached unto the spirits in prison." ‡ But perhaps it is not so plain as this learned writer seems to think it was, that the old

---

¶ Lord Barrington's dissertation on this text, at the end of his essay on the several dispensations of God to mankind.

‡ Mr. Hallett's note on Heb. 11. 40. in his continuation of Mr. Pierce's paraphrase.

old testament saints slept till the coming of Christ, many passages of scripture look the other way; and the Jews used to express their belief of the happiness of the righteous immediately after their death, by saying they were carried to Abraham's bosom. Our Saviour countenances this opinion when he says of Lazarus, that " he died and was carried by the angels into Abraham's bosom. * Our Lord's argument from God's saying of himself, " I am the God of Abraham, and the God of Isaac, and the God of Jacob," naturally leads us to conclude not only that there would be a glorious resurrection of the saints, but that they did in the mean time exist and act in a separate state. " God is not the God of the dead, but of the living." † Besides, who can imagine, that when Christ is said to have preached to the spirits in prison, it was intended that he went and preached to persons in a state of absolute insensibility? or that, by those who were disobedient in the days of Noah, we are to understand all the saints who had lived before the coming of Christ.

I shall only add the interpretation of the excellent archbishop Leighton. He supposes, that our text refers to " the mission of the Spirit, and preaching of the gospel by it, after his resurrection, preaching to sinners and converting them according to the prophecy, which he first fulfilled in person,

and

* Luke 16. 22.   † Matthew 22. 32.

and after more amply in his apostles. That prophecy Isaiah lx. 1. The Spirit upon him, and it was sent from him on his apostles, to preach to spirits in prison, to preach liberty to those captives, captive spirits ; and therefore called spirits in prison, to illustrate the thing the more, by opposition to that Spirit of Christ, the Spirit of liberty, setting them free ; and this to show the greater efficacy of Christ's preaching than of Noah's, though he a signal preacher of righteousness, yet only himself and his family, eight persons saved by him, but multitudes of all nations by the Spirit and preaching of Christ in the gospel." † This sense of the words is very agreable to scripture language, and might easily be admitted, were it not that our Saviour's preaching to the spirits in prison is expresly limited to the days of Noah, and to the time when the ark was preparing ; and therefore can by no rules of interpretation be understood of Christ's personal preaching after he had assumed a body, or of his preaching by his Spirit in the apostles.

Having given an account of the interpretations of this text, which we think ourselves bound to reject, ¶ it remains that we endeavor to show what is

the

---

† Leighton's comment on 1 epistle Peter, vol. I. p. 91.

¶ Other solutions of this passage may be seen in Dr. Benson's judicious dissertation annexed to his paraphrase on the first epistle of Peter.

the true meaning of the words; and they seem to be rendered difficult, more by the attempts that have been made to explain them, than by any obscurity in the text itself.

The most general and obvious interpretation of this passage is, that " by spirits in prison" the apostle means the spirits or souls of the wicked inhabitants of the earth, who lived before the flood, and who are now shut up in some part of Hades, as in a prison; and are reserved to the judgment of the great day. We observed before, that it is not usual in scripture to call living men by the name of spirits, but this word is often used of those who are in a state of death. " The spirit shall return to God who gave it."‡ " The spirits of just men made perfect." ‖ It is not said in our text, the spirits that *were* in prison, as it is said they *were* sometimes disobedient, but the spirits *in* prison, now in prison; who after their death were imprisoned, and still remain in custody. The words speak their present condition in consequence of their former disobedience. It is not said that Christ preached to them while in prison, he preached to those who are now in prison, while they were upon earth, not in hell, purgatory, or any other place in the invisible world. —The place where wicked men are confined after death is, with great propriety, called a prison, as

they

‡ Eccl. 12. 7.   ‖ Heb. 12. 23.

A a

they are held there in safe custody, so that there is no escaping. 'Tis said, § "When the thousand years are expired, Satan shall be loosed out of prison." The same Greek word is used as in the text—Of this prison, this receptacle of separate spirits, Christ hath the keys. "And hath the keys of Hades and of death." ‡

We are to enquire in the second place—How Jesus Christ "went and preached" to these spirits in prison. There is no reason to suppose that our Lord preached to the antediluvian sinners in person, or in a visible appearance; on the contrary, the apostle, after having spoken of Christ, as "quickened by the Spirit," says, "by which also," i. e. the Spirit, "he went and preached to the spirits in prison."—When it is said he went, it doth not necessarily imply a removal from one place to another, the apostle seems to use this expression in conformity to the phraseology of the old testament, when God remarkably appeared in any work of his providence, especially when he was pleased miraculously to interpose. Thus it is said, "the Lord came down to see the city."—"And the Lord said— "let us go down."‖—"I am come down to deliver them." ¶ So Christ went and preached in the days of Noah, he gave the antediluvian sinners the plainest

§ Rev. 20. 17. ‡ Rev. 1. 18.
‖ Gen. 5. 7. ¶ Exod. 3. 8.

est and clearest warning by that holy patriarch, it was as if he had himself come to declare their danger to them. The apostle Paul uses the same kind of language, when he says of our Saviour, he " came and preached peace to you which were afar off." † He came by his apostles, as in our text he went by Noah, who had the influence of that Spirit which dwelt in Christ without measure.

By a number of passages in the old testament, it seems as if the kingdom of grace was, even from the establishment of it after the apostacy of man, under the direction of the Logos, who was " in the form of God," and thought it not robbery to appear in the character of God—of the infinite Jehovah; as he afterwards " took upon him the form of a servant" and was " found in fashion as a man;" He was the LORD—Jehovah, who sometimes condescended to make a visible appearance to the patriarchs—He was the Angel of the covenant, who presided in every dispensation of the kingdom of God, who sent his prophets and messengers from time to time to bear testimony to the truth of religion, to instruct and reform mankind. He inspired Noah, who is called in St. Peter's second epistle "a preacher of righteousness," ‡ most probably, because he was sent to warn the antediluvians of the approaching catastrophe, to exhort them to repentance and the practice of righteousness. It is

† Ephesians 2. 17. ‡ 2 Peter 2. 5.

no very distant construction, to say Christ did what he sent his servant Noah to do, whom he inspired and assisted in his preaching. And what can be more natural than to suppose, that while the holy patriarch was, by the direction of heaven, preparing the ark for the security of himself and family, he frequently testified against the impiety, dissoluteness and vice of the men of that generation, and warned them to flee the wrath that was to come? This is what his own benevolent mind would naturally prompt him to, and we might reasonably expect that he would be imployed on this errand by the God of heaven, as this is perfectly analogous to his usual method of dealing with sinful men. He warns them of their danger, before he executes his vengeance upon them; and calls them to repent, before he overwhelms them with destruction.

Thirdly, We are told the inattention of these sinners to the divine admonitions, and their misimprovement of the long suffering of God. That infinite Being, who is not willing that any of his creatures should perish, but had rather they would turn and live, did not deal with the anted luvian sinners as he justly might have done. They had corrupted their way, and were guilty of the grossest enormities; but he was kind and gracious to them, and used means to reclaim them from their vicious practices. The Spirit of God strove with them;

Noah

Noah preached to them: But they would not be reclaimed, they turned a deaf ear to the kind warnings of heaven, and continued in their difobedience, this afforded an opportunity for the exercife of the patience and "long-fuffering of God which waited in the days of Noah." It is an awful account which is given of the moral ftate of the antediluvian world in the fixth chapter of Genefis, "The earth was corrupt before God; and the earth was filled with violence. And God looked upon the earth, and behold it was corrupt, for all flefh had corrupted his way upon the earth. And God faid unto Noah, the end of all flefh is come before me; for the earth is filled with violence through them: and behold, I will deftroy them with the earth." But even when they had arrived at this height of wickednefs, and feemed quite ripe for deftruction, God forbore to punifh them, "And the Lord faid, "my Spirit fhall not always ftrive with man, for that he alfo is flefh, yet his days fhall be an hundred and twenty years." The Chaldee paraphrafe has it, "A term fhall be given them of one hundred and twenty years, if they will convert." ¶ So long God would defer the judgment with which he had threatned them. So long he would give them a fpace for repentance, by which their ruin might be prevented. In all this time Chrift preached to them by his Spirit, under whofe infpiration, Noah faithfully fet before them their fin and
the

¶ Vid. Ainfworth's Ann.

the danger they were in of the righteous judgment of God.

Fourthly, We are to take notice of the amazing catastrophe these sinners brought upon themselves. God waited long on the old world, but the time of his patience was limited, at the end of one hundred and twenty years the flood came and swept them all away. "In the second month, the seventh day of the month, the same day were all the fountains of the great deep broken up, and the windows of heaven were opened. And the rain was upon the earth forty days and forty nights. And the waters prevailed exceedingly upon the earth; and all the high hills, that were under the whole heaven, were covered, and all flesh died that moved upon the earth.—And they were destroyed from the earth. And Noah only remained alive, and they that were with him in the ark." * God gave them a space to repent, and they repented not; and at length sudden destruction came upon them. It was sudden though it had been so long predicted, because they despised the warning, and gave no attention to the admonitions of that faithful preacher of righteousness whom God sent unto them. They went on in their business, their diversions, and their sins, till they found themselves actually involved in the ruin they had made light of. "They did eat, they drank, they married wives,

* Genesis 7. 11. &c.

wives, they were given in marriage, until the day that Noah entered into the ark; and the flood came and destroyed them all." † Happy for them, had this been the whole. Alas! this amazing judgment put an end to their time of probation, it did not put an end to their existence. Like the evil spirits whom they had resembled in their impiety, they were reserved in chains unto the judgment of the great day. Our text speaks of them as " spirits in prison," *now* in prison, it affords no glimmering of light, no reason to expect that the prison doors will be opened, till they are opened to bring them before the tribunal of their judge.

Fifthly, Our text leads us to observe, the salvation of Noah and his family in this general devastation. " Wherein few, that is, eight souls, were saved by water." Out of the water—in or amidst the water—by water—by the means of the water—were carried safely through the water—or were saved during the time of the deluge by water, thus variously are the words rendered by critics. Whatever is the exact translation of the original words in this place, the plain meaning is, that these eight persons were preserved, when the rest of the world were destroyed in the deluge. However others despised the prediction of the judgment which God would bring on an ungodly world,
Noah

† Luke 17. 27.

Noah believed the divine threatning, and repaired with his family to the ark, which by the direction of heaven he had prepared, and by this wife conduct saved himself and his house. " Noah only remained alive, and they that were with him in the ark." ‡ " By faith," says, the author of the epistle to the Hebrews, § " Noah being warned of God, of things not seen as yet, moved with fear, prepared an ark to the saving of his house." This temporal salvation was an emblem and a type of that eternal life to which by the grace and mercy of God he became entitled, for while by his faith and obedience he " condemned the world," he " became an heir of the righteousness which is by faith." The like figure whereunto, even baptism doth now save us," as in the words following our text, " not the washing away the filth of the flesh, but the answer of a good conscience towards God." As the ark was the means of preserving Noah and his family, so baptism, if accompanied with inward holiness, or the answer of a good conscience, will save christians from eternal ruin through the resurrection of Jesus Christ.

Having endeavored to illustrate the words of our text, I am now to lead you to some practical reflections.

And in the first place, Behold the goodness and forbearance of God! He " saw that the wickedness

‡ Genesis 7. 27.   § Hebrews 11. 7.

wickedness of man was great on the earth, and that every imagination of the thoughts of his heart was only evil continually." So that it is said, " it repented the Lord that he had made man on the earth, and it grieved him at his heart." The words are exceeding strong, and emphatical, and were designed to express God's infinite displeasure at their flagrant and enormous guilt; which was such, that he determined to cut them off from the face of the earth; and yet he forbore to punish them, he seemed loth to give them up, and to enter on his work, his strange work; and bring to pass his act, his strange act. ·He defer'd it that they might have opportunity to repent, and so prevent the threatned evil.

You have in this instance a striking display of the goodness of God, and a specimen of his method of dealing with sinners. The whole course of his moral government shows that he loveth righteousness and hateth all the workers of iniquity. The perfection of his nature disposes him to testify against a thing so vile and detestable as sin is; his rectoral holiness obliges him to punish it. But justice doth not immediately seize the offenders. God bears with their perverseness and ingratitude, and even waits to be gracious. To this his patience and long-suffering it is owing, that we are any of us on this side the grave, that we are out of everlasting burnings: To this it is owing that you still have

B b   the

the advantages of the gospel, that you enjoy the means of grace, are favored with the strivings of the Spirit, and, after all your provocations, are invited to the happiness of the gospel. God's infinite abhorrence of sin serves to illustrate his goodness in bearing with the sinner, he bears with those who continually affront and dishonor him, he bears with them and continues their existence, when with infinite ease he could punish—he could destroy them. This is not after the manner of men. Their patience is soon exhausted; they know not how to put up affronts, or to bear injuries, especially from those whom they have obliged by acts of kindness and love. But God always acts like himself, like a Being of boundless goodness and grace. " My thoughts, are not your thoughts, neither are your ways my ways, saith the Lord. For as the heavens are higher than the earth, so are my ways higher than your ways, and my thoughts than your thoughts." ‖ Especially his thoughts of goodness are unutterably—infinitely superior. How ought such amazing benevolence, such vast obligations to affect our souls, and to melt them into penitence, love and obedience ! How base ! how ungrateful is it, to make no other return to our kind benefactor, than rebellion and disobedience ! And yet is not this too much the temper, and the practice of mankind ? The goodness of God doth not lead men to repentance.—On the contrary, by contemplating

‖ Isaiah 55. 8, 9.

templating his love, his grace, and forbearance we are naturally led to reflect,

In the second place, on the obduracy and ingratitude of human nature. Though God waited on the old world all the while the ark was preparing, and Noah reasoned with them of righteousness and the judgment that was coming upon the world; yet how few were wrought upon! only the preacher's own family; none others repented; none others fled to the ark for safety. We are ready to wonder at their stupidity, and to condemn their unbelief and impenitence. But how nearly do we resemble them! We have continual admonitions, not of a flood of water, not of any general temporal judgment approaching, though we are not secure from public or private calamities; but we are told, that the Lord is at hand, that death is nigh, even at the door, and that after death is the judgment. At the same time, we are pointed to an ark of safety, Christ Jesus is preached in our streets, we are invited to partake of the blessings of his kingdom, through this man are preached to us repentance and remission of sins. How few attend to these calls! Do not the most put far away the evil day, and encourage themselves in their impenitence, because judgment is delayed? Do not some presume on the divine goodness, and harden their minds against the warnings they have in the word and providence of God? because he is patient and long suffering? " Because

cause sentence against an evil work is not executed speedily; therefore the heart of the sons of men is fully set in them to do evil."

Forbear then to cry out of the antediluvian sinners; turn all your resentment against yourselves, condemn your own ingratitude, your own obduracy, your own impiety. What should you think of one of your fellow-men who should conduct towards you, as you conduct towards the blessed God? Should you not think, you ought to despise, reject and punish him?—It is not possible, that one of your fellow-creatures should treat you with such base ingratitude as you discover to this greatest and best of beings; because you have never been able to confer such vast obligations. How ought you then to abhor yourselves, and to repent in dust and ashes! How readily! how heartily should you return to him through Jesus Christ! Notwithstanding all your provocations, he is not willing that you should perish, he is still ready to receive you into the arms of his mercy, to bestow eternal life and happiness upon you. How unreasonable! how ungrateful! to misimprove this his goodness to a purpose directly contrary to it's genuine tendency, and his gracious design! to continue in sin because his grace abounds! Nor is such a conduct more criminal than it is dangerous. God is merciful and gracious, but he is also holy and righteous: he bears long, but he will not bear always: His Spirit strives with man, but this Spirit may

may be refisted, he may be grieved, he may depart so as never to return. God may say with respect to you, as he said when provoked by the sinners of the old world, "my Spirit shall not always strive with man." They had their day of grace, they did not improve it, and the most awful destruction came upon them.

Which leads us to remind you,

In the third place, of the power, the justice and severity of God. What a dreadful day was it when the flood came, when "the fountains of the great deep were broken up, and the windows of heaven were opened," and the rain poured down in cataracts forty days and forty nights, and the world was involved in one general ruin! Parents with their children, husbands and their wives, brethren and their sisters! Those who had been companions in wickedness were now companions in distress! Think—you heard one calling to another for help, but none able to help himself in this scene of misery. Imagine them climbing the highest rocks, and ascending the loftiest mountain for safety; but soon finding the loftiest summits, and the tallest mountains covered with the waters, which continually increased, till all was destroyed! and while they could find no hope of relief, beholding the ark conducted safely by an almighty invisible Pilot, through this universal devastation. Now they saw the wisdom of righteous Noah, who had repaired to the
only

only place of security—They reflected on their impious scoffs at that holy man, and their contempt of his warnings—They view him secure under the divine protection, but find themselves devoted to inevitable perdition—sinking into death—into eternity. What a dreadful picture is here!—Whose hearts doth not recoil!—Who doth not tremble at the sight when it rises up in his imagination!

But remember, that the world is reserved for a yet more awful destruction, as we are taught by St. Peter, 2d Epistle, iii. 5, &c. " By the word of God the heavens were of old, and the earth standing out of the water, and in the water: whereby the world that then was, being overflowed with waters perished. But the heaven, and the earth which are now, by the same word are kept in store, reserved unto fire against the day of judgment, and perdition of ungodly men." You now live at ease, you are laying schemes for futurity.—Your Lord delayeth his coming, he bears with your impiety and folly; " he is long-suffering to us-ward, not willing that any should perish, but that all should come to repentance." This is his design, this is the tendency of his goodness.—You perversly abuse his patience, and encourage yourselves in a life of dissipation and vice. " But the day of the Lord will come as a thief in the night, in the which the heavens shall pass away with a great noise, and the elements shall melt with fervent heat, the earth also and the works that are therein shall be burnt up."

Image to your minds the aftonishing scene which is here defcribed. Can you conceive any thing more tremendous? When we fee the heavens in a blaze, when the arrows of the almighty are darted around us, and the peals of thunder found loudly in our ears—When the earth fhakes under our feet, and we fear left it fhould open and fwallow us up, or left our dwellings fhould fall and bury us in their ruins, we have fome idea of the majefty and power of God. But thefe are only faint emblems of the amazing terrors of that day, when all nature will diffolve, and the fire of an angry God will be enkindled on the earth!—What is the moft near and penetrating lightning to a world in flames, and all confuming in one general conflagration!—What is the moft violent fhock of an earthquake, which caufes our habitations to reel and totter, or perhaps lays wafte a town, a city, or country, to the crufh of a world, and the entire overthrow of all the works of nature and of art!—When we think of this dreadful cataftrophe, inadequate as our conceptions are, well may our flefh tremble for fear of God, and we be afraid of his judgments!

"There is in general," fays Dr. Burnet, "a great analogy between the two deluges, that of water, and that which will be of fire. At the flood, the windows of heaven were opened above, and the abyfs was opened below; and the waters of thefe two joined together to overflow the world: In like manner,

manner, at the conflagration, God will rain down fire from heaven, as he did once upon Sodom; and at the same time the subterraneous store-houses of fire will be broken open; which answers to the disruption of the abyss: and these two meeting and mingling together, will involve all the heaven and earth in flames.—Where are now," he adds, "the great empires of the world, and their great imperial cities? Their pillars, trophies, and monuments of glory? Shew me where they stood, read the inscription, tell me the victor's name. What remains, what impressions, what difference or distinction do you see in this mass of fire? But it is not cities only, and works of men's hands, but the everlasting hills, the mountains and rocks of the earth, are melted as wax before the sun; and their place is no where found. Here stood the *Alps*, a prodigious range of stone, the load of the earth, that covered many countries, and reached their arms from the ocean to the *Black Sea*; this huge mass of stone is softened and dissolved, as a tender cloud, into rain. Here stood the African mountains, and *Atlas* with his top above the clouds. There was frozen *Caucasus*, and *Taurus*, and *Imaus* and the mountains of *Asia*. And yonder towards the north, stood the *Riphæan* hills, clothed in ice and snow. All these are vanished, dropped away as the snow upon their heads, and swallowed up in a red sea of fire. " Great and marvellous are thy works, Lord God Almighty; just and true are thy ways, thou King of saints." † In the midst of this general devastation, they will behold the Lord in the air,

† Burnet's Theory, vol. 2.

air, coming to take vengeance on a guilty world, not by depriving finners of their exiftence, but by dooming them to hell, to dwell in everlafting burnings. This fecond death will be the principal object of their fear. Gladly would they be confumed in the general burning—Gladly would they hear a fentence of annihilation—But to appear before their Judge—Before a Judge, whom many of them have defpifed and rejected—A Judge, who comes to execute the threatnings of his word, and to overwhelm them with irrefiftible deftruction—What terror and diftraction will feize their guilty breafts!—They will be ready in their aftonifhment and defpair, to fay to " the rocks and the mountains, fall on us, and hide us from the face of him that fitteth on the throne, and from the wrath of the Lamb: For the the great day of his wrath is come; and who fhall be able to ftand?" But ah! where will be the rocks to fall on you? or the mountains to cover you, when all will be melted with fervent heat?— You muft appear before an omnifcient Judge, and at his tribunal give an account of the things done in the body. You muft hear a black catalogue of your fins, every one of which will be as a dart ftriking through the liver—a fword piercing to the heart. Yes, thofe fins you are not now afhamed to commit, which, perhaps, you pride yourfelves in, will give you the moft uneafy reflections, when you find that for them you are bro't into judgment. Your guilt will ftrike you dumb, you will wifh, but wifhes will be in vain, that you could recall the unhappy moments of your paſt life—that you might have another ſpace for repentance.

But, miſerable ſinner, doſt thou, like the ſcoffers ſpoken of by St. Peter, make a mock at religion, and ridicule the expectation of Chriſt's coming to judgment? or doſt thou ſay in thine heart, " my Lord delayeth his coming ;" and on this preſumption indulge to ſenſuality and wickedneſs? Hear the warning which our Lord hath given; " the Lord of that ſervant ſhall come in a day that he looketh not for him, and in an hour that he is not aware of, and ſhall cut him aſunder, and appoint him his portion with hypocrites, there will be weeping and gnaſhing of teeth." Several paſſages ſpeak of the coming of Chriſt to judgment as a thing ſudden and unexpected, and which will ſurprize the ſinner in his ſecurity, his mirth, and his wickedneſs. Our Lord tells us, " as it was in the days of Noah, ſo ſhall it be alſo in the day of the Son of man, they did eat, they drank, they married wives, they were given in marriage, until the day that Noah entered into the ark, and the flood came and deſtroyed them all. Likewiſe alſo as it was in the days of Lot, they did eat, they drank, they bought, they ſold, they planted, they builded, but the ſame day that Lot went out of Sodom, it rained fire and brimſtone from heaven and deſtroyed them all, even thus ſhall it be in the day when the Son of man is revealed." But be this as it may, the ſovereign Lord of life may ſay, " thou fool, this night thy ſoul ſhall

shall be required of thee." And death will be the end of the world with you. If it find you unprepared, it will put an end to all your hopes and endeavors; your souls will be kept in prison, in safe custody, like the spirits of the antediluvians, to the judgment of the great day. Then they will be loosed, not to renew their crimes, but to receive the punishment of them—to receive their final sentence, and to enter upon their everlasting doom. It will aggravate their misery to behold the righteous secure under the divine protection, and happy in the smiles of their Judge. They will see the dead in Christ arisen, and with those saints that shall be alive at his coming, caught up to meet the Lord in the air; where, at a distance, they will behold the desolation brought on the earth, and with humble gratitude give glory to him that hath loved them and washed them in his blood. This amazing distinction will give them the most pungent sense of their own folly; while they will be obliged to own the wisdom of those who have in time provided for eternity. Which leads me

In the last place, To contemplate the safety of those who believe and obey the messages of God. At the same time that God executed his vengeance on the impenitent world, he discovered his paternal care of those who believed his threatnings, and put themselves under his protection. They were saved and reserved to replenish the earth. So those who are admitted into the true church, not only by

an

an external washing, but by the renewing of the Holy Ghost, will be finally saved by Christ. Not only eight souls, but an innumerable multitude, which no man can number, will be found among the triumphs of divine grace, and will, by their grateful acclamations, add to the magnificence of that glorious day; which will be the day of their redemption from the grave—the day of the gladness of their hearts—the day of their entrance into the joy of their Lord.—Blessed be the God and Father of our Lord Jesus Christ who hath provided for our salvation from sin and death, as he did of old for the preservation of Noah, by commanding him to prepare an ark. Noah would have lost the security which God designed for him, if he had disbelieved God, and had not entered into the ark. So if you neglect Jesus Christ, if you continue in unbelief and impenitence, you will miss the salvation of the gospel. You will soon leave this world, it is of infinite importance, that when you become separate spirits, you may not join the spirits in prison, but may be admitted into the society of the spirits of just men made perfect, and be forever happy with the Lord. It is an important admonition with which St. Peter concludes his discourse on the second coming of Christ, " seeing then that all these things shall be dissolved, what manner of persons ought ye to be in all holy conversation and godliness, looking for and hastening unto the coming of the day of God."

SERMON

Revelation V. 9.

Thou waſt ſlain and haſt redeemed us to God by thy blood.

IF you deſire to ſee a perfect character, read the hiſtory of our bleſſed Saviour. You behold in this illuſtrious perſonage an aſſemblage of virtues, without the leaſt fault or blemiſh. Image to yourſelf any thing that is lovely, any thing that is excellent, you find it in him. If any one excellency ſhine with diſtinguiſhed luſtre, it is love. It was goodneſs, pure diſintereſted goodneſs that brought him into the world—he exhibited the moſt amiable benevolence during the whole time of his continuance

ance on earth—he gave the highest proof of love in the closing scenes of life. All the sufferings he underwent were for us. Our sins were the cause, our benefit was the end, of all he endured. The love of Christ is the admiration of angels: How ought it to affect us, who are so deeply interested in it! With what sacred gratitude should we remember, that he was slain to redeem us by his blood!

Our text is part of a song, which the saints and angels above are represented as singing in heaven, in honor of our blessed Redeemer. St. John saw in vision a sealed book in the right hand of him that sat upon the throne. When no other person was found " worthy to open the book," our Lord Jesus Christ, under the representation of " a Lamb that had been slain for sacrifice, approached the throne, and took the book out of the right hand of him that sat on the throne." And when he had received the book, the heavenly church prostrated themselves before him ; " and they sung a new song, saying, Thou art worthy to take the book, and to open the seals thereof ; for thou wast slain, and hast redeemed us to God by thy blood, out of every kindred, and tongue, and people, and nation ; and hast made us unto our God kings and priests ; and we shall reign on the earth."

We are to discourse at this time upon that clause only, " Thou wast slain, and hast redeemed us to God by thy blood." It is proper,

First,

First, To inquire what we are to understand by redemption. And then,

Secondly, To show how we are redeemed by the blood of Christ.

First, We are to inquire what we are to understand by redemption.

This word, in it's original sense, intends the paying down a valuable consideration for the recovery of something which was once our's, but is now in the possession of another. We buy it again— we purchase it a second time. If it is freely given to us, there is no redemption; but if we lay down an equivalent, we redeem it. The scriptures do not always use the term in this strict and proper sense. It is often transferred from it's original meaning to a sense which contains only a part of it; or rather, it is applied to things which come under the same general notion, though they do not agree in every particular. It is used, where the person or thing was never their's who are said to redeem it, but they only lay down a price to purchase it of another. A slave is said to be ransomed, when a sum is paid for his deliverance from bondage. And by an easy transition the word came to signify deliverance in general, where there is no price at all paid, but it is a mere act of power. "The angel," says dying Jacob, " which redeemed me from all evil." Agreably, God saith to his people Israel, " I will bring

bring you out from under the burthen of the Egyptians, and I will rid you out of their bondage, and I will redeem you with a stretched out arm." It follows from the various senses in which we are said to be redeemed in scripture, as well as from the different words which are used in the original texts, to express Christ's purchase, that nothing can certainly be determined by these particular terms, except that he hath wrought some great deliverance for us. But if we cannot determine, from it's being said that Christ bought and redeemed his church, that there was a price paid for it's redemption; most certainly, we cannot determine that there was not. And however we might be at some uncertainty, if it was only said in general that we are redeemed by Christ, yet it is very strange reasoning, because redemption is sometimes used in a large sense for deliverance from any kind of slavery, subjection, or distress, without any mention of a price or equivalent; that therefore it must be so understood, when a price is particularly mentioned; which is the case with respect to our redemption by Christ. We are not only said to be bought, but to be "bought with a price;" * what this price is we are told, † "Ye were not redeemed with corruptible things, such as silver and gold, but with the precious blood of Christ, as of a lamb without blemish and without spot." And " the Son of man is said to give his life a ransom for many." ‡

Whatever

---

* 1 Cor. 6. 20.   † 1 Pet. 1. 18, 19.   ‡ Mat. 20. 28.

Whatever makes it confiftent with the perfections of God, and the honor of his government, to pardon and fave man, may be fitly ftiled the price of our redemption—This price may be confidered as paid to God, as it was what he demanded and accepted, and was pleafed to make the ground or reafon of his forgiving our fins and admitting us into favor. On account of this, God confiders us as if we had not finned; or rather, he accepts of what Chrift hath done and fuffered as an equivalent for our fuffering, fo far as to put us into a capacity of efcaping future punifhment. Nor is this all that Chrift hath purchafed for us. In this refpect "where fin abounded, grace did much more abound." We are not only by the mediation of Chrift delivered from condemnation, but are accepted in the beloved, we have peace with God, and have the promife of eternal life and happinefs. All the bleffings which Chrift hath purchafed, or which God hath promifed through him, are included in the fcripture notion of redemption. But we are not to fuppofe, that thefe bleffings are actually beftowed on all the children of men. The gofpel makes it evident they are not. "The fpecial way, terms, and conditions," fays Dr. Owen, "whereby and whereon finners may be interefted in this fatisfaction made by Chrift, are determined by the will of God, and declared by the fcripture." Jefus Chrift hath made the falvation of men a poffible thing, but they only are actually faved, who fubmit to Chrift, and are

D d brought

to a conformity to the nature and will of God; these have an interest in the promises, and become heirs of eternal life. The price of their redemption was paid by Jesus Christ; they are made partakers of it when they become believers: But their redemption is not compleat till the resurrection, when they who sleep in their graves will be awakened, and be admitted to glory, honor, and immortality. Therefore the resurrection is called " the day of redemption," ¶ and " the redemption of the body." † In that glorious day it will be seen how great blessedness Christ hath purchased for his people, he will own and applaud their piety, faith and obedience, and reward them with joy, and everlasting honor—Joy that is now unutterable—glory which cannot be conceived in this present imperfect state.

Secondly, I am to show, how we are redeemed by the blood of Christ; or how this blood becomes the ground or price of our redemption. In order to give you some just idea of this important truth; I observe,

First, That man had by sin exposed himself to punishment. Every creature is under law to the Creator. The least breach of this law makes him a sinner; I need not add that man is a sinner, " there is not a just man upon earth that doeth good and sinneth not." Who is not conscious of a heart prone to sin, and of innumerable transgressions

¶ Eph. 4. 30. † Rom. 8. 23.

transgressions of God's holy law? As soon as we form ideas of God at all, we conceive of him as a holy Being. He hath an infinite love of order and harmony, of every thing which tends to promote universal good. He hath an infinite satisfaction in that which he himself does, because it is right and fit, agreable to his nature and character; and he is pleased with every thing in his creatures, which resembles his own infinite rectitude. Sin directly contradicts the nature and will of God; it mars the beauty of the creation, it tends to introduce disorder and confusion: The blessed God must therefore be infinitely offended with it. In proportion to the degree of his displeasure, he must be disposed to make his offending creatures feel the effects of it. But every such disposition in God is under the direction of infinite wisdom. He hath the most wise and good ends in all he does. He is never displeased without the highest reason, and he expresses his displeasure because it is fit and right that he should. It is an injurious reflection on the divine character, to suppose that he inflicts evil on any of his creatures, for the sake of gratifying any angry passions, or furious resentment. This is to make him a man like ourselves. He doth not punish any for punishment-sake, nor is it likely he would have suffered any of his creatures to have sinned, if he had not known how to have bro't good out of evil, as he hath done, with respect to man, by the mediation of Christ. If punishment is not likely to answer some

valuable

valuable end, we cannot suppose God will punish. The mere misery of his creatures, however they may deserve it, cannot yield any satisfaction to this infinitely benevolent Being.

We are to consider the glorious Jehovah as the all-wise Governor of the world; who hath given his creatures a rule of conduct, a law which is holy, just, and good. This sovereign Lord sets on an exalted throne, from whence he hath an intire view of universal nature, and orders all things so as to accomplish the wise designs of his own infinite mind. From hence he observes his subjects in their various situations, he surveys their moral conduct; and to what their actions tend; whether they reverence adore and obey him as they ought, or whether they renounce his authority and rebel against his government. When they sin against him, he is to be considered not merely " as an offended person, but as an offended ruler." In this character, it seems necessary, it becomes his divine perfections, to testify against the violations of his law, and to manifest his rectoral holiness. It is right and fit in itself, it is suitable to the honor and majesty of the supreme Governor, it would be unbecoming his dignity to act otherwise. " The punishment of sin is not a matter of arbitrary appointment, but of reason, equity and justice." " The same reason that there is, why honor and obedience should be at all paid to the laws of God; the same reason there is,

that

that this honor should be vindicated, after it hath been diminished and infringed by sin. To imagine, that God requires obedience to his commandments, and yet that he will not support their authority, against the contempt and disobedience of men; to suppose that God has constituted just and righteous laws to be obeyed by his creatures, and yet that he will not maintain that constitution, by vindicating the honor of those laws whensoever it shall be insulted by any wilful transgression; is contrary to the wisdom, and altogether inconsistent with the government of God, and with the nature of government in general." If God should show no regard to the honor of his law, nor give any testimony of his displeasure against moral evil, would men have a due reverence and respect for the divine commandments? or could they possibly think disobedience to them was so very displeasing to him as it had been represented? Would not this embolden them in sin? And might it not encourage others to transgress? Of how great weight this last consideration may be, it is impossible for us to say. God doubtless has other creatures under his government besides men; and who can determine what reference the different parts of his system have to each other; or how his conduct to an apostate world may affect, or influence other parts of his dominion? It is plain from scripture, that we have some connection with angels both good and bad; and perhaps, there is some general scheme carrying on in innumerable

numerable worlds, to the completion of which man is designed to contribute. An indiscriminate bestowment of favors would evidently sap the foundation of moral government, or rather it would prove that there was none at all; and 'tis difficult to say, what would be the consequence of such a general relaxation of the reins of government in a world of free intelligencies; tho' it is easy to conceive it might introduce great disorder and confusion. Probably, every created intelligence is formed with the passions of hope and fear; and the evil which will be the consequence of it, is one of the motives which God makes use of to keep moral agents from sin. 'Tis certain, God hath in every revelation he hath made of his will to mankind, threatned death and destruction to those who break his law, or violate that constitution he hath placed them under. Now the same reason which made it necessary to threaten these evils, shows the expediency at least, if not the necessity, of inflicting them upon the offenders, unless some other way could be found out, which would equally secure the honor of the divine government. Justice took place on the angels which fell, who are " reserved in chains under darkness, to the judgment of the great day." And man, when he had fallen from God, had no reason to expect the interposition of mercy. He had sinned—Sin exposed him to death—This was the threatning which God had made a sanction of his law—and this was the sentence pronounced. God would have been clear from any charge of injustice,

if

if he had inflicted this punishment, or any other which he hath at any time threatned. If it had exceeded the demerit of the offence, a Being of infinite rectitude could not have threatned it. And if it did not exceed, there was the utmoſt reaſon to think God would inflict it. Certainly there was nothing to neceſſitate him to remit a puniſhment which he might juſtly inflict. God could not be obliged to ſet aſide his original conſtitution, and to accept of ſatisfaction from another: Or if there had been any ſuch obligation; where was the perſon capable of making this ſatisfaction; or of doing any thing which might be conſidered as a good reaſon for his paſſing by the ſin of man—any thing which would make this conſiſtent with the ends of government; or exhibit the divine Being in his true character, as righteous Governor, at the ſame time that he pardoned the ſinner? And if this could not be done, what ground of hope could ſinful man have? what proſpect of mercy? or of any thing but indignation and wrath, tribulation and anguiſh? This was the ſituation into which man was brought by ſin—a ſtate of guilt, and expoſed to death.

Secondly, In this ſtate of wretchedneſs, there was a diſpoſition in the divine Being to ſhew mercy, to deliver and ſave ſinful man. This diſpoſition is manifeſt from that which hath taken place. The cauſe appears by the effect. That God was determined to ſave man is evident from his ſending his

Son on this important errand; and he could be moved to this only by goodnefs. If man had come up to the demands of the original conftitution, he would have done no more than his duty, he would have had no merit, the continuance of his life would have been an act of goodnefs. Surely then he could not deferve any favor in his finful apoftate ftate. The divine goodnefs, or mercy, is the fource of all thofe bleffings, which are defigned and provided for man in the plan of redemption. His own infinite benevolence was the only motive—there could be no other. The plan of man's redemption was laid before he had an exiftence : The purpofe of grace was declared without any follicitation on the part of the offender : The firft covenant or original conftitution abfolutely condemned the tranfgreffor : It made no provifion of a furety : It contained no promife to the penitent : It gave no encouragement to repent : It offered no affiftance to the returning finner. The fending a Mediator, his obedience, his fufferings, his death, all the hopes man now has, all the promifes that are made thro' Chrift, have their foundation in a new conftitution or fecond covenant. That fentence was not immediately executed upon fallen man ; that God hath provided a Saviour ; that he is willing to be reconciled to the children of men through Jefus Chrift, is wholly owing to himfelf : He hath appointed this method of conveying bleffings to man who had offended him.

We

We do not express ourselves with accuracy, however good the meaning may be, when we say the death of Christ renders God propitious to to us. It is by means of the obedience and death of Christ that God acts propitiously towards us: He makes them the ground or reason of his communicating good to us sinners; but he was propitious before; he had kind dispositions or intentions; he was inclined to make up the breach, or there had been no Mediator between God and man —Christ had not died. This constitution hath it's foundation in the goodness of God. This is the language of scripture—" God so loved the world, that he gave his only begotten Son, that whosoever believeth in him, should not perish, but have everlasting life." The sending a Saviour was not the cause, but the effect of divine love. It was an evidence that God did not delight in the death of sinners, that he was not willing that any should perish, and that he had the most kind and gracious designs to the children of men. I go on to observe,

Thirdly, The wise method God hath taken to shew mercy to man, and at the same time shew his infinite displeasure at sin. To inflict the punishment threatned would leave no room for mercy. To pardon the offender without any regard to the demands of the law would seem to be an encouragement to disobedience. In this state God was pleased to take a way of reconciling the world to himself,

himself, infinitely becoming him as Governor of the world, becoming his goodness, his rectitude, his wisdom. This was by appointing one to suffer in the room and stead of the sinner. The more innocent this substitute was, the more near and dear to God, the better would the ends of government be answered: The more would God's hatred to. sin, his good-will to sinners, and his high regard to his sovereign authority, be shewn by appointing. him to this office. For this end therefore God constituted his Son to be a Prince. and a Saviour—to be a propitiation for the sins of the world. Here

First, It is impossible there should be a person of more perfect innocence. He was a partaker of the divine nature, in such a sense as no creature ever was, or can be; therefore he is denominated the only begotten Son of God. When he became a man, a most extraordinary method was taken, that he might be free from the moral imperfections which are become natural to human nature. He was conceived of a virgin by the immediate power of the Holy Ghost; on which account he is called " that holy thing." And his whole life was answerable to so extraordinary a beginning; he was " holy, harmless, undefiled; separate from sinners." He not only did nothing amiss, but he always did the things that pleased the Father. " Such an High-Priest became us, who needeth not daily," as those high-priests who were appointed by Moses, " to offer

fer up sacrifice first for his own sins, and then for the people's." If Christ had been a sinner, he would have needed a sacrifice of expiation for his own sins, and therefore his sacrifice could be of no avail to us. But having no sin of his own, and voluntarily offering himself for such important ends, as the illustration of the divine perfections, and the procuring the greatest good to man, what he did might well be transferred to us, or made a reason for God's remitting our sins, and bestowing the greatest blessings upon us. Especially if we consider,

Secondly, The dignity of his person. He is called the Son of God, he is so in a higher sense than is any man or angel. " To which of the angels said he at any time, thou art my Son, this day have I begotten thee?" He was not only " with God." but he " was God." We read, that he was " in the form of God," and that he " tho't it not robbery to be equal with God." and it is mentioned as an extraordinary instance of love, that God " spared not his own Son but delivered him up for us all." The substituting such a great and glorious person, as the Son of God, to die for us, or in order to our deliverance from death, answered all the ends which would have been answered by our death. The sufferings of Christ clearly discovered God's abhorrence of sin, and his disposition to testify against it. The inflicting such great evils on so glorious a person, and in such a cause, set the

rectitude

rectitude of the divine government in a more conspicuous light, than would even the punishment of the offender himself. If man had suffered the penalty of the law he had violated, justice 'tis true would have had it's course, and the consequence had been terrible enough. But it would not have appeared that goodness at all interposed, or that there had been any disposition to relieve and save us. But as the case now stands, God appears on a throne of grace, willing to shew mercy to sinful man, and yet such is his regard for the honor of his government, that he would not pass by the sin of man, till one of the most exalted dignity had laid down his life a sacrifice. Such weak unknowing creatures as we are, could not possibly have conceived, how the justice and the goodness of God could both have their demands; how the sinner could be saved, and God appear at the same time the righteous Governor of the world. But the wisdom of God found out this admirable expedient which reconciled all; that the Son of God should assume our nature, suffer and die for us; that God should accept his sufferings; and on account of them release us from punishment. None but a Governor who had the highest regard to his law, and was unalterably determined to assert and vindicate his sovereign authority, would have taken such a method, or have insisted on such an atonement. If goodness hath prevailed, it hath not prevailed against justice. God is just, he appears just,

just, when he passes by the sin of man, receives him into favor, and bestows upon him eternal life and happiness. "Whom," as the apostle argues, "God hath set forth to be a propitiation through faith in his blood, to declare his righteousness for the remission of sins that are past, through the forbearance of God; to declare, I say, at this time his righteousness: that he might be just, and the justifier of him which believeth in Jesus." How could there be a more full demonstration of the righteousness of God, than his sending his Son to be a propitiation, to endure the most astonishing sufferings, before he would receive man into favor? How could the Law be more highly honored, than it is by God's taking this extraordinary method to testify against the violation of it, when he saw fit to pardon the offender? Who can take encouragement from the forbearance and mercy of God to sin against him? Who must not see the danger of disobedience? And how perfectly doth the mediation of Christ secure the honor of the divine government, in the pardon and salvation of men?

This subject hath been often happily illustrated by the story of Zaleucus prince of the Locrians. Zaleucus made a law, that adulterers should lose both their eyes; it fell out, that his own son, the heir of his crown, was convicted of this crime, the people, who greatly respected him for his amiable qualities, came and interceded for him. Zaleucus, in a conflict between zeal for justice, and affection for his son, took but one eye from him, and parted with one of his own, to answer the demands of the law. Now I enquire, did not this conduct of Zaleucus discover even a stronger regard to justice, than if he had punished his son according to the law? Did it not as effectually secure the honor of his government? and equally tend to deter others from transgressing? You observe I bring this story as an illustration of the subject, and not as an exact parallell to the sufferings of our Saviour in our room and stead. It shows that there may be a wise composition of mercy and justice in dealing with an offender, or that a law-giver may demonstrate his righteousness, and show a tender regard to his law, when he doth not precisely inflict the penalty on the transgressor.

I shall conclude at present with some practical reflections.

First, We are led to a most humiliating view of human nature. Man hath revolted from God; and is in a state of rebellion. There is a native proneness in all that descend from apostate Adam to sin. It is shocking to think, to what a degree of wickedness human nature would proceed, if left wholly without restraint. And though a great part of mankind are, by the force of reason and natural conscience, by education, by circumstances in providence, and the influence of divine grace, in some

measure

measure preserved from such extremity of vice; yet, every one, who is capable of moral action, is guilty of moral evil. Every one is more or less sensible, of an opposition to that pure virtue to which the gospel calls us; and, that he hath been led away and enticed by the allurements and temptations of a vain world. In many things we offend all, and come short of the glory of God. How melancholy a situation is this! When we look into ourselves, when we reflect on our past lives, what a lesson of humiliation may we learn! When we look into another world, what a scene of terror presents itself to our minds! We behold a God of unspotted purity, of inflexible justice, of irresistible power—A God, who is the righteous Governor of the world, and who hath made the most awful declarations against those who disobey and affront him. Can we know that we are in this number, and not tremble for fear of God? and not with the deepest sollicitude make that enquiry, What shall we do to be saved? Blessed be God, this is an enquiry we may make in hope. There is a possibility of our deliverance from that wretched state to which we are reduced by sin. We, who are too justly stiled enemies to the blessed God, may be reconciled by the blood of Christ.

Secondly, How should the wisdom and grace discovered in the scheme of man's redemption fill our hearts with admiration and praise! Man had

fallen,

fallen, and seemed lost for ever. The heavenly hosts were waiting to hear our condemnation, and the attendant spirits stood ready to execute the vengeance of an offended Deity. They knew well that God could not contradict himself, or dishonor his own perfections; they saw no way in which he could act like a wise Governor, secure the honor of his government, and pass by the transgression of his law; and pronounced our deliverance impossible. But the God of heaven pronounced otherwise! I have found a ransom—one who is able to save— and one who can save without the least infringement on the rights of justice—who can deliver from the curse of the law, and at the same time magnify the law and make it honorable—My own Son is the Saviour!—He shall be incarnate—He shall be made under the law—shall obey it's precepts—shall suffer and die a sacrifice for sin—thus shall he redeem them by his blood—shall deliver the rebels from guilt and from punishment—shall reinstate them in my favor—and procure for them an admission into these mansions of rest and happiness. Heaven stood amazed at the wisdom and grace of this wonderful plan!—The heavenly arches resounded with their anthems of praise— and the blessed inhabitants sang a new song, "Glory to God in the highest, because there is peace and good-will towards men." And ever since, the angels have been prying into the mysteries of redeeming love, and while they contemplate, they discern new

new marks of wisdom—new matter for admiration, joy, and praise. Let us unite with them, in admiring and adoring this astonishing display of the divine perfections. If the angels above, rejoiced at the news of a Saviour provided for man, who could only have a more distant concern in this event; shall not we, the children of men, rejoice and be exceeding glad, for whose immediate benefit this Saviour was provided—who are by the mediation of Christ rescued from the lowest misery, and raised to the hope of a blessed immortality! Great was the infelicity which sin had brought upon man: Great is the salvation which Christ hath purchased for him. A dispensation this, which we ought to review with the closest attention, and to improve with the greatest diligence.

We see the glory of God in the works of creation, and of providence; but He hath given the brightest view of himself in the work of redemption. Here we see unspotted purity, perfect rectitude, and boundless goodness, reconciled and glorified. What exalted ideas ought we to entertain of the infinite wisdom of that Being, who could thus bring good out of evil, and derive glory even from that, which, in itself, is most displeasing and dishonorable to him!

Let us give glory to him, who hath loved a sinful world, and sent his only begotten Son upon a design so full of grace and benevolence.—Let us be thankful and bless his name, that the word of salvation is sent to us, and that we hear offers of peace and reconciliation.—Notwithstanding all Christ hath done, we cannot be saved—we cannot partake of that blessedness which is promised through him, unless we believe the truths, and practise the precepts of the gospel.—We are guilty of the basest ingratitude, and expose ourselves to the most aggravated punishment, if we do not hearken to the reasonable proposals made to us.—Let us immediately accept of Christ and the blessings which he offers.—We may expect to find much opposition from our corrupt hearts, many objections will naturally arise in our minds, against the way of salvation by Jesus Christ. But we ought carefully to suppress all opposition, and to silence every objection. The gospel will always furnish us with arguments every way sufficient.—The more we contemplate it, the more surprizing manifestations of divine wisdom and goodness will open to us.—Angels, who excel in wisdom, could see enough to excite their praise. It is because we have not the knowledge and purity of angels, if we do not join with them in their joyful ascriptions to him who sitteth upon the throne, and unto the Lamb for ever and ever.

SERMON

SERMON X.

The Connection between the Duties and Comforts of Religion.

Acts IX. 31.

----------*Walking in the fear of the Lord, and in the comfort of the Holy Ghost.*

IN this chapter we have an account of Saul's sudden and miraculous conversion. The verse which contains the text mentions the happy effect of this surprizing event. " Then had the churches rest throughout all Judea, and Galilee, and Samaria, and were edified." They were confirmed in the truth; and by a wise improvement of their outward peace and liberty, they made progress in holiness and

and in comfort; by which means the church was greatly increased. "Walking in the fear of the Lord, and in the comfort of the Holy Ghost, were multiplied." Others, observing their holy walk, and that blessed peace and serenity which they enjoyed, were induced to embrace christianity; reasonably concluding that to be the best religion, which influenced it's votaries to lead such holy and unblameable lives, and which afforded them such observable comfort and satisfaction of mind.

It is proposed, at this time, to consider those two clauses which were first recited, not as they are related to the context, but as they stand connected with each other. It is not without design, that the fear of the Lord and the comfort of the Holy Ghost are thus placed together by the sacred writer. It plainly teaches us, how these christians attained to that peace of mind which is here ascribed to them, and which had such happy influence on those who beheld them. They first walked in the fear of the Lord, and then in the comfort of the Holy Ghost. And this is the way, in which only, christians in all ages are to expect the comforts of religion. Agreably, we shall endeavor,

First, To illustrate the phrases here used; which will naturally lead us in the

Second place, To observe the connection there is between the duties and comforts of religion.

The

The first thing proposed, is, to illustrate the phrases used in the text. " Walking in the fear of the Lord, and in the comfort of the Holy Ghost."

First, We are to say what it is to walk in the fear of the Lord.

Fear, in it's original meaning, is a passion of the mind, arising from an apprehension of evil. Agreably, the fear of the Lord, in scripture, sometimes signifies the uneasiness which a sinner feels, who is conscious that he hath offended God, and is apprehensive of the punishment which God hath threatned. But the phrase is not always to be taken in so harsh a sense. There is a fear of God which is consistent with the highest love, and which they may exercise, who do not consider God as an angry Judge, but as reconciled to them through Jesus Christ, and sustaining the character of a kind Friend and tender Father. Their fear is still exercised about sin, but they are not so much affected with the penal consequences annexed to it by a holy and just God, as with it's own evil nature; they consider it as wrong in itself, and an act of ingratitude to that Being, who is ever consulting the happiness of his creatures. They fear to displease him, because they love him, and desire an interest in his love. This fear proceeds from a belief of his perfections — a persuasion of his right to govern those to whom he hath given being, and a capacity of acting—

a sense of the great things he hath done for them, and the hope that he will do more. Such a fear as this would keep men from the commission of sin, even tho' God had annexed no punishment to it.

By the fear of the Lord in scripture, we are often to understand, not only the principle, but the effect which it has on our hearts and lives. Where there is such a holy reverential fear of God, it naturally tends to universal holiness and obedience. Therefore the fear of the Lord is frequently put for the whole of religion, both principle and practice. " Behold, the fear of the Lord, that is wisdom, and to depart from evil is understanding." † The fear of the Lord is here explained by departing from evil, which is the character of the truly good man. In like manner, the psalmist says, " Come ye children, hearken unto me, I will teach you the fear of the Lord." ‡ I will teach you, how you may serve God and be happy with him. By the fear of the Lord in our text, we are then to understand the whole of religion and virtue.

Walking, in scripture language, denotes the general course of our lives. When this term is connected with our moral conduct, it signifies a habit or course of action. Thus the kings of Israel are said to walk in the ways of Jeroboam, that is, they lived in the commission of those sins which he introduced.

† Job 28. 28.   ‡ Psa. 34. 11.

troduced. We read also, of walking in the statutes of the Lord, by which is intended a course of life agreable to them. So, when it is said in our text of the churches of Christ, that they walked in the fear of the Lord after Saul's conversion, it intends that they were under the influence of religion; that they lived in some degree answerably to their christian character and profession, practising every duty which Christ their Lord required of them.

This it is to walk in the fear of the Lord. They who come up to this character have an habitual sense of the being and attributes of God; they consider themselves as ever in his presence and under his inspection, and endeavor in their whole conversation to please and glorify him. They view the perfections of God as they are manifested by Jesus Christ, and carefully attend to those discoveries they have of the glorious God in the gospel, in which there are the kindest offers of assistance, the strongest assurance of acceptance, and the highest incentives to obedience. The fear of the Lord is a powerful principle of action in their souls, it moves them to all acts of piety and devotion, and to regard every intimation of his will; it leads them to an entire submission to Jesus Christ, to whose character and mission God hath borne the fullest testimony; it excites them to do justly in all their dealings with mankind; to shew mercy to those who need their help; and to walk humbly before

God

God and man. Senfible, that they often do amifs, and always come fhort of their duty, they are frequent in their acts of faith and repentance. They rely on the merits of Chrift for pardon, and on his Spirit to enable them to correct what hath been amifs. They labor to grow in grace, and aim at the higheft degrees of virtue and holinefs. In fine, They who fear the Lord look to the end of things, they believe a future ftate of rewards and punifhments, they think of the account they muft give up to their Judge: They humbly hope he will approve their inward piety and the uprightnefs of their hearts, and contemplate with joy and gratitude on the glory which will then be revealed; but, at the fame time, they expect none of the great and good things promifed, on account of their own works of righteoufnefs, but look for the mercy of God through our Lord Jefus Chrift.

Secondly, We are to enquire what it is to walk in the comfort of the Holy Ghoft.

The ways of religion are faid in fcripture to be " ways of pleafantnefs and all her paths peace." The chriftian life is reprefented as a life of quiet, of comfort, of joy. " Great peace have they that love thy law, and nothing fhall offend them." Our Lord promifes, " Come unto me, and I will give you reft." We read in one place of " the peace of God which paffeth all underftanding," in another of "rejoicing with joy unspeakable and full of glory." It is a direction given to the Philippians, "Rejoice evermore." One would think from such expressions, that christians were to be free from all trouble, that they were to meet with no darkness or perplexity, but to enjoy uninterrupted peace and rest; that they would have some degree of the blessedness, as well as the disposition of heaven, while they continued upon earth. Whereas it is far otherwise. We often see christians in trouble like other men; not only exercised with the sorrows and afflictions of life, which they can well enough bear if they have inward comforts. But they complain that God hideth himself from them; they have no tokens of his love; they have distressing fears and doubts about the state of their own minds, and can derive no comfort from the great and precious promises of the gospel. This is a most certain fact, which greatly perplexes weak and tender minds; and gives occasion to persons of libertine principles to reproach religion, as if it destroyed all peace, instead of affording that delight and satisfaction which we are taught to expect. Where, say they, is the blessedness ye spake of? or what profit shall we have if we be cleansed from our sin?

But they labour under a great mistake, who think that the darkness & perplexity, which good christians are exercised with, is the genuine effect of religion. Possibly, men, whose lives are only one continued series of dissipation and pleasure, or who are overwhelmed with the cares and hurries of the world, may not be disturbed with such doubts and fears. It is not likely, that they who do not meditate on God at all, will have any concern to obtain his favor; or, that they who never think of futurity will be afraid of future evils. An attention to the truths of religion, a belief of the perfections of God, a sense of the worth of our souls and the danger of their being lost forever, a consciousness of the weakness and treachery of our hearts, a high estimation of spiritual blessings, and a fear of a mistake in a matter of such importance, may be the occasion of great uneasiness to our minds.

But it doth not follow from hence, that religion tends to deprive us of any rational solid satisfaction, of any peace which we ought to desire. That ease which ungodly men seem to enjoy, proceeds from an inattention and stupidity which are quite unbecoming creatures capable of thought and reflection: And however they affect to appear, it is seldom that any are so hardened in vice, as not to have, at times, an awful sense of the being and perfections of God, and a dread of that account they must give to him of their conduct in life.—That horror and distress, which christians sometimes feel, may proceed from a natural fearfulness and diffidence— from a distempered body—from ignorance of the doctrines and truths of religion—from mistaken
notions

notions about their own integrity—or from the suggestions of a busy adversary. But in all these cases, their disquietude is not to be attributed to religion, it is directly contrary to the gospel of Christ; a skilful guide would by no means encourage such a dark and gloomy temper, but would set himself to reason them out of apprehensions so dishonorable to God, and injurious to their own souls. There is no religion in being melancholy and hopeless, or in yielding to the temptations of him who is ever [seek]ing to ruin and destroy us. Perturbation or dejection is no duty, though it may be occasioned by that which is right and fit, a conscious sense of guilt.

But though a conviction of our sinfulness and guilt may justly disrest our minds, and excite fear and anxiety; yet certainly, the religion of Christ affords consideration sufficient to quiet and compose us: And it is because it doth not operate in us as it ought, that it ever fails of this effect. Perfect love casteth out fear; and it is because our knowledge and grace are so imperfect; that our fears are so prevalent. Whatever exceptions we may make in favour of melancholy tempted persons; the general reason, that religion doth not afford christians more peace and satisfaction is, because they have so little religion, so little of the spirit of christianity in the course of their lives. In the gospel of Christ there is a happy foundation for peace and rest, but by some mistake or neglect of their's they miss of it. It

It is not easy to conceive, how there could have been a scheme more wisely adapted to afford relief and ease to the mind of man, than we have in the religion of Jesus.—Have we offended God, violated his law, and exposed ourselves to his displeasure? The gospel assures us that the King of heaven is a merciful King; that God may be just and yet justify the ungodly; and that there is no condemnation to them which are in Christ Jesus, who ⬛ not after the flesh, but after the Spirit.—Are we weak and sinful, and quite insufficient to comply with the kind and reasonable requirements of the gospel? We have a fountain of grace set open, to which we may apply with freedom, and from which we may derive constant supplies; "I can do all things," says the holy and humble apostle, "through Christ which strengthneth me".—If thro' grace we are enabled to believe in Christ, to repent of our sins, and to obey the gospel, the most great and precious promises are made to us—promises of blessings most valuable and important in their nature, and eternal in their duration. Nothing can be greater, nothing can be better, than the things which God hath provided for sinners, and which are proposed to them, as objects of their faith and diligent pursuit, in the gospel of Christ—The favor and love of God—a conformity to him in holiness—an assurance of every thing good and desirable in this world, and of a blessed state of immortality in another. What can the christian desire more? what can he have more? A believer in Christ hath

a

a univerfal grant of every thing neceffary to his happinefs. "All things are your's,"|| fays the apoftle, all things are defigned and ordered for your advantage. Well therefore may the chriftian rejoice even with joy unfpeakable and full of glory.

Shall not he rejoice, who, though confcious of innumerable faults and follies which juftly expofed him to the vengeance of an almighty Deity, hath reafon to think that his fins are forgiven, that his tranfgreffion is covered, that God will remember no more what he hath done amifs, and that his fins will never rife up in judgment to condemn him?—Shall not he rejoice, who was once in a ftate of fpiritual death, and under the government of his lufts and paffions, but now finds a bleffed change in himfelf, that he has a fupreme regard to God, a love of virtue, and a defire to do that which is right and fit, that he hath fome little refemblance of the Deity, which is the true perfection of man, and lays a foundation for his higheft happinefs?—May not he rejoice, who was once a child of wrath, becaufe a child of difobedience, but is now adopted into the family of God, fuftains the relation of a fon to the Lord of heaven and of earth, and of confequence is an heir of all thofe good things which God hath prepared for them that love him?—May not he rejoice who can look upon the eternal Jehovah as his Friend, his Father, and his Portion; who is allowed to confider every difpenfation of

|| 1 Cor. 3. 2.

of divine providence, as ordered in covenant love; who knows that even the afflictions of this present life shall work for his good, and are sent to make him wiser and better?—Hath not that man a reasonable foundation of joy, who is assured of support in every trial, of assistance in every difficulty, of protection in every danger, and of relief in every distress?—May not he rejoice, who, though he knows that he must submit to the king of terrors, can look upon death as disarmed of his sting, not as an enemy, but as a friend, a friend sent to put an end to his trials and conflicts, and to place him beyond the reach of sorrow and of trouble?—Shall not he rejoice, who can look forward to the glorious morn of the resurrection, when this mortal shall put on immortality, and this corruptible shall put on incorruption, and death shall be swallowed up in victory?—In fine, shall not he rejoice, who can look on heaven as his home, as his certain inheritance; who can view the rest which remains for the people of God, as designed for him; who can think with holy confidence, of being free, not merely from the trials and difficulties of life, but from his own faults and follies, from every remainder of moral evil; who is assured that he shall be admitted to the beatific vision and enjoyment of God, in whose favor is life, and whose loving kindness is better than life? This is part of that blessedness which God hath provided for them that love him; but how little a portion is heard of it? And shall

not

not one, who is heir of so great blessedness, have his heart dilated with joy and gratitude?—If a condemned malefactor should not rejoice at the news of a pardon—If one seized with a dangerous illness should be calm at hearing of a certain cure—We should all be astonished at their insensibility, (and yet there may be good reasons why either of these should not be pleased with such an event). Should we not have greater reason to wonder, if one, who, of an enemy, is made a friend of God; if one, who, of an heir of hell, is made an heir of heaven, should feel no pleasing emotion—should be insensible of his happiness? The men of the world rejoice, when earthly good things are increased, they take pleasure in the vain and empty enjoyments of this life; how much more reason hath he for comfort and satisfaction, who is a partaker of spiritual blessings, and is possessed of durable riches and righteousness! Well may the christian, with the pious psalmist, despise and in a sense renounce every other object, and triumph in God, " Whom have I in heaven but thee? and there is none on earth that I desire besides thee. My flesh and my heart faileth, but God is the strength of my heart, and my portion for ever."

Nor are we obliged only to say, that the christian hath reason to rejoice. Blessed be God, there have been those who have been able thus to rejoice in God their Saviour. If we look into the history of the acts of the apostles, we there see the influence of religion, and to what a noble height it is capable of raising the mind of man. With what chearfulness did they part with their estates, and lay the money at the apostle's feet ! With what patience did they bear the spoiling of their goods, and the torture of their bodies ! They rejoiced that they were counted worthy to suffer shame for the sake of Christ, and in the cause of truth. They preached the doctrine of a crucified Saviour, with freedom and intrepidity, in places of the greatest politeness, and in the midst of ridicule, persecution, and danger. They were scourged; they were mocked; they were bound; they were imprisoned; they were destitute; they were afflicted; they were tormented; they were treated like the off-scouring of the earth; but none of these things moved them, neither counted they their lives dear, so they might finish their course with joy. Religion carried them above all; they could look down with contempt on the frowns and flatteries of the world; and triumph even in the agonies of death. Knowing that God was their friend, they little minded who was their enemy. They remembered that this world was not their home, and were very willing to leave it. They had a prospect of a blessed state of perfection after this life, and earnestly desired an admission into it. They had inward peace in the midst of outward trials; and anticipated the joys of heaven by the comforts they enjoyed on earth.

Nor

Nor was this happy effect of christianity peculiar to the first age of the church. Indeed it is likely, God doth in times of persecution afford some uncommon discoveries of himself, and some special prelibation of the joys of a future state, to prepare the minds of good men for extraordinary sufferings, and to animate them to persevere in the cause of true religion. It may reasonably be supposed, that this was the case when christianity made it's first entrance into the world, and the professors of it met with so many obstacles and so great temptations. But, God be praised, religion has had it's comforts at all times; and there have been found those in every age of the church, who have been enabled to live above the world while they have lived in it; and have gone thro' the most trying scenes with patience, resignation, and joy. There are christians, even in these days, who can on good grounds call God their Father, and look upon themselves under his gracious covenant care; who can think of death with comfort and serenity; and resign their souls into the hands of the Redeemer, with a full persuasion that he is able to keep that which they commit unto him against that day.——— You are not to think, my brethren, that they who freely speak of the comforts of religion are the only ones who enjoy them. Many, having other sentiments of what is right and proper, are very cautious how they declare the secret transactions of their souls, who yet do not come at all behind the others, either in the degree of their goodness, or in the

the peace which flows from it; and would, if they tho't they were called of God to do it, publicly bear their testimony to the truth of religion from what they have felt of it's influence. We, who are frequently called to visit sick and dying beds, with pleasure find many who have long before this important period devoted themselves to God; and can appeal to the great Searcher of hearts that they have sincerely desired to serve him. Tho' conscious of innumerable faults imperfections and sins, they can, with some degree of holy confidence, commit themselves into the hands of him who hath loved them and given himself for them; and are able, in the near view of eternity, to testify, that religion yields a peace which the world cannot give or take away—a peace, which they have long enjoyed, tho' the enjoyment was never known, except to God and their own souls. But whether the instances of those who have experienced the comforts of religion are many or few, is not so much to our present purpose—If there are any, it proves that religion is capable of yielding peace and satisfaction to the mind of man—that it affords considerations which are a reasonable foundation of comfort—and that it is possible to attain this great blessing. If this is the case, the defect is not in religion, but in themselves, when christians are destitute of it—it is owing to some neglect or fault of their own.——In what sense this is the *comfort of the Holy Ghost* we shall endeavor to show in the next discourse.

SERMON

The Connection between the Duties and Comforts of Religion.

Acts IX. 31.

----------Walking in the fear of the Lord, and in the comfort of the Holy Ghost.

THE point now before us is to show, in what sense that peace of mind which religion tends to inspire is denominated the comfort of the Holy Ghost. By this expression we are to understand that this glorious and divine Person is, one way or another, the Author of that peace which christians enjoy. And it is ascribed to him from these several considerations—As the Spirit of God hath in the word exhibited the marks of grace, and taught us what are the proper grounds of religious comfort and peace—As the Spirit produces that holy temper

temper and strengthens to that right conduct, which the scripture makes the mark or evidence of a good state towards God—And, as He, by enlarging, strengthening, and enlightning our minds, enables us to discern those gracious fruits and effects which he hath produced in us.

First, The comforts of religion are ascribed to the Holy Ghost, as this Divine Person hath in the word taught us what are the proper grounds of religious comfort and peace.—The christian's joy is not an accidental emotion of the passions; a mere mechanical elevation of mind; or a sudden kind of ease which a person feels he cannot tell why, nor for what reason. It is a sober rational thing, and may be defended upon all the principles of reason and religion. It arises from an inward persuasion that we are in a state of favor with God, and have a title to all the blessings of the new covenant. Now in order to determine that this is our happy state, it is necessary we should know upon what terms we may obtain acceptance with God, and be admitted into his favor. We cannot know this without an express declaration; because no gracious disposition, no act of obedience, nor any course of holy living, can of themselves give us a title to the favor of God, and to that immortal state of happiness which the gospel reveals and offers. This title is conferred only by the promises of the new-covenant. Neither faith, repentance, nor any other duty or
virtue

virtue is meritorious of the divine favor, they are conditions of falvation, only as God is pleafed to connect falvation with them. God who was not obliged to fave us at all, was at liberty to make his own terms in faving us. There is indeed a fuitablenefs and fitnefs in thofe virtues and graces which God hath made the condition of our falvation; but that fo great happinefs is connected with them is owing to the appointment of God, and the conftitution of the covenant of grace. Had man repented, believed, and performed all other acts of duty which the gofpel requires, yet had there been no promife annexed to them, God had been under no obligation to beftow eternal life and happinefs upon him. Since therefore all the influence, which any grace or duty hath in our falvation, is derived from the declaration and promife of God; we muft look into that revelation which contains thefe promifes and declarations, to know whether we have an intereft in them or not. If we find that we have thofe graces wrought in us, which the fcripture makes the marks of God's elect, or that we perform thofe duties which are prefcribed in the word, and in the manner which is there directed, and to the performance of which the promife of falvation is made, we may rejoice in hope of the glory which fhall hereafter be revealed in us. But if not, if we cannot find thofe tokens or evidences of grace, which are declared in the fcripture; whatever elfe we find in ourfelves, we may reafonably

bly conclude, we are yet alienated from the life of God, and are deftitute of an intereft in the great Mediator. No one hath authority to conftitute any new way to falvation. There is—there can be no way, but that which God hath appointed—There can be no terms or conditions of final happinefs, but thofe which are determined by the will of God —There can be no fatisfactory marks, but thofe which he hath pointed out in his word, or which by plain confequence are deduced from them. God hath promifed pardon and eternal life to thofe who believe in Chrift, repent of their fins, and fincerely obey the gofpel. If therefore we know that we have believed, repented, and fubmitted to the divine government, we may be confident that we are in a ftate of favor with God, and may enjoy the comfort which is the natural effect of fuch a conclufion. So great, indeed, is the treachery of our hearts, and fuch is our imperfection in faith and holinefs, that it is not an eafy thing to determine whether we are true penitents, or whether our fubmiffion to Chrift is fincere or not. There is fo great danger of our making a miftake, and fo many contrary reafonings, that many are at a lofs what to think or judge of themfelves. To help us therefore in the determination of our ftate, we have particular rules of trial, by which we are to fearch and examine ourfelves. Thus for inftance, we read of fome, that God purified their hearts by faith. ‡ Do we then fuppofe that we are believers in Chrift?

‡ Acts 15. 9.

We

We are to enquire, what effect our faith hath on our hearts, whether we see the moral turpitude there is in sin, so as that we desire and endeavor to abstain from it entirely and universally; whether we see the reasonableness and excellency of holiness, so as to press towards a perfect conformity to the law and will of God. Again, it is said, " we know that we have passed from death unto life, because we love the brethren." † We are to enquire, whether we have universal benevolence to mankind, and a special regard to those who bear the image of God, and walk agreably to his commandments. Further we are to enquire, whether we are meek and patient, forgiving and forbearing; whether we do justly, love mercy, and walk humbly with our God; whether our affections are placed on things above and not on things on the earth; whether we grow in grace, in our love to God, in our regard to Jesus Christ, in a devout, humble, serious, christian temper. These are some of the marks which the scripture gives of the true christian; and if our conscience bear witness that they are to be found upon us, we may safely determine that this character belongs to us. " If our heart condemn us not, we have confidence towards God," and a scriptural foundation for comfort, peace, and joy. And this comfort, which arises from comparing our hearts and lives with the word of God, may properly be called the comfort of the Holy Ghost, as the scripture was given by inspiration of the blessed Spirit.

† 1 John 3. 14.

Holy men wrote as they were moved by the Holy Ghoſt. Whatever comfortable words we find there, or whatever comfort we derive from any thing that is written there, may fitly be called the comfort of the Holy Ghoſt. For had not the Spirit in the word declared, what the conditions of the covenant of grace are, and what are the marks of God's children, our finding ever ſo many graces and virtues would not have been a juſt foundation for that peace and reſt, which a conformity to the chriſtian rule may now reaſonably afford us.

Secondly, The chriſtian's comfort may be aſcribed to the Holy Ghoſt, as the gracious diſpoſitions and holy converſation which are the proper evidence of his good ſtate, are the fruit and effect of the Spirit's influence on the mind. Under the laſt head we have proved, that nothing can be an evidence of our having an intereſt in the favor of God, but what is declared to be ſo in his word. Now if we look into the holy ſcriptures, we find, that men are repreſented as ſinners, tranſgreſſors of the law, and under a ſentence of condemnation—We are told, that God is in Chriſt reconciling the world unto himſelf, not imputing to them their treſpaſſes: They who were ſunk into the loweſt depths of miſery are raiſed to the higheſt hopes. But it is plain from the oracles of truth, that before men can have any title to the bleſſedneſs promiſed in the goſpel, it is neceſſary they ſhould paſs through a great moral change,

change, or that the powers and faculties of their minds should be renewed with respect to moral good and evil. So great is this change, that it is called a new creation, and they who experience it are said to be new creatures; the meaning is, they think and act as if they were quite different persons; they have other principles views and aims; they have a holy temper and disposition, and endeavor to live in conformity to the rules of the gospel. Agreably, christians are ever described as holy persons, by something which belongs to the work of sanctification. All the marks or rules of trial, which we have in the word of God, imply the exercise of some grace, or the practice of some virtue. " I know," says Dr. Sherlock, " no sign of grace, but grace itself; no sign of faith but believing; no sign of temperance, but the government of our sensual inclinations; no sign of being righteous, but doing righteousness." It is from the exercise of grace, we are to determine that we have grace. A filial disposition proves that we are the children of God; an imitation of the example of Christ proves that we are his disciples; he that is sanctified may be certain that he is justified; he who hath the temper of heaven may conclude he is an heir of heaven. —This is the proper scripture evidence, nor are we to look for any other.

No one hath any reason to expect an immediate testimony from heaven, either by a voice, or by inspiration. You no where find it written in the sa‑
cred

cred oracles, nor can you conclude from any thing there said, that you are in a ftate of favor with God, if you have a particular audible declaration, or a whifper, a fecret fuggeftion, a ftrong impreffion, a firm perfuafion, that this is your happy privilege. Nor are you to draw this conclufion, becaufe you have fome encouraging text, or gracious promife, brought to your mind, as that your fins are forgiven, that God is your Father. The fcripture doth not point out the particular perfons whofe fins are forgiven, or to whom the promifes are made, but only reveals the character, marks, or qualifications, by which they are diftinguifhed from others; and therefore no one ought to determine that he is of this bleffed number, unlefs he find that he hath this character, or thofe qualifications, which the fcripture makes the marks of the children of God. He whofe foul is conformed to God's law, may know that his name is enrolled in the Lamb's book of life. A ftory we have in one of the Roman hiftorians agreably illuftrates this point. A Senator relating to his fon, the great honors decreed to a number of foldiers, whofe names were written in a book, the fon was importunate to fee the book. The father fhewed him the outfide, it feemed fo glorious, that the fon defired him to open it; by no means, fays the father, it is fealed by the council. Then, faith the fon, tell me if my name be there; the names, faith the father, are fecret to the fenate. The fon ftudying how he might get fome fatisfaction,

tion, defired his father to declare the merits of those infcribed foldiers, which the father doing, and the fon confulting his own heart, found himfelf to be none of them. The names of thofe whom God hath determined unto life are not revealed unto us; but the qualifications of thofe who fhall enter into heaven are made known to us in God's holy word. It is plainly enough declared, that they are in a juftified ftate, who love God, who delight in his law, who are pure in heart, who aim at a conformity to the nature and will of God in all things, who have a fincere regard to Jefus Chrift, carefully imitate his holy example, and ftrive to be fuch as his gofpel requires them to be, without any limitation or referve. Holinefs in heart and in life is the only genuine evidence that we are chriftians, the children of God, and heirs of eternal happinefs; nothing without this ought to give reft and eafe to our minds, but this is a good foundation for comfort peace and joy. " Our rejoicing," fays the holy apoftle, † " is this, the teftimony of our confcience, that in fimplicity and godly fincerity, not with flefhly wifdom, but by the grace of God, we have had our converfation in the world."

The comfort which we enjoy, in confequence of this holy temper and conduct, is juftly afcribed to the Spirit of God, as it is by his influence we become holy, or do any thing as we ought to do. He
converts

† 2 Cor. 1. 12.

converts the sinner; He impresses the truths of God upon the mind; He causes them to have their genuine effect, and strengthens to those acts of virtue and holiness which men perform. Christians are therefore said to be "born of the Spirit," to be "led by the Spirit," to "walk in the Spirit," we read of the sanctification of the Spirit, of the indwelling of the Spirit, of the fruits of the Spirit, and many other expressions are used in scripture, which make it plain, that whatever holy disposition there is in us, or whatever good is done by us, is the effect of divine grace, and owing to the agency or influence of the Spirit of God. What the Spirit doth in us, or enables us to do, is that, from whence we conclude, that we are the children of God, and have a title to eternal life. This blessed conclusion is an act of our own minds, but it is ascribed to the Spirit, and called the comfort of the Holy Ghost, because the matter of our comfort, or that by which we determine our state to be good, proceeds from Him. The Spirit doth not immediately reveal to us that we are in a state of grace, but we are to know this, by perceiving that we have the Spirit in his gracious fruits and effects within us. "Hereby we know that we dwell in him, and he in us, because he hath given us of his Spirit." ‡

'Thirdly, The peace of mind which the christian enjoys is called the comfort of the Holy Ghost, as this

‡ 1 John 4. 13.

this Divine Person enables us to discern those gracious fruits and effects which he hath produced in us. Although God hath testified in his word what are the marks of grace, or what is the proper ground of religious comfort and peace—Altho' every christian hath more or less of that holiness, which is the scriptural evidence that he is in a state of favor with God ; 'tis yet evident, that many christians walk in darkness and have no light. The general reason of this is some defect in the christian. But we have scripture warrant to conclude, that some special agency of the Spirit of God is necessary, to our enjoying that rest and peace of mind, which religion lays a happy foundation for. The Spirit not only furnishes that which is the matter of the evidence, but he convinces by the evidence. The matter of evidence is for substance in every christian, but every christian hath not the comfort which is the genuine effect of it. Every christian hath grace, but every one, to whom this character belongs, doth not know that he is thus happy. He is indeed sensible of his own actions, he knows what he thinks, and what he does ; but he is uncertain, whether his acts are gracious, or such as prove him to be in a state of grace.

A good man sees so much in himself that is contrary to what he ought to be—so great a want of love to God—so little faith in Christ—such an undue attachment to the world—so much formality mingled

mingled with his highest acts of devotion, that he often hath fears, whether his heart is right, and his state good—Many suspicions, doubts and objections arise within him, even in his best frames. The more he encreases in holiness, so much the more doth he abhor sin, and so much the more uneasiness doth the sin which he perceives in himself occasion him—The more lively views he hath of the excellency of Christ, and of spiritual and eternal blessings; so much the more concern doth he feel, that he hath not a greater value for this glorious Mediator, and left he should miss of those blessed privileges, immunities, and enjoyments, which his disciples have a right to expect—The more strong his faith in things that are future and invisible, so much the more anxious is he about every thing which makes his title to them uncertain and dubious—This being the case, christians are often hesitating and doubting; if sometimes ready to hope they have an acquaintance with religion, from some sensible actings of grace, and an habitual regard to God in their conversation; yet a consciousness of sin—sin dwelling in them, and committed by them, makes them fearful of drawing so comfortable a conclusion. Such fears are, as hath been observed, owing to some weakness in them—To a weakness of grace, there is so little conformity of heart to God, that it is scarce discernible—or to a weakness in their understanding, which keeps them from making a right judgment of their state.

To

To relieve them under this difficulty is part of the office of the Holy Spirit; to resolve their doubts, and bring them to a comfortable determination in this great point. Without this, he would not answer the character of a Comforter, whatever else he might do in them, or for them. It could afford a christian but little consolation, that he had the marks of God's children upon him, if he did not arrive at the knowlege of them. The Holy Ghost is a Spirit of consolation, as he causes men to experience the comforts of religion, and sometimes to " rejoice with joy unspeakable and full of glory." Perhaps, our text hath a special reference to this particular agency of the Spirit, though by no means to the exclusion of his testimony in the word, and his sanctifying influence on the mind, separate from which there can be no reason for peace.

If any one enquire, How doth the Spirit bring us to discern the truth of grace? I answer, one way in which he doth this is, by quickning us in the exercise of grace, and exciting us to greater diligence and activity in the work of the Lord. It is the nature of grace to evidence itself. The Spirit of God makes us feel the power of religion, and strengthens us to such lively actings of love, of faith, of repentance, of obedience, as are evidential. " While " grace," says one, " lies, as it were, dormant in the " soul, it is not so visible, but eminent actings of " grace, in such duties as are attended with peculiar

labor

"and self-denial, carry with them their own evidence,
"with a more satisfying clearness.—When chris-
"tians are enlarged in any duty or grace, as trust
"and resignation to God, or charity to men; it
"affords them the happy occasion of observing
"something of the Spirit of God in them, some
"discernible lineaments of his image, something
"that speaks them his children, the objects of his
"favor, and the heirs of his kingdom. The emi-
"nent acts of grace carry light in them as well as
"heat, and tend to settle in the conscience a per-
"suasion of divine approbation and love."

But it hath been with reason supposed, that the Spirit enables christians to discern the truth of grace in a still more direct way; that is, by enlarging, strengthening, and enlightning our understandings, in judging concerning our moral or spiritual actions. Why should this be thought at all more irrational, than his shining into our hearts to give us the knowledge of the truth? While the saints are desirous to know their state towards God, and are enquiring into the foundation of their hope, the Spirit may give them a more clear understanding of the covenant of grace, may lead them to more just sentiments of the nature of grace or evangelical holiness, may enable them to discern their sincere acquiescence in the method of salvation by Jesus Christ, their desires after God and a conformity to him: He may scatter their doubts, silence their objections,

objections, bear down their contrary reasonings, and encourage them to believe, not only, that such sinful unworthy creatures as they are, may partake of those great and comprehensive blessings which Christ hath purchased, but, that what now passes in their minds is real holiness, and of consequence that they are gracious persons, or in a state of grace.

All this the Spirit may do in a secret imperceptible way, while they are in the exercise of their reasoning powers, so that they may be unable to distinguish his operations from the acts of their own minds. He doth not fill christians with joy and peace they know not why, nor without their perceiving any reason of the hope that is within them. He strengthens their holy dispositions, assists to holy practice, and then helps them to perceive and determine, that these holy exercises are the true scripture marks of God's children. And it is not easy to conceive, how there can be a more reasonable ground of rejoicing, than the firm persuasion of this high relation to the blessed God ; and a lively view and hope of the blessedness that is connected with it in the word. This persuasion is in itself highly delightful, it is an earnest of heaven, a prelibation of that felicity which awaits the saints in another state and world. Therefore the apostle prays for the Romans, " The God of hope fill you with all joy and peace in believing, that ye may abound in hope, through the power of the Holy Ghost."

I have now said why the christian's comforts are ascribed to the Holy Ghost. I only add under this head, that by *walking* in the comfort of the Holy Ghost, it is intimated, that the christians spoken of in the text enjoyed for a space of time, or a season, the blessed tokens of divine love, or a joyful sense of their interest in the favor of God through Jesus Christ. It intends that they had something more than a sudden flow of passion, or some transient pleasure ; that as their christian temper continued, so their peace and comfort continued likewise. A happiness this beyond expression ! They only who have had experience of it know how great it is ! A stranger intermeddleth not with this joy.

I proceed to the Second general head, which is to consider the connection between walking in the fear of the Lord, and in the comfort of the Holy Ghost—or between the duties and comforts of religion. Our text connects them together, and thereby, as I observed in opening the words, intimates, that this is the most likely way to attain that peace and rest, which is most desirable in itself, and which we in vain pursue in any other way. And I presume, after what hath been already said, very little need be added to prove this point.———If the religion of Christ is adapted to afford relief and ease to the mind of man—If it is from the exercise of grace we are to determine that we are heirs
of

of the promises—If the only way to attain the comfort of the Holy Ghost is, by his enabling us to discern those holy dispositions which he hath produced in us, and which he hath in the scripture made the marks of God's children—If this is the true state of the case, then certainly the best way to know our state, and to have the comforts of religion is to keep our graces in a constant and vigorous exercise, or to walk in the fear of the Lord. —The more we act under the influence of religion, and walk answerably to our christian character, the clearer is the evidence that we are in a state of favor with God—The more we grow in grace, the stronger is the proof that we have grace—The more we have of a filial temper, the more certain it will be that we are the children of God. "The work of righteousness shall be peace, and the effect of righteousness, quietness and assurance forever." Peace in our own minds is the proper genuine effect of the practice of righteousness, as the practice of righteousness proves, that we have an interest in the promises, and a right to eternal life and happiness. Therefore the psalmist, speaking of the commandments of the Lord, says, " In keeping of them there is great reward."*

Further, while we walk in the fear of the Lord, or live in the practice of holiness, we are most likely to have those special influences of the Spirit, which

---

* Psalm 19. 11.

which are necessary to our discerning the grace of God in our souls, and to our having the comfort of such discernment. "Thou meetest him," says the prophet, "that rejoiceth, and worketh righteousness, those that remember thee in thy ways." ¶ We must follow after holiness if we would enjoy the comforts of religion. It is a just punishment upon those christians who are negligent and slothful in the work of the Lord, that they are in doubt and perplexity about their state. It is only the fruitful that can expect to be the comfortable christian. As it is in temporals, so also is it in spirituals, the diligent hand maketh rich. And certainly, nothing could be more wisely ordered: We are exceeding apt, notwithstanding this powerful motive to diligence, to slacken and grow remiss in our christian course, would not this criminal temper be more prevalent, if we met with no difficulties in our way, but enjoyed uninterrupted ease and quiet, whether we were diligent or not?—But on the other hand, what a stimulus is it to the greatest vigor and activity, when by a stedfast adherance to the rules of our holy religion, and in this way only, we have reason to expect that peace, comfort and joy, which the gospel lays a blessed foundation for! Whether therefore, that is the immediate sense of the apostle Peter or not, it is certainly a very good sense, in which most expositors understand the exhortation, "Give diligence to make your calling and election sure." †

This

¶ Isaiah 64. 5. † 2 Peter 1. 10.

This perfuafion of their good ftate is not to be obtained merely by reflecting on what is paft, there muft be continued action; the apoftle fpeaks of chriftians, as "forgetting the things that were behind, and reaching to thofe that were before." This expreffion doth not mean, that a chriftian is to take no notice of the experience he hath had of the power of religion on his foul; it muft be a great advantage in forming a judgment of himfelf, to have had opportunity to try his graces, especially in fcenes of great difficulty and felf-denial; to find that he hath been able to withftand peculiar temptations, and to endure uncommon trials of his faith and virtue. The recollection of fuch victories cannot but afford great fatisfaction to the mind; but there will arife, even in the midft of fuch pleafing reflections, many doubts and fufpicions of his fincerity, unlefs he finds a prefent correfpondence to the law and will of God. Our paft experience of the efficacy of religion may give us fome hope that we have paffed from death to life; and where there is the prefent activity of grace, will abundantly ftrengthen the evidence, that we are fincere difciples of Chrift; but it cannot alone carry the mind above all fear of a deception, and afford that fettled peace and comfort which every good man afpires after. Unlefs I can fay with the pfalmift, " I love the Lord," or with the apoftle, " I know in whom I have believed." · Unlefs I find a prefent regard to God and to his law, and a difpofition to

prefs

press towards the mark, to encrease in grace and holiness, I have reason to suspect whether I know any thing of religion, and have not been deceived in what is past, that hath had a goodly appearance. It is the prevalence of love that casts out fear; if divine love decays, doubts naturally arise. And as much imperfection attends the highest exercise of grace in our present imperfect state, many good divines have questioned whether absolute assurance, or such as excludes all doubts, is attainable on this side heaven. "The highest assurance in this life," says Mr. Willard, "is that which needs strengthing. A believer's grace is imperfect, and his corruptions potent; and perfect assurance is not consistent with imperfect grace. Hence believers are ever put on the work of self-examination."——"If there be such absolute assurance," says Mr. Flavel, "as to be no doubt nor danger, there is no place nor room for examination, or further endeavors to make it surer than it is."——"Such an evidence, conviction, or persuasion of our acceptance with God," says Dr. Owen, "as are exclusive of all contrary reasonings, that suffer the soul to hear nothing of objections, that free and quiet it from all assaults, are neither mentioned in the scriptures, nor consistent with that state wherein we walk before God, nor possible on account of Satan's will and ability to tempt, or of our own remaining unbelief." There is, notwithstanding, such an hope through grace, a hope so far preponderating all doubts, as may, without any great impropriety, be term'd assurance, as

it

it very much answers the end for which any one would desire an absolute certainty; to encourage the christian in his spiritual conflicts, to enable him to take comfort in the promises, to fill him with joy and peace in believing, and to give him some prelibation of the blessedness of heaven. " These things," says our blessed Saviour, " have I spoken unto you, that my joy might remain in you, and that your joy might be full." ‡ And with what confidence doth the apostle Paul speak, " I know whom I have believed, and I am persuaded that he is able to keep that which I have committed to him against that day !" §

I am sensible, some of you will be ready to object against the account I have given of the christian's joy, that it seems to suppose a long course of reasoning, whereas God hath sometimes shed abroad a sense of his love, as it were, at once. Good men have had an immediate witness of the Spirit, that they were the children of God, and have been suddenly filled with comfort peace and joy.

To this it may be replied,—If by an *immediate* witness is intended, a testimony from heaven without any means, or any thing intervening, it can be nothing else than an immediate revelation, that they are in a pardoned sanctified state, which the scripture gives us no reason to expect: Christians are
not

‡ John 15. 11.   § 2 Timothy 1. 8.

not to know their filial relation to God by an *immediate* declaration, or secret suggestion; they can know it only by the declarations and promises of the word, and therefore only by their finding in themselves that evidence of their regeneration which is agreable to the scriptures.—If by *immediate* is intended no more than instant, or present with regard to time: I deny not, that christians have sometimes had such witness or evidence, of their being born of God. But even here, I see no reason at present to suppose, that they have attained an assurance of their good state, without any regard to the word, or without their discerning the exercise of any grace in themselves. The case may be thus, the christian being before well acquainted with the rules laid down in scripture, and which are there made the marks and signs of God's children, hath some lively exercise of the christian temper, or finds a holy love to God excited to such a vigorous exercise, as leaves no room to doubt, that it is what it appears to be; it carries it's own evidence, and gives full and immediate conviction, that it is the very temper, which in the word is made the mark or character of God's children. This instantly fills him with a sacred divine joy, with the peace of God which passes all understanding. Here is no long reasoning—no course of argumentation—nothing which may not pass in an instant, almost a moment of time.

If

If in this account of things I differ from some eminent Divines, I can truly say, I have delivered what appears to me the sense of scripture; sure I am, I have no design to limit the holy One of Israel, where the word of God gives us the least warrant to look for his divine influence.

IMPROVEMENT.

First, How much reason have we to be thankful for the new covenant; which lays such a happy foundation for peace with God, and for peace in our own minds! The law of our nature required indefectible obedience—an absolute conformity to the nature and will of God. When we compare ourselves with this law, in how many instances do we offend daily? And in what one instance do we perfectly answer it's demands? This law therefore condemns us. All the assurance the first covenant gave of the favor of God was to those who never violated it:—To the sinner, it breathes nothing but indignation and wrath. A gracious God hath looked upon us with pity in our state of imperfection and sin; and hath provided a kind Deliverer—an almighty Saviour. He hath sent his Son, in our nature, to atone for our offences, and to make way for our reconciliation to him. Pardon is proclaimed—& not pardon, only—We may thro' the grace of the gospel, expect every thing necessary to the perfection of our nature in holiness and happiness.

This happiness is not dispensed promiscuously to all the children of men, it is promised to them who believe, to them who are pure in heart, to them that do his commandments. But when the gospel speaks of holiness in general, or any particular grace, as a qualification for the blessings of the new covenant; it doth not—it cannot intend perfect holiness, or the exercise of grace without any mixture of sinful imperfection: It intends, that we aim at that which is right—that we have a sincere regard to God in our moral conduct—that our love is supremely fixed on him, so that no other object hath an equal place in our hearts, tho' we do not love him so much as we ought—that we allow ourselves in nothing that is contrary to the will of God—are heartily grieved when we do amiss—and daily press after higher attainments. Where there is such godly sincerity, we may be assured we are in a state of acceptance. Though all the connection there is between any goodness of our's, and any favor we receive from God, is owing entirely to his mercy and grace, yet the connection between true evangelical purity, and the blessings of the new covenant, is quite certain, being founded on the promise of the true and faithful God. A holy love to God, exhibiting itself in a correspondent temper and conduct, proves that we are christians, in a state of favor with God, and in the number of those whom he will receive to glory. One who hath a full persuasion of this may reasonably
rejoice

rejoice in God, and believe that his redemption draweth near. How much reason is there from this view of things, to bless the name of God, for that covenant of peace which is the foundation of all!

Secondly, From what hath been said, the most of us may learn the true reason why we have not the comforts of religion. Whatever other causes there may be of that darkness which afflicts the minds of many, yet have we not reason to judge and condemn ourselves? Can we wonder that God hides his face from us, when we have had so little of a holy filial fear of him—have been so unmindful of him—and so negligent of our duty to him? If we have any grace, ah! how languid! how almost imperceptible is it! May we not justly suspect, and be diffident of ourselves? Have we not often grieved that good Spirit, whereby christians are sealed to the day of redemption? Can we expect the Holy Ghost will favor us with his comforting visits, when that temple which ought to have been devoted wholly to him, hath harboured so many disorderly passions, and impure lusts, which are directly opposite to his holy nature? Our own consciences can bear but a feeble testimony for us, who have, in many instances, neglected duty—in many, acted in contradiction to it—and in our best actions have been greatly deficient. And if our own minds and consciences do not testify in our favor,

how

how can we have the witness of the Spirit of God, who is said to witness with our spirits? If our hearts condemn us, how can we have confidence towards God?

Thirdly, What hath been said teaches us how to prove and to try our comforts. Examination is a great and important duty; but in order to our having any advantage from it, it is necessary that we examine by a right rule: Our general directory is the word of God: This contains all those signs and marks by which we are to prove ourselves: They all amount to this—a conformity, in some degree, to the holy nature and will of God. We must therefore look into ourselves to know our true state. If we are reconciled to God, we shall find in ourselves a change from what we were— we shall have the exercise of grace in our souls— and we shall bring forth the fruits of the Spirit in our conversation. Is this the case with us? if it is, what better evidence can we have that we are true christians.—If the Spirit enable us to discern his work, we have no reason to question our right to his consolations.—But if you do not walk in the fear of God, in vain do you pretend to walk in the comfort of the Holy Ghost.—Are you the children of God, where is your child-like temper? Are you created anew in Christ Jesus, where are your good works? Are you the disciples of Christ,
where

where is your self-denial—your meekness—your refignation—your purity—your contempt of the world—your zeal for God—and your love to mankind?—There is no peace, faith my God, to the wicked.

Fourthly, Would you walk in the comfort of the Holy Ghost, be very careful to walk in the fear of the Lord. You must be justified by faith, and have peace with God thro' our Lord Jesus Christ, or you cannot rejoice in hope of the glory of God. You must have grace, before you can know that you have it. Make it, therefore, your constant prayer, "Create in me a clean heart, O God, and renew a right spirit." Be ever watchful over your heart, and careful of your life. Attend every duty in it's place. Be frequent and regular in the exercises of piety and devotion. Shew a proper regard to the great Redeemer and Saviour of men. Repent of your sins. Be holy in all manner of conversation. And continually labor to be wifer and better. This is the way to attain that peace and rest which a christian cannot but desire, though it is not the main thing he ought to desire. It is of more importance to be in a state of favor with God, than to know that this is our happy privilege—It is better to be religious, than to be assured that this is our just character. "There is many a one who might have been in a much more

more comfortable ſtate than he is, if he had minded his comfort leſs and his duty more ; if he had ſtudied more the pleaſing of God, than the pleaſure, peace, and ſatisfaction of his own mind ; if he had labored more to be a true obedient child of God, than to know that he is ſo." However, no one ought to be contented—no chriſtian can be contented, without knowing his true character. This is not only neceſſary to a life of comfort and joy, but tends greatly to promote a life of holineſs.

Laſtly, If you are ſo happy as to have the comforts of religion, give to God the glory of his grace, praiſe him for what he hath done, and for what he hath promiſed to do : Being confident of this very thing, that he which hath begun a good work in you, will perform it until the day of Jeſus Chriſt. To him be glory forever—AMEN.

SERMON

SERMON XII.

The Obligations to Family-Religion.

Joshua XXIV. 15.

------ *But as for me and my house, we will serve the Lord.*

THIS is the close of Joshua's noble and spirited addreſs to the people of Iſrael. Having given them an hiſtorical account of the great things God had done for their fathers and for them, he concludes with this very ſolemn application—" Now therefore fear the Lord, and ſerve him in ſincerity and in truth: And put away the gods which your fathers ſerved on the other ſide the flood, and in Egypt; and ſerve ye the Lord. And if it ſeem evil unto you to ſerve the Lord, chuſe you this day whom ye will serve; whether the gods whom your fathers served that were on the other side of the flood, or the gods of the Amorites in whose land ye dwell:—But as for me and my house, we will serve the Lord." Though all Israel should prefer some other god, it was his fixed resolution to serve Jehovah, and to command his house to adhere to him. He and his family would maintain the cause and worship of the true God, tho' there should be none to join them. Joshua could not answer for his family, that they should have an inward veneration of the supreme Being; but he could determine, that no one should reside with him, who would not unite in a visible acknowledgement of the God of Israel.

This great and good man first determined for himself, that he would serve the Lord. Heads of families should themselves set an example of piety, or all their endeavors with those under their care will be to little purpose. But the resolution of Joshua extended further; he considered himself as the Master and governor of a family, and obliged to something more than personal religion, and therefore says, "as for me and *my house*, we will serve the Lord;" intimating his firm resolution to maintain the worship of God in his house; and to make use of the authority with which God and nature had invested him, to oblige his houshold to attend upon

upon it. These words are therefore a proper foundation for a discourse upon family-religion.

Agreably, my present design is to show, that it is incumbent on every one who is at the head of a family, to maintain the worship of God in his house, or to serve the Lord with his houshold.

Upon this point, I am persuaded we shall have very few to oppose us, except those, who from their disinclination to religion itself, and to every expression of it, desire to frame excuses for their neglect. If social worship is ever reasonable, nature itself will lead us to family religion. Who are so adapted to unite together in exercises of devotion, as they who are united together in some very near relation, or in the most intimate bonds of friendship? one of which, we must suppose, is the case with all who are of the same family. These, in ordinary cases, best know each other's circumstances, cares and difficulties, and therefore can more properly join in praying with and for each other. They must have many common wants, which they may, in a united manner, seek to have supplied—They have many common mercies, which demand their thankful acknowledgments—They are usually affected with the same afflictions, which ought to lead them to God for help and support. The more devout heathen had their houshold gods, to whom they committed themselves; and will it not be a shame to christians, if there is a less appearance of religion in their houses, than was to be found in the houses of those who knew not the true God. There is a particular obligation on heads of families to promote the everlasting happiness of those under their care. But how poorly will the duties of instruction, of counsel, of a constant watch over their early steps, be performed, if we never pray with them. And it is much to be feared, that those parents and masters who wholly neglect to pray *with* their children and servants, do scarce ever pray *for* them, or even, I had almost said, for themselves. That they have an habitual spirit of indevotion, and very little regard to God and religion.

The scriptures do, in a very clear manner, intimate family worship to be a duty. We do not assert, that there is any precept, which, in plain and direct terms, enjoyns this practice; the reason of this omission is not, because family-worship is not a duty, as some would argue; but, because it is so plain a duty, and so evidently approves itself to the consciences of those who have a just sense of religion, that there was no need of an express injunction. There are some truths, and those of great importance, taken for granted by the sacred writers, or which are only implied in what they deliver. These truths so readily strike the mind, that there was no occasion for their being proposed in any other way. When Moses was about to give the history of the creation,

creation, he doth not say in express terms, there is a God, which is the foundation of all revelation, and all religion: He goes upon the hypothesis, that his readers believed the existence of an all-perfect Deity, and begins with saying, "In the beginning God created the heavens and the earth." We are not explicitly commanded to pray in secret at any particular times, but are only directed with respect to the manner in which secret prayer is to be performed, "Thou when thou prayest, enter into thy closet, and when thou hast shut thy door, pray to thy Father which is in secret." It is a point taken for granted, that good men would have their seasons for prayer, and the taking it for granted in this manner is, perhaps, the strongest way of expressing the expectation of the God of heaven.

This is the case with respect to family prayer; It is no where expressly injoined as a duty, but it is plainly intimated that it is. We read, § "Likewise ye husbands, dwell with them" (your wives) "according to knowledge, giving honor unto the wife, as the weaker vessel, and as being heirs together of the grace of life, that your prayers be not hindered." The most natural construction of these words is, that husbands should treat their wives with tenderness and respect, lest any uneasiness should arise, that would disturb their minds, and render them unfit for those exercises of social worship, which it was supposed they would maintain.

§ 1 Peter 3. 7.

The apostle aimed to encourage these nearest of earthly relatives in frequent acts of social worship, as the best method to preserve them in holiness and virtue, and particularly to promote a mutual regard and affection for each other.

We find this was the practice of those, whose names are recorded with honor in the sacred oracles.———When we are told of the removes of the Patriarchs, we read also of their building an altar to call on the name of the Lord ; and it was very seldom that any devout men offered their sacrifices in private ; it is much more probable, that their families were called to unite with them in these exercises of piety.—It was Joshua's resolution in our text, " as for me and my house we will serve the Lord," in which, as hath been already observed, he must refer to that religious worship, which he had determined to maintain in his house, for no otherwise could he engage for his house, that they should serve the Lord.—And it is observable, that, amidst all the festivity and pomp of that illustrious day, when David brought home the ark, and notwithstanding the holy transport to which this pious Prince was raised on this joyful occasion, he retired from the public solemnity, " to bless his houshold." * What can this intend, but that he went to pray with his family, and to implore the divine blessing upon them ? In no other way could
" he

* 2 Samuel 6. 20.

" he blefs his houfhold." It is probable, that when he found the time for his family worfhip was come, he left the facred feftival in which he had been engaged, that he might attend this more private exercife of religion.—It is reafonably fuppofed, that the devotion of Daniel, which he fo fteadily attended, notwithftanding the wicked decree contrived on purpofe to deftroy him, was family prayer. " He went into his houfe, and his windows being open in his chamber towards Jerufalem, he kneeled upon his knees three times a day, and prayed, and gave thanks to his God, as he did aforetime." † Had this been fecret or clofet prayer, it might eafily have been concealed from his enemies; however they might fufpect, they could not prove his violation of the king's edict; and it is hardly fuppofable, that he would make his fecret devotions public, on purpofe to furnifh evidence againft himfelf. It is faid, his windows were open towards Jerufalem, this was his ufual practice, not for oftentation, or that others might hear, but to fhow his regard to the God of Ifrael, and to ftrengthen his faith and confidence in Him, by looking towards his holy temple, the place where God had recorded his name, and where his prefence had been wont to refide.— We read of Cornelius, " He was a devout man, who feared God, with all his houfe." ‡ It was a religious family, a houfe in which God was worfhipped. Cornelius was at prayer in his houfe, §

or

† Daniel 6. 10. ‡ Acts 10. 2. § Verfe 30.

or with his houshold, when an angel was sent from heaven, to testify God's approbation of him, and to direct him to further means of instruction and improvement.

Family worship having been the practice of good men in all ages, we may reasonably suppose the apostle intended to include it, when he directed christians to pray " always with all prayer." ‖—Nor is there any reason to think this was a duty peculiar to those days, or which was practised only by saints of an eminent character. It is a duty so fit —so reasonable—and so agreable to the first notions of religion, that I cannot easily conceive of any objection which a devout mind can have to it.

It is not for me peremptorily to fix the seasons when this duty is to be attended: In this every master of a family hath an undoubted right to think and judge for himself. But nature itself seems to direct to the morning and evening.——When we have been carried through the passages of the day; and are met together in our common habitation, that we may again separate for our necessary repose; what can be more fit and decent, than that we should, with one heart and voice, bless God for the favors and protections of the day—humble ourselves for our miscarriages—and implore *his* care, through the silent watches of the night, of whom it is said, that

He

‖ Ephesians 6. 18.

He neither slumbers nor sleeps?———When in the morning we arise from our beds, how natural is it, before we enter on the business of the day, to return our thanks to Him who hath protected us in our defenceless hours—to ask the direction, care and blessing of our heavenly Father—and to commit ourselves to his guidance and influence, thro' the business and temptations of the day?—How beautiful is prayer in these returning seasons?—How pleasing must it be to God to observe our devout acknowlegements? Next to the satisfaction which He hath in himself, and in his own divine excellencies, He takes pleasure in the homage and obedience of the creatures which He hath made; Both, as by their right conduct they honor Him; and as, at the same time, they advance their own happiness. Whenever we approach Him in our acts of religious and social worship, we own Him as the greatest and best of beings—as the fountain of all good—and as ready to extend his goodness to his creatures: We acknowlege our dependance upon Him, and our obligations to Him. This is to shew forth his glory. What a happy effect is such a devout practice like to have on our own souls, and on the souls of those who are under our care!—What honorable sentiments of God will it naturally introduce into the minds of children, and other young persons, who generally constitute a great part of families, when, every morning and evening, a sacrifice of prayer and praise is offered up to Him!

What

What venerable conceptions will they form of this all-perfect Being, when they hear their parents and masters, whom they are taught to honor and reverence, daily acknowleging his superintendency over us, and all our concerns! How doth it tend to fix in their breasts, a sense of the presence, the perfection, the government of God; when they observe, that we dare not engage in business, nor retire to rest, without a solemn address to Him, devoutly imploring his favor, protection, and assistance! But at the same time, what an amiable representation doth it give of the Lord and Father of all, when they consider Him, as admitting us guilty sinners into his presence, allowing us to breathe out the desires of our souls before Him, and giving us the greatest encouragement to hope for audience and acceptance!

While family religion hath this happy tendency to produce in us and our's, just thoughts of the blessed God, it may also greatly advance our mutual ease and comfort. Our united devotions will naturally unite our hearts in love and affection: They tend to suppress all unchristian wrath, fierce resentment, and indecent murmurings; to promote a spirit of tenderness, and forbearance on the one part—duty and submission on the other—kindness and benevolence in all: They are happily calculated to make those under our care truly religious, and religion will make them whatsoever else they ought to be—obedient children—faithful servants,

servants. It will make every one good in every relation, and will secure the faithful performance of every social duty.

In speaking of Family-religion, I have confined myself to the article of devotion, not because this contains the whole of the duty; family instruction —reading the word of God—counselling, warning, and restraining those under our care—and every kind of family-government, come under this head; but as a single discourse would not allow of a distinct consideration of these particulars, so I look on family-prayer to be the leading duty. Where this is neglected, the other are like to be neglected also. Where this is attended with seriousness and solemnity, the other will seldom be omitted.

Your time will not allow me to enter upon a particular consideration of the manner, in which God is to be worshipped in our houses. Doubtless, those prayers which are offered up from pure hearts, and in the exercise of suitable graces, are most acceptable to this All-perfect Being; and, in a strict sense, these are the only sacrifices that will be acceptable to Him. But as it is a principle, which may have very dangerous consequences, that they who are not in a state of acceptance with God are not obliged to pray at all; so is it also, that they are not obliged to pray in their families. A neglect of family-worship is a direct affront offered to the

Majesty of Heaven, and puts us out of the way of a blessing. There is a principle of conscience in unregenerate men, a sense and impression of duty, which often leads them to do that which is in itself right; which awakens them to attend the means of grace and the exercises of religion; gives them a degree of seriousness and solemnity of mind; and excites in them desires after spiritual blessings: and it may be of advantage to attend family prayer from such principles, when there is no higher. Their prayers may serve, by the blessing of God, to make those who lead in these religious exercises, wiser and better, and they may have a happy effect upon others. Besides, if they who are heads of families are not themselves sincere christians, yet there may be sincere christians in their families, and these may offer up spiritual sacrifices, they may lift up holy hands, when they join in the addresses of those who are not holy; God may hear them praying by others; and, in answer to their prayers, bestow blessings on the families to which they belong. I proceed to the

APPLICATION.

And in the first place, I shall address those who practice the duty of family-worship. Beloved Brethren, continue, instant in prayer. As often as the stated seasons return upon you, and these, I hope, are as often as the return of morning and evening, let your prayers be going up to God—Let not a light matter, or a trivial excuse, prevail with you to put by your family devotions. I own, there may be some extraordinary occasions which afford a sufficient reason for omitting them; as when our temporal interest is likely to be very greatly injured, or when our neighbours, whom we are to love as ourselves, are in great danger. But we should be very careful, not to make excuses for omitting this important duty, when there is not a real exigency, or the call to some other duty is not quite apparent. In most cases that occur, we may have our family devotions, and either by shortening them, or by attending them a little earlier or later, may do what necessity or charity requires.

But let us not content ourselves with a bare attendance on these duties of religion. If the prayers of his people are acceptable to God, it is as they are spiritual sacrifices. The more our hearts are engaged in them, so much the more agreable they will be to that God, who hath pleasure in uprightness. If we are not very watchful, these frequently returning exercises will degenerate into mere form and custom. Too many, it is to be feared, content themselves with the performance, without attending to the frame of their minds. Their hearts are far from God, while they draw near to Him with their lips; and there is no inward devotion, when they profess solemnly to address Him. They hurry over a few good words, in a careless

and

and irreverent manner, and call it family worship. But this is not prayer—it is not religion—such sacrifices cannot be pleasing to the heart-searching God, altho' they should be offered by those whom he loves: for it must be owned that good men are often faulty in this respect, they are too slight and perfunctory in their family-devotions. Whenever we address the God of glory, the amazing distance between us should impress our minds, with a holy awe, and the most profound humility. That we may be in the best frame to attend family worship, it will be well for those who are engaged in business, to order things so, as to have this duty over in the morning, before they enter on their worldly affairs; and so seasonably in the evening, as that neither they who lead, nor they who join in the devotions, may be in a sleepy drowsy frame, the consequence of which will be inattention, and irreverence.

Secondly, I am to apply myself to those head of families who live in the habitual neglect of family worship. If this is a duty, the neglect of it must be infinitely displeasing to a holy God. He requires that you acknowlege Him in all your ways, but you live, as if there were no God to be acknowleged, or you were under no obligation to obey and serve him.—If there are any such prayerless heads of families now present before the Lord, (and would to God there were none) I must plainly ly tell you, the sin of such neglect lies at your door. To you it belongs, to set up the worship of God in your houses, and to take effectual care that all who are committed to your charge, whether children or servants, attend upon it.

It may be difficult to bring yourselves to attend this duty, when you have lived any time in the omission of it. You are ashamed, to let your domestics see that you have neglected what you ought to have practised—to confess, by an alteration of your conduct, that you have been wrong heretofore. But remember those words of our Saviour, " whosoever shall be ashamed of me, and of my words, of him shall the Son of man be ashamed, when he cometh in the glory of his Father, with his holy angels." * Are not you among those who are ashamed of Christ, who omit a known duty, lest you should be despised for having neglected it ? How terrible the thought of being raised to shame and everlasting contempt !—If you could be prevailed upon to begin, the main difficulty would be over ; you would find the work easy and pleasant. —You object, that by entering on family religion now, you shall implicitly condemn your-self—your children and servants will despise you. But do not your own consciences condemn you, while you live without any religious acknowlegement of God in your houses ?—Should you be called before the tribunal

* Mark 8. 38.

bunal of a holy and juſt God, have you not reaſon to fear he would condemn you?—Thoſe very children and ſervants, by whom you imagine you ſhall be lightly-eſteemed, if they have any degree of ſeriouſneſs—if they are not, by your example, made forgetful of God, and thoughtleſs about religion, cannot but look upon you as negligent of your duty to God, and to them; which will of courſe leſſen that reverence and regard they would otherwiſe have for you. I ſay, if they are not forgetful of God and unconcerned about religion;— But conſider, what a dreadful tendency your irreligious courſe of life hath to harden their minds, and to render them proof againſt every conſideration that can be propoſed to them!

Children are very apt to form themſelves by their parents, and to think all is right which they ſee them do. Eſpecially are they ready to follow them when their example doth not contradict their natural propenſities. It is difficult for pious parents to reſtrain their children, and to keep them within the bounds ſet by reaſon and religion, but it is not difficult for wicked parents to lead them aſtray— Melancholy is the influence which the bad example of parents and heads of families hath upon thoſe who are under them!—If children ſee their parents vicious, is it not to be feared they will be vicious too?—If their parents neglect God, is it to be wondered at that they alſo neglect Him?—And can

can you wish to be!—can you bear the thought of being—the inftruments of the future ruin of thofe you brought into being—of thofe fouls which were committed to your charge! You love your children, and will you not do all you can to preferve them from everlafting burnings? What an aggravation will it be of your mifery, if you have the guilt not only of your own, but your children's fins lying upon you!—Methinks, thefe confiderations, if you fuffer them to have their due weight, muft abundantly preponderate the thought of appearing contemptible in the eyes of thofe who are placed under your care, by owning you have done amifs, fuppofing they would really defpife you.—But this is fo far from being certain, that it is probable, the effect would be quite contrary—that they would rather efteem and honour you. It is impoffible, but they fhould take notice of your neglect; and if they come to years of thought, they will know it to be a neglect of duty: They will obferve, you do not live and practice as your neighbours do; and will naturally think, it is becaufe you are not fo good as your neighbours are; and will defpife you in their hearts. If you do not render to God that honor, which, as your Father and Mafter, He expects and claims from you; how can you reafonably expect, that your children and fervants fhould yield you that refpect which you demand from them! Think with yourfelf, when about to rebuke or correct a child for irreverence and

disobedience—

disobedience—What a wretch am I!—Who withhold from my heavenly Father that homage and respect, which is infinitely more justly due from me to Him, than any honor can be due from this child to me! And let this reflection lead you to amend your conduct towards God, as you expect your child should correct what is amiss in his behavior to you.—Oh! should our children behave towards us, as we do towards the glorious God, how should we resent and punish their ingratitude and disobedience!—How justly doth He say of himself, "My thoughts are not your thoughts, neither are your ways my ways, saith the Lord. For as the heavens are higher than the earth, so are my ways higher than your ways, and my thoughts than your thoughts." ¶

Are there any who object their inability to keep up family worship?—How can you know you have not ability, if you have never made the trial? Perhaps, if you should engage in the duty with seriousness, you would find your tongue like the pen of a ready writer. Or if you should not express yourself with so much exactness and propriety as some others do, God requires according to that which a man hath, and not according to that which he hath not, and accepts our prayers, not according to the elegance of the expression, but according to the sincerity of heart with which they are offered.

And

¶ Isaiah 55. 8, 9.

And they who attend on your devotions muft be very bad indeed, if inftead of uniting with you, they fpend the time in critically obferving the diction or language, in order to make their profane remarks afterwards. Such as thefe will be like to banter every expreffion of religion, and you muft either banifh them your families, or treat them with the neglect and contempt they deferve while they are there.

They who complain of their want of ability for family worfhip fhould endeavor to attain fome better acquaintance with religion, to know more of God and of themfelves; they fhould contemplate their mercies, confider their dangers, and think of their wants—Such meditations would foon fupply them with proper matter for prayer, and when the heart indites matter, words will feldom be wanting. " Every one can tell, how eloquent neceffity is wont to make beggars, that are pinched with want and hunger; they do not ufe to want words to reprefent their cafe." Let me efpecially recommend to fuch heads of families a conftant ferious perufal of the holy fcriptures; thefe are not only able to make them wife to falvation, but they are peculiarly adapted to help them in their devotions; they will furnifh their minds with futable fentiments, and their mouths with words proper for almoft every occafion.—If you cannot prevail with yourfelves to perform this duty in any other way, it is better to pray in the use of some plain familiar forms than not to pray at all. At least, you may use these, till by practice, and a more thorough acquaintance with religion, you have gained courage to pray without them; and then it seems more eligible to dismiss them. Possibly, I may be influenced by custom and the prejudices of education; but it appears to me, that the stated use of forms, especially in our more private exercises of religion, hath a tendency to damp our devotion, and leads to formality. They may not always have this effect, and I doubt not but many good christians, who chuse to make their addresses to God in this way, have the true spirit of prayer. We ought to bear with one another in our different sentiments on such circumstantial points; and to love and esteem those, who serve God sincerely, though their way of worship differ from our own.

Heads of families should take particular care, that all in their houses do, as far as may be, attend on these social exercises of religion; and to order the other affairs of the family so as that the meanest servant may not be excluded. How ill doth it look, when a family is called together to worship God, to find one half of it dispersed, and engaged in other business, as if they had no part nor lot in this matter!

I shall not pretend to dictate how much time is to be allotted for family devotion. Wisdom is profitable

fitable to direct in this, as in many other cases. There are two extremes which should carefully be avoided. The one is, when we hurry over the exercise in an indecent irreverent manner, as if we attended it only for form's sake, and wanted to have it at an end. The other extreme is, when we run out to a tedious length, as if we expected to be heard for our much speaking. " I reckon," to use the words of the judicious Mr. Howe, " that one quarter of an hour or less, spent with spirit and life, is a great deal better than hours together spent in nauseous flatting repetitions; (which was the pharisaical way) in such a tedious fulsome way, as tends to make religion a burthen and grievance. I think that is applicable to the purposes of religion, which hath been applied to meaner, much meaner purposes; that it is good to come from a meal with an appetite; that it is good to come so too from an exercise of religion, with those pleasant relishes left upon one's spirit, as may make him long for the return of such a season.

It is highly proper, when the family comes together for morning and evening devotions, to read some portion of God's holy word. This may be greater or less as suits our other affairs. By this practice, we put an honor on the scriptures—we may hope for great spiritual advantage—and we may be sure that all under our charge will get an acquaintance with the sacred oracles, although
there

there may be some who wholly neglect them at other times. The strict charge which God gave the Jews remains on record for our instruction; "Thou shalt teach them diligently unto thy children, and shalt talk of them when thou sittest in thine house, and when thou walkest by the way, and when thou liest down, and when thou risest up." †

I have now delivered my thoughts concerning the nature and importance of family religion. I make no apology for my freedom and plainness, because I have not said any thing that I did not think myself obliged to say.

Let me once more beseech you, oh! prayerless heads of families, to consider what hath been said. Think what account you shall be able to give to the great God—Think what is likely to become of your children's souls, while you set them such an awful example of irreligion—While you live without prayer, you live the life of an heathen; yea, you are worse, in this respect, than some even among the heathen—You bring discredit on the religion of the blessed Jesus—You are injurious to the community of which you are members. While you should be deprecating the judgments of heaven, you rather help to bring them down. No longer cast off fear, nor restrain prayer before God. Begin this evening. The sabbath is a good season to enter upon this duty; when, it is to be hoped, some serious impressions are made on your minds by the exercises of the day. This also is a time

† Deut. 6. 7.

when

when you are likely to meet with the least interruption. The serious consciencious performance of this duty will afford you a satisfaction you cannot enjoy while you neglect it. And who can tell what blessings you may prevail with a prayer-hearing God to bestow—on yourselves—on your families—on the land?

I shall conclude with some passages of an eminent author, only adapting them to ourselves and the present state of this community. "Do not you desire that the world should mend? that you may see better times; and to see your country flourish? If trade languish, every one is sensible. If your civil rights are in danger, there is a general alarm—Methinks we should not be insensible, if religion languish, if the power and spirit of the gospel are lost. But how shall religion live, if not in families? There is the great failure—and any place, that hath long been the seat of religion, when it comes to decay in that respect, will decay in other respects too. "Be instructed, O Jerusalem, lest my soul depart from thee; lest I make thee desolate, a land not inhabited." If that, which is the very soul of any people's good estate, even of the political body; if that retire, all moulders. How desirable a thing is it to see New-England in a prosperous flourishing condition! But never expect to see it so, if religion shall be in a languishing decaying condition, gradually from day to day. This will be a dreadful foretoken. The cry of wickedness is loud among us: If the cry of prayer shall prevail and be louder, this will draw down bleſſings. The cry of wickedneſs is calling for wrath and vengeance, for the vials to be poured out upon us; but if ſo many houſes as there are in this town, in this land, wherein religion is profeſſed, ſhould really become ſo many oratories, houſes of prayer, it is to be hoped there will be ſo many louder cries aſcending up into heaven for mercy. If there had been fifty, forty, thirty, twenty, nay ten righteous perſons in Sodom, that would have prevailed for mercy for that city. If ſo many as profeſs religion in New-England would but practiſe it, and family religion in particular, in this reſpect *vox populi* will be *vox Dei*, the voice of a praying people will be as the voice of God bleſſing us from above; and telling us that you have prevailed, the courſe of wrath is ſtopped, the decree reverſed, you ſhall ſee " the city of your ſolemnities a quiet habitation." This is ſaid by the prophet in a way of anſwer to the people who were brought in † praying, "O Lord, be gracious unto us, we have waited for thee; be thou their arm every morning, our ſalvation alſo in the time of trouble." Here was daily prayer aſcending and going up. It follows, § "Look upon Zion the city of our ſolemnities, thine eyes ſhall ſee Jeruſalem a quiet habitation, a tabernacle that ſhall not be taken down, not one of the ſtakes thereof ſhall ever be removed, neither ſhall any of the cords thereof be broken." AMEN!

† Iſa. 33. 2. § Verſe 20.

SERMON

SERMON XIII.

The Usefulness and Importance of Religious Education.

GENESIS XVIII. 19.

For I know him, that he will command his children and his houshold after him, and they shall keep the way of the Lord, to do justice and judgment.

ABRAHAM was a very eminent personage. He was distinguished by his situation and circumstances in life; but he distinguished himself more by his virtues. He had the signal honor of being called the friend of God. He sat a bright example of faith and obedience in many trying instances. But, at this time, when God was about to treat him with an uncommon degree of intimacy and condescension, the reason He is pleased to give is—

is—" I know him, that he will command his children and his houshold after him, and they shall keep the way of the Lord." You see how acceptable Abraham's pious care to transmit true religion to future generations was to God. It shows the very great Importance of parental endeavors to form children to virtue and holiness. God, as it were, singles this out among those virtues, which constituted the character of this illustrious Patriarch. Them that honor him, he will honor.

These words are a proper foundation to discourse of the duty of religious housholders, to instruct those under their care in the principles of religion and virtue; or, in the words of our text, to " command" their " children and houshold to keep the way of the Lord."

In the first place, I shall shew what we are to understand by keeping the way of the Lord.

Secondly, In what sense parents and heads of families are to command their children and houshold to keep the way of the Lord.

Thirdly, I shall endeavor to prove, that this is the character of every religious housholder, which will lead me to speak of the importance of the duty, and how peculiarly acceptable it is to God.

First, I am to shew what we are to understand by keeping the way of the Lord; it is added in the text, " to do juſtice and judgment." The phraſe includes univerſal moral rectitude, or the whole of that duty which creatures owe to God their Creator and Lord. This duty is, in ſome reſpects, different, under different diſpenſations. The foundation of moral virtue is always the ſame, the nature and perfections of God. But ſome particular circumſtances in religion, have been ſubject to alteration. For wiſe and good reaſons, God hath required, that men ſhould expreſs their regard to him, at one time, by rites and ceremonies, which have not been neceſſary at another. Religion hath been the ſame, but ſome appendages of religion have varied. As it is not my deſign critically to explain the text, but only to improve the example of Abraham for the quickening and encouragement of Chriſtian Parents, I ſhall not enquire into the ſtate of religion under the Abrahamic diſpenſation, but ſhall confine myſelf to what we are taught under the much clearer light of the goſpel.

The New-Teſtament plainly teaches us, that we muſt be ſaved in the way of faith, and in the way of holineſs. This is the " way of the Lord"—the way which is pleaſing to Him—the way which he obliges us to walk in—and with which He hath been pleaſed to connect eternal life. We are to believe the record which God hath given of his Son, and to yield him that tribute of homage, reverence,

verence, truſt, and obedience, which are juſtly due to his perſon and character. We are to ſubmit to his inſtructions—rely on his merits—and obey his commands. This is our duty. So far as we practiſe our duty, we "keep the way of the Lord." We do not walk in his way, when we reject his truths, or neglect the duties of our holy religion. However contemptuouſly ſome men ſpeak of faith, yet the goſpel lays great ſtreſs upon it, a belief of the truth is a fundamental principle in religion, and is neceſſary in order to juſtification and life. "He that believeth," ſaith our Saviour, "ſhall be ſaved; but he that believeth not ſhall be damned." On the other hand, in whatever high terms the goſpel ſpeaks of faith; it always ſuppoſes, that it is a vital operative principle, that it purifieth the heart, and is productive of univerſal holineſs. "Faith, if it hath not works, is dead, being alone."

To "*keep* the way of the Lord" intends continuance, or perſeverance in duty. It is not enough, that we believe the teſtimony of God concerning Jeſus Chriſt, at this or that particular time; it muſt be a continued exerciſe, a prevailing habit. A chriſtian is not perfect in this life; he daily ſins, and contracts new guilt; he can obtain pardon and comfort only by the view of a crucified Saviour, and an hearty acquieſcence in the goſpel ſcheme of ſalvation. This is the fountain ſet open for ſin and for uncleanneſs. This is what alone can pacify the conſcience

conscience of a sinner. Therefore christians are said to " live by the faith of the Son of God." Faith may be increased, it may grow stronger and stronger. It is by exercise that this and every other gracious habit is increased or strengthened. The most sublime acts of virtue will not prove that we are in the way to eternal life, unless, by patient continuance in the ways of well-doing, we seek for glory, honor, and immortality. He that endureth to the end shall be saved. Whatever change we may think we have experienced at any particular time, if the temper of our minds and the course of our lives be not correspondent, we know nothing of religion, and our trust is that of the hypocrite, which is " a spider's web," and will disappoint us when we have most need of support.

I am, secondly, to consider, in what sense parents and heads of families are to " command" their " children and houshold to keep the way of the Lord." Mankind do not naturally walk in the right way. There is too often seen in early life a propensity to sin. It discovers a strange unacquaintedness with human nature, to suppose that it is as much inclined to virtue as to vice. All the pains we can take are but just sufficient, they are often insufficient, to restrain the passions and appetites of those who are under our care, and to keep them from forbidden paths.———What would become of children?———What would become of families?———What would become of the world? if every one was left to walk after the inclinations of his own heart, without any check or restraint. This earth would probably become a scene of disorder and wickedness; men would abuse and devour one another; and a virtuous character would scarcely be found. The God of nature hath therefore constituted a kind of natural subordination; hath entrusted one to the care of another; and hath particularly fixed the relation of parents and children. Parents, from the natural affection which they have for their children, desire to keep them from things that would be prejudicial, take upon them to guide their early steps, and to point out the way in which they should go. This is the plan of Providence: and agreably to this plan, parents should endeavor to form the minds of their children to a love of virtue and goodness, and to preserve them in their tender years from those practices, which will make them the bane of society in this world, and expose them to the curse of God in the other.

There is certainly a distinction between right and wrong, virtue and vice. But how shall children find out this difference? We must not expect theywill be taught it by immediate inspiration: and if we leave them to the exercise of their own reason, and to that only; is there not room to fear, that before this is mature enough to guide them, if that should ever be the case, they will have contracted such habits of vice, as reason will never be able to eradicate

eradicate? Parents ought therefore to take them by the hand, and lead them in the way everlasting. God and nature have made this their duty. They are to " command" their children and houſhold to keep the way of the Lord.—Parents are rulers in their own houſes. They have authority over thoſe whom Providence hath committed to their charge. They may not enjoin any thing unreaſonable; but they may enjoin the commands of God, becauſe they are founded in the higheſt reaſon. They may forbid—they ought, as far as in them lies, to prevent whatever is contrary to the divine law. They have a right to inſiſt on the attention of their children, while they ſet before them the neceſſity and reaſonableneſs of a ſubmiſſion to God, their Maker and Lord. They ought to watch for the dawnings of reaſon, and to inſtruct them in the great truths and duties of our holy religion, as they are able to bear them. They ſhould endeavor to impreſs on their minds a ſenſe of the being and perfections of God, of his univerſal preſence, and moral government. They ſhould teach them the difference between good and evil, and ſtrive to beget in them, while they are yet young and tender, an abhorrence of ſin, and a love of virtue and holineſs. They ſhould labor to awaken conſcience, and to keep it active and vigilant. They ſhould obſerve their faults, correct their miſtakes, and warn them of their danger. They ſhould open to them the doctrine of a Mediator; ſet before them, in the moſt

engaging

engaging light, the aſtoniſhing love of Jeſus Chriſt, in taking our nature, to inſtruct and reform a vicious world, and to lay down his life a ſacrifice, that he might reconcile us to God. They ſhould teach them, that God will pardon the offences they commit, only on account of the merits of this glorious Redeemer, the reaſon they have to hope in the mercy of God through Chriſt, and the mighty encouragement there is to the practice of virtue, from the gracious declarations of the word. They ſhould endeavor to alarm their fears by the awful threatnings denounced againſt the impenitent and unbelieving, to melt their hearts into gratitude and love by the goodneſs of God, and to quicken their obedience by the glorious proſpects which the goſpel preſents. They ſhould make them ſenſible of their moral weakneſs and inſufficiency to that which is good ; this they may be early taught to obſerve, from their love of vanity, the tranſitory effects of their good reſolutions, and their frequent violations of their moſt ſolemn vows and promiſes. They ſhould ſoon make them acquainted with the treachery of their own hearts; and warn them of the ſnares and temptations with which they are continually ſurrounded. From all theſe conſiderations, they ſhould be led up to God as the ſource of all good ; they ſhould be taught the neceſſity of divine influence, and the importance of maintaining a conſtant intercourſe with the Deity, by frequent acts of devotion. Theſe are ſome of the truths and duties we

are

are to inculcate on our children. We shall doubtless often find great backwardness and opposition in them; and shall have frequent occasion to mourn the little effect of our instructions and endeavors; but we may not give way to discouragement; We should follow them with continual counsels; We should vary our methods of application; and use every just art of address, till we win them to God.

If the truths of religion were subjects of doubtful disputation; if the practice of virtue was a thing quite indifferent; we might leave children to themselves, and permit them to chuse this way or that, without taking any pains to influence their choice. But as this is a matter of the last consequence, as they will probably meet with innumerable allurements and temptations, and are in danger of being seduced by reason of their unacquaintedness with the world, the men and the things of it, we may well be allowed to improve all the means with which God hath furnished us, to preserve them.

It would be wrong and unjustifiable to use any deceitful arts, or to fill the minds of children with imaginary terrors. And what need can there be of our taking any such method? We need no arguments besides those which reason and religion afford us. These, and these only, we are to improve: These we are to set before them in the strongest light, and to press with unceasing perseverance.

But

But how ineffectual are our endeavors like to prove, if we do not exemplify the duties we inculcate! Children, as we have had occasion to mention in the preceding discourse, soon learn to observe their parents: They are apt, while they are young, if not afterwards, to form a high opinion of them, and are fond of treading in their steps. And if they see us careless in our walk, loose and vain in our conversation; if we are passionate, quarrelsome, intemperate, evil-speakers, profane; or are given to pleasure and dissipation; if we neglect God, mis-spend the sabbath, or are indifferent in our attendance on public institutions, in vain shall we enjoin on them the duties of religion and virtue. They will not think themselves obliged to observe those precepts, to which we pay no regard ourselves. They will look on our instructions as only matter of form, and of little importance, or that a very small degree of goodness is all that is necessary. It is an old maxim, but which contains a great deal of truth and justice, " The greatest reverence is due to children." They are so apt to form themselves by us, that we cannot be too cautious of our behaviour before them. They are ready to think that which is lawful for their instructors, is lawful for them, and to excuse themselves if they come a little short. If, therefore, a parent desires his children should aim at an exalted degree of piety, he should be an example of it himself; he should behave with the utmost circumspection and care,

and

and be sure never to practise himself what he condemns in them. In this way of instruction and example, a parent may do much to gain his children to virtue and a sober conversation. But something more is necessary. It is not enough that children are civil and moral in their deportment. This is good—it will prevent the uneasiness which a contrary behaviour would occasion—it will make them useful in the world. But, in order to their being happy in a future state, they must have an inward principle of holiness, a supreme love of God reigning in their hearts, and be governed by the peculiar motives of the gospel of Christ. You cannot but be sensible your power doth not reach so far—You cannot give your children a spiritual discernment of divine truths—You cannot captivate their hearts to the love of holiness—You cannot produce true repentance—You cannot, though you exhaust every topic of persuasion, compel them to devote themselves to God, and to maintain a constant regard to Him in their moral conduct. They may chuse, from respect for you, to avoid those things that would grieve and offend you, and to behave as they think will please you; but you cannot make them sincere christians—You cannot produce right principles—or bring them to act from those exalted motives which christianity proposes.——This is the work of God. He hath the most intimate access to our minds, and is able to work in us both to will and to do of his good pleasure. By the internal

ternal operation of his Spirit, he gives such a view of divine truth, as changes the heart, produces right dispositions, and leads to an answerable practice. He impresses such a sense of the reality and importance of religion, that Satan tries his arts in vain, the soul is fixed on God, and a conformity to this All-perfect Being is the height of its desire. This is a state of mind human nature is capable of. It is not an exalted pitch of virtue, which we may only view at a distance, and wish we could attain; it is what the gospel encourages us to aim at. Christ hath purchased the Spirit, we are directed to ask this great and comprehensive blessing, and are allowed to expect the bestowment of it. Our Heavenly Father is infinitely more ready to give the Holy Spirit to them that ask him, than the most affectionate parents on earth are, to give good things to their children. Parents therefore, besides all other means, ought to be frequent and earnest in their prayers to the God of all grace, that he would give their children a just concern for themselves, renew and sanctify the powers and faculties of their souls, and keep them in the love of God. They should, at the same time, endeavor to give their children such a rational conviction of the truths of religion, in their nature and importance, as will influence them to pray for themselves. They should set before them the condescending notice God takes of early piety, and the gracious promises he hath made to it, "I love them that love me, and they that seek me early shall find me." §

I proceed in the third place, to evidence the importance of the duty we have been explaining, how right it is in itself, and how peculiarly acceptable to God.

First, Hereby the glory of God is advanced. Every one reduced from the paths of sin is a new subject gained to Christ—The greater the number of those who are recovered to him, the less sin is committed, and the more good is done in the world—The less there is of sin, so much the less is God dishonored—The more there is of virtue, so much the more is God glorified. This cannot but be a powerful motive with one who hath sincere love to God, to exert himself to do good to all within his sphere; especially, to such as are most intimately connected with him, as with these he hath the greatest prospect of success.

Again, This is the best way of testifying our regard to our children. Religion was not designed to extirpate our natural affections: It tends to confirm those social ties, which are so necessary to the peace and good order of the world. But religion teaches us to turn our affections into the right channel, or to express our love in a right manner. Love naturally leads us to consult the interest of

the

§ Prov. 8. 17.

the object beloved; and we shall always look on that to be the interest of our children, which we value and chuse for ourselves. If we are earthly-minded, we shall be follicitous that they may be rich and great. If we have chosen God for our portion, we shall endeavor that they may make the same happy choice. A good man cannot, without the utmost distress, see his children, whom he loves as his own soul, immersed in sin, abandoned to vice, and going in the broad road to destruction. The thought, that they are the enemies of God, will be like a dart piercing through his heart. It will be an allay of the joy he feels from the prospect of being ever with the Lord, that these dear parts of himself will be excluded this blessedness, and must dwell in blackness of darkness for-ever. This consideration will give fervor to his prayers, and quicken his endeavors, that he may save their souls from death.

Once more, a concern for his own soul ought to influence every parent to do what he can, that his children may " keep the way of the Lord." They were given to him by God, the great Lord of all; they were committed to his care, that he might bring them up for God. This is an important part of our duty; and if we neglect their souls, we so far neglect our own. They will be in danger of perishing, but their blood God will require at our hands. This neglect will scatter darkness in our paths,

paths, and make a death-bed uncomfortable. Whereas, by inculcating the truths and motives of religion upon our children; we shall, probably, feel the weight of them on our own minds, and shall imperceptibly make advances in the christian temper; and there is reason to hope, that if we discharge our duty with fidelity, God will succeed our endeavors; and we shall have the unspeakable joy to see " our children walking in the truth."

It is observable, that God not only says of Abraham, " he will command his children and houshold after him;" but adds, " and they *shall* keep the way of the Lord," as if this was the certain effect: He will faithfully instruct them, and they will learn and practise what he teacheth. So we read in Proverbs, " Train up a child in the way he should go, and when he is old, he will not depart from it." † Such expressions, though not to be taken in a strict and absolute sense, are yet a great encouragement to a religious education. But if, after all, our children should prove refractory, dissolute, and vicious; as, alas! the case may be, we shall be clear of guilt, God will accept our faithful, though unsuccessful, endeavors; He " is not unrighteous to forget your work and labor of love, which ye have shewed towards his name." He speaks with peculiar approbation of Abraham's pious care of his houshold, and makes it a reason

for

† Prov. 22. 6.

for revealing his purpose concerning Sodom. It is pleasing to God, when his servants manifest a regard to him, and are careful of every part of their duty. It is pleasing to him, when parents bring up their children in the nurture and admonition of the Lord, as this puts their children in the way of a blessing, which they will not miss of, if they be not wanting to themselves. God delighteth not in the death of sinners, but had rather they should turn and live. He would have all men to be saved, and to come to the knowlege of the truth; and therefore he is pleased with every thing that tends to promote their salvation.

On the whole, If children are neglected, they are in danger of being dissolute and vicious—If this is their just character, they will be the disgrace of their parents, the bane of society, and the objects of the divine displeasure in a future world—If parents exert themselves to promote their best good, they may humbly hope, their children will be a comfort to them, a blessing to the world, and forever happy after this life; or, if they are incorrigible, their blood will be on their own heads.

And what possible objection can be made, to our treating our children as reasonable creatures?—to our endeavoring to make them feel that they are so?—and persuading them to think and act rationally

ly? Is it not right and fit to make them acquainted with truth, and to conduct them in the way that leads to life and glory? How incongruous is it to all the principles of reason, as well as religion, for parents to be anxious and distressed about the temporal interest of their children, and thoughtless about their eternal welfare? How careful are most parents to get their children instructed in some useful art and business, that they may be able to live in the world! They caution them, when they see any danger of their making a mistake—They advise and assist them—They inculcate care, industry, and frugality—They give them line upon line, precept upon precept, whether they will hear or whether they will forbear. And ought they not to have a greater concern for their souls, which are of infinitely more value than their bodies, and which are in continual danger of being lost—ruined forever?

IMPROVEMENT.

First, What hath been said may well lead parents to the most humbling and serious reflections. Alas! are there not many who stand in this relation that have no concern for their own souls? Such as these cannot be expected to have much concern for the spiritual welfare of their children. They cannot guide others in a way which they are unacquainted with themselves. If they attempt to admonish and instruct their children, how justly may their own hearts upbraid them? How pungently will their consciences, if they are not quite callous, expostulate? "Thou that teachest another, teachest thou not thyself?" When they reprove their children for not attending to the things that belong to their peace; how must their own hearts reproach them—"Thou art the man"—Thou art guilty of that very thing which thou condemnest in them! How can parents exhort their children to pray, when they never make their addresses at the throne of grace themselves! How can they inculcate sobriety and virtue, when they are sensual and wicked themselves! Their children will be ready to despise their instructions and to set at nought their counsels, however good in themselves: It will be well, if they do not contract a prejudice against religion itself, and think it all a delusion—a mere farce, when they find their teachers and instructors live in direct contradiction to their own precepts. Such evil examples, especially in parents, do more hurt, than all their counsels can possibly do good. They tend awfully to harden the minds of young persons, and to embolden them in those evil practices, which tend to perdition. And so far as you, who are parents, lead your children into the paths of vice, you will have the accumulated guilt of their sins to answer for at the bar of God. What additional horror will seize you, to see your sons—your daughters—at the left hand of their Judge, and to hear them accusing you

in

in that awful day ; I was committed to this father —to this mother—They were appointed by God and nature to be the inftructors of my childhood— They ought to have taught me the truths and duties of religion—But they neglected this important charge—They never prayed with me, nor taught me to pray—They did not counfel, warn, nor reprove me—I never heard from them what God expected from me, nor was urged to flee the wrath to come—They did not bring me to an acquaintance with the holy fcriptures, which might have made me wife to falvation—They did not teach me to reverence fabbaths, nor to prize the inftitutions of religion——On the contrary, I faw them carelefs and vain, fenfual and worldly, and I only followed the example they fat me—and by their means am now involved in endlefs, remedilefs ruin. —Curfed be the father that begat me ! and the mother that gave me fuck !—With what anguifh will you hear fuch dreadful accufations ! and how terrible the tho't of having thofe your companions in the place of torment, and of being inftrumental of bringing them there, whom you were under peculiar obligations to lead in the ways of truth and holinefs ! Oh ! be awakened, ye guilty parents, reflect with deep contrition on your paft neglects, and amend your ways and doings before it be too late, that neither you, nor your children may come into condemnation.

But, I fear, the charge doth not terminate here. Thofe parents, who have been wholly forgetful of

God, are not the only ones, who have reason to remember their faults with respect to the education of their children. Many, who have some sense of religion may find much in themselves to blame. Alas! have we, any of us, done our duty?—We have been careful, that our children might make a good external appearance; but have we been as sollicitous, that they might be adorned with the graces of the Spirit?—We have been anxious that they might live agreably in this world; but have we had equal anxiety that they might live for-ever in a better?—We have been distressed when they have met with difficulties, losses, and disappointments; but have we been as uneasy when we have seen them indifferent about religion, immersed in sin, and in danger of losing their immortal souls? And yet, we are convinced that the soul is of more worth than the body, and that eternity is of infinitely greater importance, than the short, the fleeting time of our continuance here.—We are persuaded of these great truths, we venture our all upon them; but we are too closely attached to this world; we are too sensibly affected with earthly things; we do not look at those eternal things, which are not seen, as we ought, and as we desire.—We complain of the badness of the times—of the degeneracy of the age—of the prevalence of vice and irreligion—and in particular, of the vanity and dissoluteness of our youth—and God knows, we do not complain without reason. But is not much of the levity and wickedness, we see in our children and young people,

ple, owing to ourselves? Have not they learned to think lightly of sacred things; because they have seen us careless in our attendance on the duties of religion, or because we have not more warmly pressed these duties on them? It cannot be supposed that a parent, who hath any, the least degree of goodness, can wholly neglect those under his care; but might we not have done more—much more, than we have done?—Surely we might. If we are heirs of the promises, how much reason have we for shame and remorse, in the reflection that when our Heavenly Father hath done so much for us, we have done so little for Him! that we have discovered so little affection for those who came out of our own bowels! that we have not been more industrious in our endeavors to promote their everlasting welfare!

The next head of Improvement is, to awaken parents to a sense of their duty, and to persuade them to attend it with the greatest diligence and care. "They should command their children and servants to keep the way of the Lord."—It becomes you, in the first place, to walk in this way yourselves. If you have a just concern for your own souls, you cannot be indifferent about the souls of your children. To neglect them is to endanger yourselves.—Consider, with seriousness and attention, your obligations to teach your children the truths and duties of our holy religion—You owe this to God—You owe it to them—The time is
short—

short—quickly—very quickly—your opportunities to instruct and counsel your children will be at an end.—Perhaps they may be taken from you by death ; and how amazingly distressing will be the parting, if you have reason to apprehend they have no acquaintance with God and divine things ; and that this fatal ignorance is owing to your neglect ! —If they are not taken from you, you must soon leave them, you must leave them in an ensnaring world, surrounded with temptations and dangers. Improve the time you have with them, to instruct them, and to lead them in the way in which they should go : Do what in you lies, to form their minds to religion and virtue, and to prepare them for a blessed immortality. With what comfort will you leave the world, if you have reason to think, that you leave those behind you, and who have proceeded from you, who will do more for God than you have done ! What delight and satisfaction may you have in the thought, that, though you are to be separated for a time, you shall again meet, never to be separated, but to rejoice together through eternal ages !—You may carry your tho'ts still further—What ineffable joy will it afford you, to see your children at the right hand of Christ ; and to hear that glorious, but condescending Savior, approving your care of them, accepting your endeavors to promote their good, and publicly declaring that all the happiness they now enjoy, all the glory they expect, is, under God, owing to

your

your piety, fidelity, and diligence ! How will it add to the felicity of that happy day, to hear your children, now perfected spirits, blessing and praising God, that they were born of parents, who devoted them to God, and followed them with their instructions and prayers ; and bearing testimony, before the assembled universe, to your faithful discharge of the trust reposed in you by the great Lord of all ! It will be an addition to your own blessedness, to find that you have been happily instrumental of increasing the number of Christ's disciples, of the heirs of glory ; and that not only you, but your children are to be admitted to the inconceivable joys of heaven. With what ecstaric delight will the glorified parents celebrate that infinite love, which hath distinguished them and theirs from the unbelieving world—from those unhappy wretches, who stand trembling at the bar of Jesus Christ; waiting to hear their doom ! With what holy gratitude will they cry out, Lord, here are we, and the children thou hast graciously given us ;—given us, not merely to be a transitory comfort in the world we have passed through ; but to be an addition to our joy through eternity !

Oh parents ! How ought such thoughts to rouse your souls, and animate you to the most vigorous and constant endeavors, to bring your children to the love and fear of God !—Lead them betimes to God—never rest, till you have reason to hope they are believers in Christ, and heirs of the kingdom—

Pray

Pray for them, and learn them to pray for themselves—Counsel them to begin with God, and to dedicate the morning of life to his service—Restrain them from bad company, and bad practices—Teach them to deny all ungodliness and worldly lusts, and to live soberly, righteously, and godly in the world—Enjoin upon them a sacred regard to the Lord's-day.──────

While our Rulers are taking laudable pains, to prevent the open profanation of this holy day ; ¶ or rather to prevent *their* being disturbed who would gladly keep it holy ; while they who are appointed to see our laws duly executed, are endeavoring, at the expence of their ease and comfort, to discharge their trust; methinks every religious housholder ought to second their endeavors, or rather go before them, and prevent all occasion of their exercising authority upon him, or upon those that belong to him. Most of the disorders on our sabbaths might be prevented, if heads of families would keep at home themselves, and restrain those who are under their care, from going abroad. If they have no scruples themselves, yet tenderness to us who have, and who think we ought to keep one day in seven holy to the Lord, should prevent their doing any thing to disturb and offend us. Although an external observation of the sabbath doth not prove that we are sincere christians, yet an open contempt of it gives a good deal of reason to fear we are not.

But

¶ This sermon was preached, by particular desire, the Lord's-day after a new election of wardens.

But to return.———Often remind your children of a future state—Admonish them of death, judgment and eternity—Charge them, in the name of God, to give diligent heed that they may be found of their Judge in peace. To all your counsels and endeavors be careful to add your own good example. Let them see by you, that religion is practicable, is amiable, and that you require no more of them, than you are willing to submit to yourselves. Let them see, that you esteem the service of God no unreasonable restraint, but rather a privilege; that you attend duty with delight and from choice; that you serve God with both a perfect heart and a willing mind.

While you take care of your children, do not forget the rest of your houshold. "I know him," as it is said in the text, "that he will command his children and houshold after him, and they shall keep the way of the Lord." Masters of families should inspect the manners of all in their houses, and inculcate upon them the nature and importance of religion. The meanest servants have souls, and are probationers for immortality. This consideration ought to come with peculiar force on those, who think they have a right to keep their fellow-creatures—their brethren, in a state of perpetual slavery. One argument, often used in favor of this practice, is, that these persons are, by means of this merchandize of slaves, brought to the light of the gospel. To give this argument the least appearance of weight, masters must take pains to instruct them in the principles of religion, and to make them partakers of the glorious liberty of the sons of God. Then *they* will have reason to rejoice in their otherwise unhappy lot. They will love and esteem you, they will serve you with chearfulness and fidelity, and bless God for you to eternity. But, if you neglect their souls, there is danger of their becoming more the children of disobedience than they were before; and their being brought into a christian land will be their greatest misfortune.

Thirdly, Let children be attentive to their parents, while they instruct and counsel them. Your piety and holy conversation will afford them the highest satisfaction: And when you consider how much they have done for you, if you have any ingenuousness of mind, or the least spark of gratitude, you cannot but wish to afford them all the comfort in your power. But whatever pleasure they have in you, or from you, your conformity to the nature and will of God will be of the greatest advantage to yourselves: Religion is a never-failing source of rest in this world, and will be followed with unceasing joy and glory in another.

Your pious parents are grieved, when they see you take to evil courses; and can you have the heart to do any thing to trouble those, to whom you are so obliged, and who think no pains too great to serve you! They are distressed to see you going in the paths of the destroyer, but your's will be the destruction.

destruction. You will feel the misery, the very thought of which makes them to tremble. They tremble for you now, but if they are faithful to your souls, they will be above being affected with your infelicity hereafter. They will be glorious, though you be not gathered. They will have none of that uneasiness, which your faults and miscarriages occasion them, in the present imperfect state. They will be swallowed up in God. His pleasure will be their's—his choice their choice. They will have no affection to created beings, further than they discern in them a conformity to God, the supreme object of their love. They will see those, who were once their nearest relatives, doomed to perdition, without any uneasy emotion—without a wish that it might be otherwise. They will acquiesce in their condemnation.—But as for you, all the advantages you have had in your education, all the light you have been favored with, will rise up in judgment against you, and be so many circumstances to aggravate your guilt. They will increase the horror of your own mind; and add to the fierceness of those flames, that will never be extinguished.

Lastly, Are any of you so unhappy, as to be left in your early days, under the care of parents or masters, who take no care of your best interest, who never instruct or pray with you; but, on the contrary, set an example, of levity, of profanness, of intemperance, of sabbath-breaking, and a disregard to religion; you have the more reason to watch over yourselves, and to pray to God for his grace to preserve you. You know you have souls of infinite worth—souls which are now upon their probation for eternity—You hear of Christ—You have the holy scriptures—You can find opportunities to attend the institutions of religion—You have means sufficient to leave you without excuse, if you neglect God, and live in sin. If you have not so many advantages as some others have, you ought to be the more diligent in improving the advantages you have. Your adherence to God, when you have so many temptations to forsake Him, will be peculiarly pleasing to Him. He will remember all your trials, discouragements, and self-denial. The favor of God is not confined to the children of his covenant servants; He is able even of stones to raise up children unto Abraham; there was some good thing toward the Lord God of Israel found in a son of Jeroboam, who made Israel to sin; very unworthy parents have sometimes been blessed with pious and virtuous children. As none will be admitted to the blessings of Christ's kingdom, because they have had the honor to descend from religious parents; so none will be excluded, because their parents were profane and wicked. Whatsoever good thing any man doth, the same shall he receive of the Lord. God is no respecter of persons, but in every nation, and in every family, he that feareth God, and worketh righteousness, shall be accepted of Him.

SERMON

MALACHI I. 7.

Ye say the table of the Lord is contemptible.

THE altar and table of the Lord are used as words of the same import in several of the prophecies. We read in the prophetical description of the temple, " The altar of wood was three cubits high, and the length thereof two cubits—and he said unto me, This is the *Table* that is before the Lord." §

God expected from the Jews a sacred regard to his institutions; that they should approach them with

§ Ezek. 41. 22.

with that purity and preparation which the law required, and attend them with that seriousness, decency, and humility, which became them, when in the presence of the Divine Majesty. "Ye shall keep my sabbaths, and reverence my sanctuary; I am the Lord:" † A neglect here God esteemed an affront offered to Him. To despise his ordinances was to despise Him. Accordingly, in our context, God declared himself highly displeased with their offerings, and pronounced an awful curse on those who presented them. "A son honoreth his father, and a servant his master, if then I be a father, where is mine honor? and if I be a master, where is my fear? saith the Lord of hosts unto you, O priests, that despise my name." Instead of pleading guilty to this charge, and correcting their faults, they are represented as standing upon their justification, "And ye say, wherein have we despised thy name?" Notwithstanding the insolence of this reply, God condescended to enter into particulars, "Ye offer polluted bread upon mine altar." They enquire again, "Wherein have we polluted thee?" They either denied that they offered such polluted things; or, that the imperfections of their services any way affected the All-perfect Deity. He replies, "In that ye say the table of the Lord is contemptible." It is not likely they ventured to say this in express words, but this was the language of their practice. They attended on the institutions of religion with levity and indifference, so as to shew that
they

† Levit. 19. 30.

they set no value on them; or, their general behaviour was profane and wicked, whereby they led others to despise ordinances, which had so little good effect on those who pretended to observe them.

The spirit of our text reacheth to gospel times. Although the particular rites and sacrifices of the Mosaic dispensation are abrogated, yet God hath still his sacred institutions, which are designed to keep up an intercourse between the great God of heaven, and us his indigent dependent creatures; and are most wisely adapted to make us more holy and spiritual. As they are appointed by the wise Governor of the universe, we ought to have the highest sense of their importance—To attend upon them with the utmost reverence and respect—and to avoid every thing which would look as if we despised them ourselves, or might lead others to despise them.

I might profitably discourse on all the parts of instituted worship, and caution you to take heed how you observe them. But my design is to speak particularly of that ordinance, to which the letter of our text naturally leads our thoughts.—Had the Lord a table under the Jewish Œconomy? He hath also a table under the Christian dispensation. We read in one place, of " eating the Lord's supper," This is expressed in another place, by partaking of the Lord's table: Both phrases refer to that sacred entertainment, which Christ hath prepared,

pared, and by which we are to shew the Lord's death until he come. This entertainment is spiritiual, the blessings it was designed to convey are spiritual, & we ought to be spiritual in our attendance upon it. "God is a Spirit, and they that worship Him," should "worship Him in spirit and in truth." Did the Jews say; "the table of the Lord is contemptible?" and is not this the language of christians? Is not this the language of our practice? If an infidel was to observe the conduct of most among us with respect to the Lord's table, would he not suppose we despised the institution, and thought it of no importance at all?—The most wholly neglect it—Some rush carelesly to it—Others attend upon it with a calm indifference—Too many take no care to behave agreably to the profession which they make there. All these practically say, "The table of the Lord is contemptible." You would, perhaps, tremble at the thought of using such profane language; but if you say this by your behavior and conduct, surely you are not free from this impiety.—It may not be amiss to set before you, in its proper colors, the contempt you cast on this ordinance, that you may be awakened and led to repentance—And as my design is, by the blessing of God, to reach your consciences, you will suffer me to speak with all possible plainness.

First, They say "that the table of the Lord is contemptible," who neglect to attend on the supper of the Lord. There is scarcely any thing plainer in the

the sacred oracles, than the obligations christians are under, to commemorate the love and grace of JesusChrist at his table. OurLord says," Do this in remembrance of me." St. Paul says, " Thus are ye to shew forth the Lord's death till he come ;" and yet, how few are there, comparatively, who obey this command, or attend this sacred institution? It begins to be a rare thing to see any coming to the table of the Lord. They, who have been given up to God in baptism, neglect to devote themselves to Him, when they come to years. Not only dissolute and profane persons turn their backs upon this ordinance ; but persons of character, who make conscience of their ways, and appear to have a serious sense of religion on their minds. Parents, who ought, as their children grow up, and their rational powers expand, to take them by the hand and lead them in the ways of piety, set them an example, in this instance, of a criminal neglect. Our young people, as soon as they are capable of observing, see so many of a superior character omitting this duty, that they naturally conclude it is a matter of indifference, whether they perform it or not. And they, who have lived long in the neglect of this ordinance, find so many as negligent as themselves, that they feel neither shame nor remorse ; they become easy, while they live in disobedience to as plain a command as any in the Bible. I appeal to all present, whether this is not a true state of things among us. The neglect of the

Lord's

Lord's supper is so general a thing, that I have no fear you will think I point out particular persons; I rather fear, particular persons will not think themselves immediately concerned, where the charge is so general, and affects so many.

But, my brethren, is not this a matter which well deserves your serious consideration? Here is a plain command of Jesus Christ, who hath the highest claim to your obedience—It is the command of Him, who hath loved you and given himself for you—It is his last, his dying command—and yet you disregard and neglect it. Is not this to say, as plainly as the Jews did, " the table of the Lord is contemptible?" Can you cast more visible contempt upon this institution, than by such an habitual neglect? Is not this to declare to the world, that you think it of no importance, whether you obey Christ or not? that his institutions may as well be omitted, and his ordinances rejected? and do not such reflections in the end fall upon him who is the Author of them?—upon him whom God would have all men to honor even as they honor the Father?

Some make a great distinction between moral and positive duties. Moral duties, they tell us, are of everlasting obligation; positive duties depend on the will of God. But is it not an everlasting truth, that God is to be obeyed, whatever he requires

quires of his creatures ? Is not the Lord's supper adapted to answer many moral purposes ? While, therefore, we endeavor to shew all possible regard to every moral duty, we are not to despise those which are called positive institutions, as if they were of inferior obligation ; or, as if the neglect of them were a matter of trifling concernment. We ought to venerate every divine appointment, tho' there is no apparent reason for it, but the will of God the sovereign Lord of all. If mercy is sometimes to be set before sacrifice, sacrifice is not therefore to be neglected, but to be observed with reverence and solemnity of mind.

It is an awful consideration, that so many live in the habitual breach of a command of God. That the careless and profane should turn their backs upon the holy eucharist, is what we expect, yea, while they retain this character, it is what we desire. But that you, who appear to have a regard to our blessed Saviour, and to make conscience of your conduct in other instances;—that you, who appear to have a sense of the worth of your souls, of the shortness of your time, and to live in expectation of an eternal state—that you should habitually neglect to do this public honor to our blessed Redeemer, is what we cannot justify, nor well account for. We cannot—we dare not think, that all, who absent themselves from the Lord's table, are strangers to the power of godliness ; it would be uncharitable

charitable so much as to suspect this. But surely religion hath not its proper influence on their minds; if it had, they could not refuse this expression of regard to Christ; their grateful souls would rejoice in every opportunity of testifying their love to this blessed Redeemer, and of commemorating his love to them. With respect to some who do not attend this ordinance of Christ, we have reason to believe, they do not turn their backs upon it without sensible grief and remorse; they are convinced of their obligations to their Saviour and Lord, but they have some mistaken notions of the ordinance, or they have doubts about their qualifications for it. They would gladly wait on Christ in this way of his appointment, but they fear they should not be worthy guests; or are jealous of themselves, that they should not walk agreably to their profession. These are much to be pitied, as they cannot but have much anxiety and distress in their own minds, and must be strangely tortured, between their desire to obey the command of Christ, and the fear lest they should not come with acceptance. Where persons have such difficulties and fears, however faulty they may be in entertaining them, their neglecting this ordinance is not to be considered as equally criminal with their's, who give themselves no thought about the matter, or think of it only with a careless indifference. A merciful God will without doubt make all gracious allowances. But as their difficulties and fears are a secret between
God

God and their own souls, or are known only to a few, their absenting themselves speaks the same language to the world, and therefore reflects the same dishonor on God, as doth the absence of those who are careless and secure. This appearance of things, and the construction which may be put upon their conduct, should make them cautious, how they give occasion for such offences, by yielding to unreasonable scruples and objections; and should give them the most serious concern, to walk in all the commandments and ordinances of the Lord blameless.

It may not be amiss to add, that by your not communicating at the sacrament of the Lord's supper, you not only dishonor God, but you greatly hurt and injure your own souls. You deprive yourselves of the advantages you might reasonably hope to receive by a serious consciencious attendance upon it; these advantages are so many and great, that we may justly excite you to it as a privilege, as well as charge it upon you as a duty. Your omitting this duty is, we are persuaded, the cause of that languor and indifference in the service of God —of that declension of religion in your soul—and of those fears about your state, which you so frequently complain of.—You do not partake of that spiritual food which Christ hath provided for his church, and therefore do not receive that nourishment from him, which is of so much importance in the christian life—You do not obey a plain pre-

cept

cept of your Saviour—your dying Saviour—and are therefore juftly apprehenfive, that as you have neglected to remember him at his table on earth, he will not remember you when he cometh in his kingdom.——A neglect of this ordinance makes death-beds uncomfortable: Many have lamented in their laft hours, that they have not obeyed this exprefs command, that they have publicly difhonored the Saviour of men, by their criminal omiffion of this duty.

Further, By abfenting yourfelves from the Lord's table, you caft ftumbling blocks in the way of others; they are difcouraged from making a profeffion, when they fee perfons afraid to engage in fuch a folemn tranfaction, who have been longer in the fchool of Chrift, and who are much better acquainted with religion, than they can pretend to be. This is a confideration which ought deeply to affect parents, and others who ftand in a fuperior relation. It may reafonably be fuppofed, that their example will have great influence on their children and fervants, efpecially where it falls in with the natural depravity and backwardnefs of the human heart. They fhould, therefore, facredly avoid every thing, which tends to give thofe under their care light thoughts of religion—to hinder them from attending their duty,—or to make them eafy in the omiffion of it.

But

But let who will neglect the institutions of religion, it is no argument that you may neglect them. Possibly, your parents have particular reasons for absenting themselves from the Lord's table, which do not affect you. Whether they have or not, your duty is plain, to have respect to all the commandments of Christ. If your parents sin, it is no reason that you should sin with them. You ought to follow their good examples, but may by no means follow them to do evil. Perhaps by performing your duty, you may stimulate them to perform their's.

You may not excuse yourself from attending on the supper of the Lord, because you are young, and are not yet settled in the world. You are not so young, but you may die; or, if you are spared in life, it will afford you unspeakable comfort, that you made the dedication of yourself to God in your early days. Whereas, if you defer this great and necessary work, new temptations and difficulties will arise, and there is danger that you will never engage in it at all. This is a consideration of great weight, with respect to the sacrament of the Lord's supper. Many young people, being deeply impressed with the truths of religion, have had serious intentions of coming to the table of the Lord, but they have put it off from time to time, till they have grown easy in their neglect, and contracted an almost total indifference about it. The danger of such an un-

unhappy effect is a good reason, why you should make haste and not delay to keep this commandment of God.

But am I to come to this ordinance, without any preparation—without any regard to God—any desires after Christ—any concern for my spiritual and eternal interest—and while I know myself to be careless and indifferent about the things of religion?—By no means. We shall endeavor under the next head to guard against rushing precipitately to divine ordinances. But if you are really unprepared, and know yourself to be so; what is to be done? Are you to sit down satisfied, and as if you had no concern with the sacrament, because, in your present state, you cannot worthily partake of it? Is not the command still to you, "Do this in remembrance of me"? Is it a sufficient reason for your neglect of this institution, that you are in so bad a frame, that you dare not make a profession of religion, or take the covenant of God into your mouth? Do you plead this as an excuse? Surely it is the worst plea you could make. Such unpreparedness is your fault; and can that which is your fault and your sin, be a sufficient excuse for your neglect of a command of Christ? Or is it any excuse at all? Methinks it ought to alarm you, that you are in such a state, that you dare not make a profession of religion; that you are shut out from communion with the people of God; that you may not partake of that

that bread and wine, which were defigned to nourifh and comfort the fouls of men. While you are unprepared for the Lord's fupper, you are unprepared for death, you are unfit for the kingdom of heaven. If you are unworthy to unite with the faints on earth, how can you have an admiffion into the general affembly and church of the firft-born, whofe names are written in heaven, or unite with the fpirits of juft men made perfect? Every time you leave the Lord's table, and are, as it were, excluded from this inftitution of Chrift, confider with yourfelf, what if I fhould be excluded from the marriage fupper of the Lamb—fhould be fhut out from the prefence of Chrift—and doomed to an everlafting feparation from Him? Is a ftate which may terminate in fuch awful deftruction to be continued in? Ought you not, with the utmoft earneftnefs, to implore the Spirit and grace of God, that you may be delivered out of it? Should you not feek every difpofition, which is neceffary to prepare you for the Lord's table, and to make you a worthy gueft there? This is the way to get thefe objections removed. But nothing can be more perverfe and unreafonable than to fuppofe, that any are excufable in their neglect of this ordinance, becaufe they are refolved not to be prepared for it. And though perfons of fuch a temper are not to be encouraged to come to the facrament, yet let them not think that their neglect is an innocent thing: A prince, who invites guefts to an entertainment, is juftly offended, if they

do

do not come; it is no excuse that they have not a suitable habit, when he alloweth them to supply themselves out of his own ward-robe. There is, oh sinner, grace enough in Christ, but if you will not accept and improve it, nothing awaits you but indignation and wrath, tribulation and anguish.

But oftentimes, they, who make these objections, are better prepared than they are willing to own, and perhaps much better than some who come to this ordinance. Hypocrites boldly presume, while many diffident trembling christians tarry away. Their fears keep them from attending an institution, which was designed as a happy means of removing them. If you find desires after Christ, and the blessings he hath to bestow, though you cannot determine these desires to be gracious, if you are determined by the help of God, to devote yourselves to Him, and to live as the gospel teaches you to live, you are the persons whom Christ invites to his table. Nor will it free you from your obligation to obey Him, that you have doubts and fears about your qualifications for this ordinance. You cannot neglect it and be blameless.

Many are deterred from the Lord's table by that passage in the epistle of Paul to the Corinthians, "He that eateth and drinketh unworthily, eateth and drinketh damnation to himself, not discerning the Lord's body." † But this text, rightly understood,

† 1 Cor. 11. 29.

understood, need not give any serious person the least uneasiness. The apostle explains what he means by their eating and drinking *unworthily*, in those words, "not discerning the Lord's body." The Corinthians, instead of coming to the Lord's table as a religious rite, came to it as to a common meal. They used the church, as one expresses it, more like an eating or a tipling house, than like the house of God. This was a notorious abuse of the ordinance, it was most unworthy conduct, it was irreverent and profane. The unworthy partaking therefore, which the apostle condemns, respects the manner in which they attended the sacrament, their behaviour at that time; and not their general state, or the habitual frame of their minds. Gracious persons may possibly, through incaution, be guilty of this eating and drinking unworthily, they ought, in some places, and under some circumstances, to be greatly on their guard. The word rendered by our translators, *damnation*, doth not at all refer to that punishment, to which the wicked will be consigned in a future state, it is rendered *judgment* in the margin; and the context plainly shews, that the judgment intended was wholly of a temporal nature; it immediately follows, "for this cause, many are sick and weakly among you, and many sleep." Their indecent profane carriage bro't such discredit on christianity, that God saw fit to testify against it, by inflicting temporal evils upon them, some were sick and some died. But as to punishment in another world, or the damnation of hell, not one word is said about it. Nor is it said, that these persons, criminal as they were, would be sentenced to it. The apostle intimates, that the very end, for which these persons were punished, was, that they might not be punished in another state. "But when we are judged, we are chastened of the Lord, that we might not be condemned with the world."

We own, that if a person partakes of the Lord's supper unworthily, in a careless irreverent manner, and never repents of so great a sin, he may expect condemnation in another state; this is a truth, tho' it is not the truth conveyed to us in this place. But what do we say in this more than we may say of any other institution? If we pray unworthily, if we hear unworthily, if we spend the time of divine worship, in laughing, whispering, if we set ourselves to sleep, or to gaze on the objects around us, so as to cast contempt on the duties we are called to engage in, these sins as certainly expose to future punishment, as unworthy partaking of the sacrament. And yet, would any one, for this reason, neglect these duties, or totally abstain from them? No; if he acts wisely, he will repent of what is amiss, and endeavor to correct it for the time to come. This is the method we should take with respect to the duty we are considering.

Are you so incumbered with worldly cares, that you cannot find time to prepare for this ordinance? Must you go to your farm and your merchandize, and

and for this reason do you neglect this institution? This is a certain evidence, that you prefer the world to Christ, and spiritual and eternal blessings; and may you not then justly fear, that he will disown and reject you another day? So the King is represented as dealing with those who would not come to his feast. §

Are any of you fearful, that, by making a profession of religion, you shall be under stronger obligations to holiness, than you now are?—It is an excuse you may well be ashamed of. There cannot be a stronger reason for a compliance with this precept of our Saviour. Rectitude of heart and life is your duty—it is your interest—it is what you pretend to see the necessity of—You find, by daily experience, the too little efficacy of the arguments and motives of religion; the disposition of your mind, and the practice of your life, are very different from what they ought to be. Can you then, convinced as you are, of the necessity of a conformity to the nature and will of God, omit any means of attaining to this blessed end? Will you live in the habitual neglect of an institution, so wisely adapted to make you what you ought to be, as is the supper of the Lord? and will you dare to give as a reason, that you shall be obliged to greater strictness and purity? You have reason to fear, not only that you are yet in an unrenewed state; but that you shall always continue so—That you shall lose all impressions of religion, and grow absolutely

§ Matt. 22. beg.

lutely careless and secure.——One reason why I am so earnest in pressing this duty is, because I am persuaded, it hath often been a check and restraint to persons through the whole course of their lives ; and a powerful excitement to holy living. The sense they have of obligation from their public profession, hath made them much more regular and watchful than they would otherwise have been, and hath fixed the principles of religion in their souls. There are, 'tis true, melancholy instances of apostacy, some have been, and are a disgrace to their profession. But it can be no reason, why others should neglect an ordinance so well adapted to promote their best good, that it hath not this effect on every one who attends it. It may well be expected, that there will be hypocrites in the church; there was a Judas even in the college of the apostles. Weak as you are in yourselves, the grace of Christ is sufficient to preserve you, and to keep you from falling.

I have now endeavored to remove the obstructions that are in the way of many, and keep them from coming to the Lord's table. It is an ordinance by no means to be neglected, and it is surprising that any serious person can live in the omission of this duty, without constant pain and uneasiness. They certainly practise, as if they tho't the table of the Lord contemptible, and lead those who observe them to despise this sacred institution. Whereas by their serious and exemplary attendance, they might quicken others to their duty.

SERMON

SERMON XV.

The Table of the Lord rendered contemptible.

MALACHI I. 7.

Ye say the table of the Lord is contemptible.

I SHALL think I have done an important service to the interest of religion and to your souls, if I may be any way instrumental, to awaken in you, my hearers, a just regard to the holy institution of the supper. With this view, I endeavored in a former discourse, to set before you the evil and danger of neglecting a religious rite, so expresly enjoined on his disciples by our blessed Lord. This is to despise the table of the Lord. But we are not less guilty of this impiety, if we rush upon a christian profession without thought and deliberation. We ought to act, in so important a transaction,

tion, with great ſeriouſneſs and ſolemnity. I go on, therefore, to obſerve

Secondly, They practically adopt the language of our text, who come to the Lord's ſupper with apparent careleſſneſs and indevotion. If you was invited, by one greatly your ſuperior, to an entertainment, you would think it a piece of reſpect, to have on your beſt attire, and to appear before him in a clean and decent habit. Every one would think you put an affront upon him, if you came to his table in a ſordid ſlovenly dreſs. The greater the perſon who invited you, the more careful would you be. If it was your Prince, with what ſollicitude would you avoid every thing indecent, every thing he would be likely to diſapprove of? And ſhall we not be much more ſollicitous to be ſuitably adorned, when we come before Him, who is King of kings and Lord of lords. The habit of the body is indeed of little importance; it is the temper of the mind He chiefly regards; and it is infinitely offenſive to this holy Lord God, when we preſent ourſelves before Him without due thought and conſideration; and the more ſolemn the ordinance in which we approach Him, the more careful ſhould we be. Here,

Firſt, They caſt contempt on the table of the Lord, who have hypocritical views in coming to that holy ordinance. By hypocritial views,

views, I intend your putting on a shew of religion, not from any regard to God—not from any sense of the authority of our blessed Redeemer, or your obligations to him:—But merely in conformity to those whom you would be thought to imitate—that you may appear to men to be religious—that the world may think favorably of you—that you may avoid any outward inconvenience—or may have some temporal advantage. Nothing can be more contrary to the great design of this institution, than to prostitute it to such unworthy purposes—to make use of it to promote sinister worldly ends. "Do this," says our Lord, "in remembrance of me." This religious rite was established, to affect our souls with a sense of the great things Jesus Christ hath done and suffered for sinful man—to remind us of his love—of our infinite obligations to him—and, in this way, to cure us of our moral disorders—to purify our souls—to promote the christian temper—and to quicken us to all holy obedience. And that it may have these effects should be our aim in attending upon it. Can any thing be more affrontive to the great Author of our religion, than to lay aside these pure and spiritual views, and to make use of this sacred institution, to carry on designs that are quite foreign from it? This is like those, who carried their merchandize into the temple, whom our Lord expelled with that severe rebuke, "It is written, my house shall be called the house of prayer, but

ye

ye have made it a den of thieves." And though He may not think it necessary to testify against our impiety in the present state, yet he undoubtedly will, unless we repent, in that day, when He will come to judge the world in righteousness. I am far from throwing discouragements in the way of such as are willing to come to this ordinance; but who can help being astonished at the hardiness of those, that venture to approach this holy institution, when at the same time they feel in themselves no serious desires or purposes, and so cannot but know they are unworthy partakers; especially, if they are conscious, that their intentions in coming are directly contrary to what they ought to be!

While upon this head, I cannot but express my grief, that this holy sacrament, which was designed only for spiritual purposes, is, in our nation, used as a test for civil and military offices; whereby multitudes of a most profligate character are laid under an almost insuperable temptation, to come to the Lord's table—to be guilty of horrid hypocrisy—a most daring profanation of holy things: And the ministers of Christ have no legal power, to refuse the sacred elements to the vilest debauchee, who demands them as a qualification for an office. Such an abuse and perversion of this ordinance hath an awful tendency to render it contemptible; and may be justly esteemed one cause of that infidelity and impiety, which are so generally ly complained of by the friends of religion and virtue. May God awaken thofe to whom it belongs, to remove this ftumbling-block out of the way, and to reform an abuſe which hath been long offenſive to the more ſerious part of the nation, both conformifts and non-conformifts! This leads me to ſay

Secondly, It makes the Lord's table contemptible, when they who are openly wicked and profane preſume to approach this holy ordinance. The only reaſon of our eating and drinking bread and wine in the ſacramental ſupper is, that Jeſus Chriſt hath commanded it. And if the will and authority of Chriſt is the only foundation upon which we obſerve this religious rite, it plainly follows that our obſerving it is an implicit acknowlegement of his authority to impoſe commands upon us; or, in other words that He is our Lord, and that we are bound to ſubmit to him in all things; for if he hath a right to our obedience in one inſtance, he hath a right to it in all other inſtances. Our coming to the ſacrament is in ſhort a profeſſion of the chriſtian religion. But how awfully contemptible is ſuch a profeſſion, when made by men who live in known ſin, and indulge to practices that are directly contrary to the laws of Chriſt and the rules of the goſpel. Can there be greater prevarication, than for a man to go immediately from the commiſſion of the moſt flagitious crimes to partake of the Lord's ſupper?

supper? This is to trifle with God in a sacred act of religion; it is worse than trifling, it is boldly to affront and dishonor him. No temptation, no worldly prospects can be any excuse for it. "The sacrifice of the wicked is abomination to the Lord." No pretended acts of devotion, no glittering appearance of religion, can be pleasing to God, which come from persons thus defiled with sin. Professors of this character can, in no sober or religious sense, be said to remember Christ; they cannot have any desires after the blessings of the new covenant, of which this ordinance is a sign or token. To them we may apply the words of the psalmist, " Unto the wicked God saith, what hast thou to do to declare my statutes, or that thou shouldest take my covenant into thy mouth? Seeing thou hatest instruction, and castest my words behind thee. When thou sawest a thief, then thou consentedst with him, and hast been partaker with adulterers. Thou givest thy mouth to evil, and thy tongue frameth deceit. Thou sittest and speakest against thy brother, thou slanderest thine own mother's son." Such as these should cease to do evil, and learn to do well, before they approach the table of the Lord.

Nor can it either be safe or decent, for one who hath been a notorious habitual sinner, to come to this holy ordinance, immediately on his finding himself awakened to some serious concern for his eternal

eternal salvation, even though he resolves to amend his life, and feels a present regard to his Lord and Saviour. There have been such numerous instances of persons greatly alarmed by the word and providence of God, and apparently resolved to seize the kingdom of heaven with violence, who have in a very little time, lost all impressions of religion, and relapsed into carelessness, irreligion, and vice; that it should make every one jealous and diffident of himself. If upon every alarm of conscience, men rush on a public profession, there is great danger of their injuring their own souls, and bringing discredit on the christian name. You are all sensible, how much religion hath suffered by such rash intrusions. Sollicitous as I am, to see the Lord's table full of guests, I sincerely desire to see it filled only with those who are worthy to be there. They who have led a life of dissipation and vice ought to give some proof of a change of disposition, both to themselves and others: They may not trust to some sudden emotions, but should take time to try the strength of their resolutions and purposes; they should count the cost of being christians. It is true, wickedness is no excuse for not coming to the Lord's table, because men ought not to be wicked; they ought to repent and reform, but while men are habitually wicked and profane they ought not to come there. They should be willing to stay away, and they who have the power of admission should take effectual

care

care to debar them, if they are hardy enough to offer themselves. Would to God, I could think there had been that care on both hands there ought to have been: The table of the Lord would not have been rendered contemptible as it now is!

Thirdly, They practically say, the table of the Lord is contemptible, who come to the Lord's supper without serious thought and circumspection. When Samuel went to sacrifice at Bethlehem, he said to the people of that city, "Sanctify yourselves, and come with me to the sacrifice." There were particular purifications required of the Jews before they attended their solemn feasts. These external purifications were designed to answer moral purposes, to lead them to seek after spiritual cleansing or a right temper of mind towards God, when they made their solemn approaches to him; and unless they were attended with the thing signified, however they might answer the Jewish law, and entitle to the privileges of that dispensation, they could not render men acceptable to God, or put them in the way of obtaining any spiritual or eternal blessings. These carnal ordinances are done away by the coming of Jesus Christ, but that to which they were designed to lead their thoughts is still necessary. God hath his institutions of religion under the gospel as he had under the law: Christians ought to approach these with caution and reverence. The Lord's supper is an ordinance peculiar to christianity, it is an explicit acknowlegement of of the authority of Jesus Christ; some particular inquiry and preparation seems fit and proper before we enter on such a solemn transaction.

The apostle says, " Let a man examine himself and so let him eat." Some have interpreted this expression, that persons who could not determine their state to be good, or that they were sincere disciples of Jesus Christ, were not to come to the Lord's supper, as if it had been said, Let a man examine whether he is a good christian, and then, and not till then, let him eat. Such an examination is a great christian duty, and no time can be more proper for it, than when we are coming to the Lord's table; but it may well be made a question, whether this is what the apostle immediately intends in this place. His meaning seems rather to be, that a man should examine himself, whether he understands the nature of this ordinance, and proposes to attend it in a manner agreable to the design of it, and so should eat, making a proper difference between the Lord's supper, and a common meal, attending it in a sober religious manner. But in whatever sense we understand this passage, it plainly supposes, that there is some previous thought and deliberation necessary to our coming aright to the Lord's table; that all who approach it should come with a humble, serious, devout temper. They should seek the influence of the Holy Spirit to make them sincere in this

this sacred transaction, and to cleanse them according to the purification of the sanctuary. It is fit and right, if not absolutely necessary, that we should give up ourselves to God in our secret retirements, before we publicly assume the character of christians.

It is for want of this serious deliberation, that too many fall away from God, and disgrace their christian profession. They enter upon it without thought, have no sense of their own weakness, and take no care to secure Divine aids. They act, with respect to this religious rite, as if it was a matter of very light and trivial concern. And by such a conduct evidence, that they look on the table of the Lord as contemptible, and they make it appear contemptible to others. The men of the world think lightly of Divine ordinances, when they observe the levity—the total indifference with which some men run to them. It is of great importance, that we shew forth Christ's death at his table; but it is equally important, that we should consider what we are about, and should have a right disposition when we draw nigh to God. Without this, it is very unlikely, that the ordinance will be of any spiritual advantage. It will make us worse rather than better.

The preparation of which I have been speaking is peculiarly necessary, when we first present ourselves at the Lord's table; but something of the same kind is suitable, if we have opportunity every

time

time we make our approach to it, tho' not of equal importance. There are certain meditations which are proper at all times, but which are particularly adapted to prepare our minds for the sacramental supper—As the nature and design of the ordinance—the wisdom and goodness of the institution—The love and grace of God in sending his Son to die for us—The great things which Christ did and suffered, that he might atone for our sins and bring us to God—The evil of sin which made such an atonement necessary—The obligations his infinite benevolence lays us under—The blessings Christ hath purchased—and the importance of our being interested in them.——There are certain actions which are proper at all times, but which seem peculiarly seasonable when we are coming to the holy supper. Such are the solemn consecration of ourselves to God, and engagement to be his—a serious solemn inquiry into our state, our principles of action, the views we have in our religious duties, our desires, our purposes, what we have been, and what we design to be—A penitent humiliation and contrition of soul for what hath been amiss—a believing application to the blood of Christ for pardon and cleansing—and fervent prayer to God for renewing and sanctifying grace.

But you will say, what if I cannot find any exercise of grace, or do not perceive, after all my examination, that gracious temper which I ought to have?
What

What shall I do then? I answer, I am saying what we ought, and what we should desire to be at all times, and in particular what are proper exercises of mind when we are coming to the Lord's table, but I by no means say, that we may not come, unless we are conscious we are entirely what we ought to be. We tell you what christianity is, and what it requires you to be; we set before you the sublime standard, that you may be excited to come as near it as you can. We say that God requires purity of heart, when you draw near to him in his holy institutions, but we do not say, that if you have not that purity which he requires, you are excusable in the neglect of them. We declare to you, that when you hear the word you should mix it with faith, but we do not declare, that unless you have faith you should not hear the word. We assert that when you pray, you ought to lift up holy hands, but we do not assert, that unless you have holy hands, you must not pray. So we say, you ought to come to the Lord's supper in the exercise of knowlege, faith, love, repentance, but we do not say, that every one who hath not these graces eateth and drinketh judgment to himself. Upon the whole, they sinfully presume, who come to the sacrament in a light careless manner: It is a solemn religious action, and we should endeavor to prepare our minds for it by meditation and prayer. Christ requires that we should thus shew forth his death, and we ought to come to this ordinance in obedience to him, and not in compliance with custom,

or

or with any worldly and sinful views. He that hath such a frame of heart is in no danger of being an unworthy partaker of the Lord's supper; and tho' he should not be in that state he was ready to hope he was, he will, according to the common course of Divine grace, be more likely to meet with God, and be in a fairer way to obtain a blessing, than if he had lived in the neglect of so plain a command.

Having said so much of preparation for the Lord's table, some may be ready to enquire, whether it is necessary, whenever they are about to come to this ordinance, to have some stated time, in a solemn manner, to prepare themselves for it? To which it may be replied, That as there is no such injunction in scripture, no one hath a right to enjoin it. However, this sacred rite implies so much professed by us, and is such a distinguishing badge of the christian religion, that they whose leisure will admit of it, do well to separate some particular time, to think what they are going about, —to implore the Divine presence—to commune with their own hearts—renewedly to dedicate themselves to God—and to employ their minds in such meditations and acts of devotion, as tend to put them in a right frame, when they draw near to God in this holy institution. But, expedient as this is, I am aware that some christians have carried their scruples upon this head even to a degree of superstition; they must have days as well as hours; and when they have not had time to prepare themselves according to their usual custom, they have turned their backs on the ordinance. It is best, where it can be, to take time for preparation; but when any are necessarily prevented, as may frequently be the case with those who are in a state of servitude, and sometimes with others, they ought to rely on the grace of Christ to supply the want of previous preparation, and by no means to affront him by putting an open slight on his institution. A particular preparation for sacramental occasions " being only a prudential thing, no where enjoined in the word of God, must not be looked upon as absolutely necessary, much less the spending such an exact portion of time in the exercises of devotion. Let us employ what time we can command, and find by experience to be of use to this purpose, and we have nothing further to trouble ourselves about, but putting our hearts in the best order we can, and so moderating our affections to all sublunary things, that as often as we are called to duty, we may be in a proper disposition for the performance of it; let us do this, and we need not doubt of our being acceptable guests at the table of the Lord."

I am in the Third place to set before you your contempt of the Lord's table, when you attend this ordinance with irreverence or vanity of mind.——It tends greatly to render this religious rite contemptible, if there is any thing indecent or irreverent

verent in our external deportment. This is what the apoftle blames in the Corinthians. They were fo far from fetting down at the Lord's table as a fpiritual entertainment, and as if they meant to improve themfelves in the chriftian temper, that they made no difference between that and their common meals; yea, their behavior was fo riotous and indecent, that it would have been a difgrace to their common entertainments. " When ye come together into one place, this is not to eat the Lord's fupper. For in eating every one taketh before other, his own fupper; and one is hungry, and another is drunken. What have ye not houfes to eat and to drink in? or defpife ye the church of God?" One can fcarce conceive of a more profane and unworthy behavior than this of the Corinthians. It is hoped, the Lord's table is not thus abufed, or the inftitution affronted, among us. Perhaps, there is very little to be blamed in the external deportment of thofe who come to the holy eucharift. The countenance of the communicants is grave, the pofture is decent, and the gefture is agreable, becoming fuch a folemn approach to God, free from levity on the one hand, and affectation and fuperftition on the other.——Would to God, the fame could be faid with truth of the inward man—that the hearts of all who partake of the Lord's fupper were right with him! But alas! when we have drawn nigh to God in this ordinance, hath there been nothing in any of us unbecoming this facred act of religion?—nothing which gives occafion for pain-

ful

ful reflections?—nothing which hath been offensive to that Being, who is a Discerner of the tho'ts of the heart? " Ye say the table of the Lord is contemptible," when it is not your constant desire and endeavor, that it may answer the ends for which it was designed: Especially, if you indulge to any thoughts or dispositions which contradict the great end and design of it. It is true, these inward motions of the soul are not visible to the world, and therefore you do not by them dishonor God before men: But they pollute the ordinance in the sight of God; they discover contempt of the great Author of it; and a disregard of the gracious design he had in the institution. When you put on a shew of seriousness which you have not, and pretend a devotion which you do not exercise, nor so much as aim at, you practically deny the omniscience of God; you act as if he did not know what passes within you; or, as if you thought it of no consequence to approve yourselves to him; you evidence that you value the praise of men, more than the praise of God, since you are so sollicitous to appear well to them, while you neglect Him, who searches the heart and tries the reins of the children of men. The language of your practice is, " the table of the Lord is contemptible"— When you content yourselves with barely attending the duty, without any concern about the frame and disposition of your hearts there—When you allow your minds to wander, and indulge to thoughts

about

about the world and your temporal affairs, to subjects, which, though they might be lawful at other times, are not suitable to the present occasion—Especially, when your thoughts at the sacrament are in themselves sinful, and such as would be offensive to God at any time—When you do not remember Christ at all, or remember him only in an indifferent superficial manner.

First, It is to cast contempt on the Lord's table, when you content yourselves with a bare attendance upon the sacramental supper, without any concern about the frame and disposition of your hearts there. It is not enough that we attend the institutions of religion, unless we come to them as means of grace; and if we come to them as means of grace, we shall look to the end more than to the means. David had great desires after the house of God, but his desires did not terminate in the mere performance of duty, he desired and sought after the presence and enjoyment of God, " O God, Thou art my God, early will I seek thee, my soul thirsteth for thee, my flesh longeth for thee in a dry and thirsty land, where no water is ; To see thy power and thy glory so as I have seen thee in thy sanctuary." If at any time christians attend upon a religious duty, and do not find those dispositions which are peculiarly suited to that duty, they come away disappointed and humbled. They think that sabbath, that sacrament lost, in which they do not gain some knowlege of divine things, nor experience some spiritual advantage. But when, on the other hand, they find the love of God improved in their hearts, when they see more of the divine excellency, and their souls cleave to him in holy affection and delight; when they are more afraid of sin and more watchful against it; when they gain strength against temptation; are more firmly persuaded of the truth of religion, and feel its influence on their hearts: When christians find these the happy effects of their attendance on divine ordinances, they cannot but highly prize and value them. And they shew their esteem of the institutions of religion, when they look for such blessed effects from them, and have these in view in the observance of them. But when men content themselves with a bare attendance, and are indifferent whether they profit by them or not, when they have no concern about their hearts and the exercises of their minds, it shows that they have no sincerity in their professions of religion. To pretend to draw near to God in the ways of his appointment, and not to desire those spiritual blessings which they were designed to convey, is not merely to despise these blessings, it is to despise God himself—to contradict the design of the duty—and to deprive their souls of all benefit thereby. I will not say that such communicants will not receive any advantage from the ordinances of the gospel, God is sometimes found of them that seek him not, but it is very unlikely that they will, and their care-

lessness

lessness in attending on duties is doubtless one reason why many find them so useless and unprofitable.

Secondly, You despise the table of the Lord, when you allow your minds to wander, and indulge to thoughts, which might be lawful at other times, but are not suited to this particular season. The situation of men in the world is such, that it is necessary often to think of worldly things, to lay plans for our comfortable subsistence, and to take proper steps to carry them into execution. Tho' we ought to seek first the kingdom of God and his righteousness, yet other things are not to be neglected. But there are seasons, when thoughts about our temporal affairs are improper and sinful. They are so, whenever we are called to an immediate intercourse with the Deity. At such times, it becomes us to dismiss the world, and to fix our minds on things above, and not on things on the earth. When we come to the Lord's table, we should be raised above the pleasures, the amusements, the profits, the honors of this world. Thinking on our secular affairs cannot be innocent when we are at this festival, because it must necessarily shut out some religious meditation which we ought to have there. Every worldly thought which enters our mind at the sacrament is an intruder, and as such we ought to treat it, immediately to exclude and reject it. If we suffer our minds to rove to the enjoyments of time and sense when we come to the Lord's

Lord's table, such thoughts will prevent that serious religious temper which ought to possess our souls there. They will erase all good impressions, and make our attendance unprofitable. 'Tis true, the hearts of the best are apt to wander, the world intrudes itself into our most sacred transactions. But there is a vast difference between our having these thoughts involuntarily, and contrary to our desire and endeavor, and our giving way to them or suffering them to dwell in us. A serious communicant, one who partakes of the Lord's supper in a right manner, looks upon all worldly thoughts as unfit while he makes this solemn approach to God; he strives—he prays against them; and it is the grief of his heart, that the world hath such a place within him, that he cannot rise above it, even when he hath such powerful incentives to a spiritual heavenly disposition, as are presented at the Lord's table. Do any of you then, when you sit down at this holy institution, apply your minds to worldly topics? Do you suffer vain thoughts—earthly desires, to lodge within you? Do you meditate on your farms—your merchandize—your secular business—or your lucrative prospects? you have reason to fear you are unworthy communicants. You treat the Lord's table with contempt, you cannot expect any spiritual advantage from the institution, or that God will look on the duty as performed to him.———The contempt you cast on this ordinance is still greater, if in the

Third

Third place, Your thoughts at the facrament are in themfelves finful, and fuch as would be offenfive to God at any other time. Worldly tho'ts are finful at this feafon, becaufe they intrude at a time when you ought to be wholly employed in fpiritual contemplations : It is much worfe—If you allow yourfelves in carnal, malicious, revengeful thoughts—If impure images and difpofitions prefent themfelves and find room within you—If your mind is filled with covetous, proud, ambitious defires, purpofes, and views. Such a temper is evil at any time. But it proves great perverfenefs and obduracy of heart, if men give way to fuch vain and wicked thoughts when they profefs to engage in a facred act of religion. They defpife that glorious Being before whom their hearts are naked and open ; and however, by their fpecious pretences, they may gain the efteem of men, they will certainly fail of the approbation of God. Their hypocritical fervices are a ftench in his noftrils, and he can have no pleafure in their offerings.

Fourthly, They treat the Lord's table with contempt, who either do not remember Chrift at all, or only in a carelefs fuperficial manner. The general defign of this ordinance is contained in thofe words of our bleffed Saviour, " Do this in remembrance of me." If then your thoughts are not ill employed, that is, if they are not employed on fubjects that are evil in themfelves, if you have religious thoughts, yet, if you do not remember

Chrift, if He is not the fubject of your contemplations, you do not comply with the defign of the inftitution; and if this is difregarded, with whatever frequency, and apparent ferioufnefs you attend upon this religious rite, you practically fay, the defign was unneceffary, and the command might have been omitted. It is very much the fame language, if you content yourfelves with fome tranfient thoughts of Jefus Chrift, which make no impreffion on your hearts. It ought to be your great concern, not only to remember Chrift, but that the remembrance of him may have its proper influence upon you, and that you may have thofe fentiments of love, gratitude, and obedience, which the inftitution tends to infpire. It fhows great contempt of the Lord's fupper, when men fatisfy themfelves with fuperficial unaffecting meditations, however fit and proper they may otherwife be—when they go to this ordinance and come from it with a lukewarm indifferent fpirit, as if there was nothing valuable to be obtained there, or they had no follicitude to obtain it.

When we think what we ought to be when we come to the Lord's table, how much reafon have many of us for humble penitent reflections!—Did we not rufh upon a profeffion with a criminal indifference, and even when we knew that our lives were a contradiction to our public declaration, diffolute and vicious?—Did we take time to deliberate on fuch a folemn tranfaction, and enter upon it with ferious meditation and earneft prayer to God

God for light and direction?" I fear some of us shall find, upon careful recollection, that we had very little concern about duty, no design to approve ourselves to God, no desire to be made wiser or better: But that our main view was to make a good appearance to men, to gratify our pride, or some other passion which was predominant.——— When we have been at the Lord's table, instead of those religious meditations which were proper on that sacred occasion, have we not indulged thoughts about our worldly business, and even irreligious and wicked thoughts? Have we not satisfied ourselves with the performance of the duty, though we have had no particular regard to Jesus Christ—no sense of that infinite philanthropy, which it was the special design of this institution to produce in our minds? Or if we have, at some times, found room for serious religious meditations, yet what a sad mixture hath there been of formality, hypocrisy, and sin! Let us call our faults to remembrance this day: The consideration of them should not lead us to neglect duty, as the manner of some is; but should excite us, to make our application to the atoning blood of the great Redeemer, and to be more watchful for the time to come. Blessed be God, the setting down at the Lord's table in an unprepared or an unworthy manner is not an unpardonable offence, tho' some are so much more distressed about this than they are about any other, that it looks as if they thought it was. The blood of Christ cleanseth from this as well as every other sin.

If

If persons, by coming unworthily to this ordinance, expose themselves to judgment, yet it by no means makes their eternal damnation necessary. Let none encourage themselves from hence, in a careless approach to divine ordinances; such levity of mind not only makes religion contemptible in the eyes of the thoughtless and profane, but tends dreadfully to harden our own hearts. And if some have too awful thoughts of the sacrament, and carry their fears even to superstition, others are in still greater danger of treating it with indifference. That our minds may be impressed with a becoming reverence; Let us remember, that Jesus Christ is here present. And shall we dare to offend and affront him who is to be our final Judge! or rather, shall we do any thing, or indulge any temper, that will displease him who hath shown such inconceivable love to us?——What shame!—what horror! must possess the mind of one, who thinks of Christ at his table, and finds his heart full—of hypocrisy—of enmity to God—or malice to his brethren!—But on the other hand, how great the pleasure of that man, who feels his heart warmed with the love of Christ, and can humbly appeal to him and say, Lord, Thou knowest all things, Thou knowest that I love Thee! Who, sensible of innumerable defects, hath such views of the glory of the Redeemer, as to venture himself in his hands; and, under the greatest pressure of guilt and unworthiness, can find rest in this Almighty Saviour!

SERMON XVI.

The Table of the Lord rendered contemptible.

MALACHI I. 7.

Ye say the table of the Lord is contemptible.

WHATEVER God commands we are sure is right. A Being who is infinitely wise and good cannot enjoin any thing, but what is agreable to wisdom and goodness. We ought to venerate every institution of heaven, to observe all the duties of religion, and to do every thing in our power to reccommend them to others. The command to attend the Lord's supper is so express, that no christian ought to be easy in the neglect of it—But a bare attendance on this institution is not enough to approve us to God, and therefore ought not

not to quiet our minds.——It becomes us to approach the table of the Lord with seriousness and reverence, we should consider and improve it as a mean of grace, and be chiefly sollicitous to attain the end, to have the same mind that was in Christ, who hath gone before, setting us an example that we should walk in his steps.—When we are at the Lord's table, we ought religiously to remember Jesus Christ, the great Author of this institution.— In our daily walk, we are to consider our christian character, and to walk worthy of the vocation wherewith we are called. It is owing, as hath been already observed, to the carelessness and indifference of christians in each of these respects, that this ordinance is despised, as it too generally is among us. " Ye say, the table of the Lord is contemptible." You say this, By a careless neglect of it—By rushing precipitately to it—By irreverence or levity of mind while you attend upon it— and by a life and conversation disagreable to your christian profession. I have discoursed to the three first of these particulars.

I am now to shew, that you make the Lord's table contemptible, when your life and conversation are not agreable to your christian profession.

When men profess christianity, and lay themselves under solemn engagements to be the Lord's, they ought to be sincere, they ought not to deal falsly with God. They prevaricate, if they have

no

no defires and intentions to be what they profefs—
If they put on religion as a cloke, to hide the wickednefs of their hearts, or to ferve fome finifter defign.
If there is any fincerity in them, they intend, by the help of God, to be chriftians, when they profefs themfelves the difciples of Chrift. They defign to do the will of God, when they folemnly promife it. I do not mean, that it is neceffary to know they are gracious perfons, when they profefs the religion of Chrift: But fuch a profeffion implies—a belief of divine revelation—a fenfe of the importance of the truths it contains—a defire at leaft that the inftitutions of religion fhould have their proper effect—and a determination, by the grace of God, to live as the gofpel teaches them to live. Where this is the cafe, men will endeavor to form their lives by the precepts of chriftianity; and fo far as they do this, they adorn the doctrine of God our Saviour. When they practife otherwife, they caufe the good ways of God to be evil fpoken of, and make a religious profeffion contemptible, in the eyes of thofe who have not felt the power of religion on their hearts.

In fpeaking to this point, I fhall firft confider what kind of converfation is agreable to the gofpel, and tends to the honor of God and religion—and then, on the other hand, when perfons difcredit religion; or, in the language of the text, " fay the table of the Lord is contemptible."

Firft,

First, I am to say, what conversation that is, which is agreable to the gospel, and tends to the honor of God and religion. You easily perceive, that this leads me to speak of such parts of the christian life as are visible to the world, at least to those who are near us and observe our conduct; and not of our secret and retired transactions. We ought, in all our deportment before others, to make the gospel our rule ; or, in the language of our blessed Saviour, to cause our light to shine before men, that they may see our good works and glorify our Father which is in heaven. We ought to evidence that christianity is something more than a name, and, as far as an external deportment can, that we are not only almost, but altogether christians. We should avoid what the law of God forbids, and practice what it enjoins. Christians should live above the world, they may not take any indirect methods to gain those things which are pleasant and agreable ; nor at any time discover an anxiety about worldly enjoyments : They should behave with calmness and resignation when they meet with things that are contrary to flesh and blood. They should endeavor to practise duty with chearfulness, that all about them may see, they do not esteem the commandments of God to be grievous restraints, or unreasonable injunctions, but that their obedience is free and unconstrained, and others may be induced to believe that Christ's yoke is easy and his burden light. I do not intend that any can be able to determine with certainty

the

the frame of the heart, by the manner in which men perform their outward actions. There is no doubt but an artful hypocrite may conduct so as to impose on the most discerning eye; and may appear to delight in those religious duties to which he hath an inward aversion. But it is no argument that a christian should put on a different appearance, because a hypocrite will endeavor to appear as he does. That man gives very slender proof of his sincerity, who pursues the enjoyments of this world with pleasure and satisfaction, and in matters of religion acts with reluctance, or so as to lead others to think the service of God is unpleasant and disagreable to him.

The christian should not, like the Syrian general, desire, that in this thing the Lord would pardon his servant, but should carefully abstain from the very appearance of evil; and be willing to abridge himself of lawful pleasures, if they are likely to prove a snare, or an occasion of sin; he should even avoid things that are in themselves indifferent, rather than offend a weak brother. It is not necessary he should put on a precise supercilious air, or assume a sour austerity of manners; this is rather an affected shew of religion, than religion itself; but he should always behave with such seriousness and circumspection, that they, who observe his course of life, may have reason to think he is afraid to offend God, and that it is his habitual desire to please and honor

honor him. Agreably, he should set a constant guard upon his lips, that he may never utter a rash or sinful word, but that his common conversation may answer some valuable purpose, and be, as the apostle expresses it, " to the use of edifying." He should keep at a distance from all indecent mirth and levity, and preserve a gravity and decorum, becoming one who hath a sense of the account he must give unto the Judge of all the earth. He should reverence " this glorious and fearful name, The Lord thy God," never using it in a light or thoughtless, much less profane manner. The sabbath of the Lord should be honorable in his eyes, and he should endeavor to make it honorable in the eyes of others. He should consider it as a day which God hath set apart for himself, and employ the time in reading, meditation and devotion. In his attendance on public worship, he should be constant and seasonable, that he may have his part in the whole of the exercise; and while he is in the house of God, he should have a reverential regard to that All-perfect Being who is particularly present in the assembly of his saints; avoiding a light careless air on the one hand, and sloth and drowsiness on the other.

A professing christian should be sober and temperate in all things, not indulging his appetites and sensual inclinations, not given to wine, not conforming to every silly and fantastic mode in his attire, but appearing with a modesty becoming saints.

Christians

Chriftians fhould deal juftly with one another; they fhould not injure or hurt their neighbours in order to ferve themfelves; and fhould defpife all little arts and clandeftine methods to raife themfelves to honor and affluence. In all their tranfactions they fhould behave with uprightnefs and generofity, fo that their conduct may bear examining, and they may not run the hazard of being detected in any mean or evil practice. They fhould be tender of their neighbour's reputation, loth to receive evil reports, much more to make or fpread them. They fhould always incline to the charitable fide, believe all things, hope all things, and be difpofed to think and fpeak well of all, fo far as there is any juft or reafonable ground for favorable fentiments and reprefentations. Their charity fhould go further than good words or fair fpeeches; they fhould abound in acts of kindnefs, and be generoufly ready to fupply the wants and relieve the neceffities of their brethren.

Again, Chriftians fhould learn the due government of their paffions. Their hopes and fears, their joys and forrows fhould all be regulated by reafon and religion, neither placed on improper objects, nor raifed to an undue pitch. They fhould be patient under afflictions, calm under reproaches, meek under injuries. Like their bleffed Mafter, when reviled they fhould not revile again, nor retaliate their wrongs even when it is in their power. They fhould be clothed with humility, and evidence in their whole deportment, that they are fenfible

sible of their own weakness, sinfulness, and guilt. They should justify God whatever he brings upon them. Conscious of demerit, their surprize, if any is expressed, will be, not that God inflicts so much, but that he doth not inflict more. They are disposed to think others better than themselves; & therefore, when their neighbours receive superior marks of respect and honor, they will not envy their prosperity or repine at their happiness, much less will they do any thing to blast their reputation or detract from their character. If in any thing a christian excel other men, he will not treat them with haughtiness, contempt, or neglect: But will behave to all with kindness, affability, respect, and condescension, as their situation and circumstances require.

Professors of religion should carefully discharge the duties of every relation—Rulers should endeavor to answer the great end of their institution, to be ministers of God for good; they should consult the public happiness in their several departments—And while *they* are employed in promoting the weal of the community, those who are placed under them should endeavor to lighten the cares of government, by due submission to authority, leading quiet and peaceable lives in all godliness and honesty.—Ministers should be faithful, diligent, and fervent in the work of the Lord—Their people should hearken to them so far as they deliver the words of truth and soberness.—Parents and heads

heads of families should instruct their children and servants in the great truths of religion, and govern their houses with firmness, discretion, and tenderness: They should be constant in their devotions and exemplary in their walk—Children should obey their parents, and servants be faithful to their masters, and each in their respective stations should endeavor to promote the peace, the comfort, the happiness of the families to which they belong.—In short, professing christians should, in their whole deportment, endeavor to glorify God, and to recommend religion to all with whom they are conversant. They should live up to the dignity of their character, be uniform in all parts of their behaviour, and maintain a close walk with God at all times and in all seasons. How lovely would religion appear, if it was thus exemplified in the lives of those who profess it! How many would be attracted by their amiable conversation! What a change should we soon perceive for the better! and what happy times might we expect!

I am, in the Second place, to shew, when persons who profess christianity do by their practice discredit the religion they profess; or, in other words, when the conversation of those who partake of the Lord's supper is such, as renders this holy ordinance contemptible in the eye of the world.— That there will be such persons in the church of Christ, he hath himself taught us to expect.— " When the Master of the house hath risen up and
shut

shut to the door, and ye begin to stand without, and to knock at the door, saying, Lord, Lord, open unto us ; and he shall answer and say unto you, I know you not whence you are ; then shall ye begin to say, we have eaten and drunk in thy presence, and thou hast taught in our streets. But he shall say, I tell you, I know you not whence you are ; depart from me all ye workers of iniquity." ‖ Although these words did not immediately refer to the Lord's supper, which was not then instituted ; yet they doubtless represent the state of men who had made pretences to religion, and had been unholy and wicked in their lives ; and they may very well be applied to those who profess to commemorate the love of Christ at his table, and take no care to do the things which he hath commanded. Would to God there were no such daring sinners to be found! But alas! are there none who name the name of Christ and do not depart from iniquity? Are there none, in these days, who call Christ, Lord, Lord, while they do not the things which he says? Are there none who eat and drink with the King at his table, and are vicious and profligate in their lives? If you are so happy as never to have known any of so flagitious a character, you must own it is possible for such persons to exist. And they who stand should take heed lest they fall. It cannot be amiss to point out what course is inconsistent with that sincere regard to Jesus Christ which you profess to have, that you may abstain from every appearance of it, may watch against every approach to it, and may shun

‖ Luke 13. 25, 26, 27.   those

those occasions of sin which have proved fatal to others. Without such continual watchfulness and care, no professor is secure from the grossest enormities.

In general, They treat the Lord's table with profane contempt, whose lives are a contradiction to the profession they make there.—They, who are careless in their walk, profane in their language, and dissolute in their manners—They, who profess their belief of christianity, but are ashamed of the gospel of Christ, can hear his Person degraded, his doctrines blasphemed, his Spirit derided, his precepts ridiculed, with silence, if not with apparent approbation—They, who, instead of being companions of those that fear God, associate with the ungodly, and sit in the seat of the scornful—who are vain and frothy in their conversation; eager in their pursuit of the world; and take mean and unjust methods to be rich and great—They, who are close and penurious to their brethren that need and perhaps ask their assistance—who oppress and extort from those whose distresses put them in their power—who speak evil of their neighbours, invent scandal, propagate slander, or take no pains to suppress it, when whispered round by the ill-will of others—They, who are proud, peevish, and passionate, indulge to envy, malice, and revenge—whose lives are among the unclean, and are guilty of chambering and wantonness, rioting and drunkenness, or any other vicious enormity; who are unfaithful

faithful to their truſt, negligent of the duties of ſocial life, and which are incumbent upon them in the particular ſtations and relations in which Divine Providence hath placed them. Such as theſe wound chriſtianity in a very tender part; their unholy lives are a ſtumbling block to others, and cauſe them to think there is nothing in that religion which the profeſſors of pay ſo little regard to. By their diſobedient lives they are likely to keep more out of the church, than their glittering profeſſion will invite into it. Such a conduct hardens men in ſin, and renders them proof againſt all the arguments which are uſed to reclaim them. They are ready to deſpiſe thoſe inſtitutions which do not purify the hearts, or correct the lives of thoſe who attend them. The table of the Lord is deſpiſed by them, becauſe they ſee bad men frequent it; and that contempt which ought to fall on theſe wicked pretenders, comes upon religion itſelf. I do not ſpeak of this as either rational or juſtifiable conduct; but I ſpeak of what is likely to be the effect, when profeſſors act contrary to their profeſſion, and walk according to the courſe of this preſent evil world; it brings reproach on the chriſtian name, and occaſions the moſt ſevere reflections on religion itſelf.

The ſubject we have been upon may very properly be applied in various ways.

Firſt, They certainly have reaſon for ſerious and very humbling reflections, who wear the chriſtian name

name, but have by the courſe of their lives diſho‑ nored their profeſſion and rendered the table of the Lord contemptible. We are all favored with the goſpel of Chriſt, have peculiar opportunities of coming to the knowledge of God, and underſtand‑ ing our connection with him. Privileges always in‑ fer obligation.———Some of us have made a public explicit profeſſion of chriſtianity ; we have called Chriſt Maſter and Lord, and therefore ought to o‑ bey his commands. The converſation of a chriſtian ſhould be holy, exemplary, and uniform, that he may ſet religion in an agreable light before others, and perſuade them to be chriſtians. But alas ! when we look back, how much occaſion do we find for grief, for ſhame, for repentance ! In many in‑ ſtances we have offended daily, and come ſhort of the glory of God. The beſt chriſtians, the moſt exact walkers, by no means come up to that ſtrict and perfect purity which is enjoined in the precepts of the goſpel. But are there not ſome whoſe prac‑ tice hath been evidently the reverſe of what it ought to be, who have indulged to vice, and whoſe lives have been among the wicked and ungodly ? They have diſhonored God—by profaning his name —by diſregarding his inſtitutions—by their injuſ‑ tice and uncharitableneſs—by their inordinate at‑ tachment to this world—by their intemperance— their laſciviouſneſs—their unchriſtian wrath—their levity—their pride—their unſtedfaſtneſs in religion —and the inconſiſtency of their demeanor. Such as these have given great occasion to the enemies of the Lord to blaspheme. And they too readily seize the occasion which is thus unhappily given them. They reproach religion on account of the bad lives of those who profess it. How little reason soever they have for their reproaches; how unjust soever it is to charge upon the gospel the faults of those who are condemned by it; yet, since it is so natural for men to judge of a cause by the character of those who embrace it, how ought they to be ashamed who have laid a foundation for such prejudices! Oh! my brethren, how have we caused the way of truth to be evil spoken of by our unholy lives and wicked practices! How many have we turned from the good ways of God! Hath not our light been darkness? or have we not rather dazled the eyes of beholders with a mere blaze, than afforded them any real help in the way of heaven? How affecting the thought, that we have not only not done the good we might and ought to have done, but have done actual disservice to the cause of Christ! There have been so many spots and blemishes in us, as that, instead of being an honor to christianity, we have brought disgrace upon it—instead of gaining men over to religion, we have prejudiced them against it.

Secondly, How detestable the character, and how dangerous the condition of a wicked hypocritical professor! " A wicked christian," says one, " is the

the moſt unprofitable creature of any upon the face of the whole earth: He ſerves for no purpoſe but only to do hurt in the world, and of that indeed he does a great deal, much more than he could have done, if he had not been a profeſſed chriſtian. For the open ſins that he is guilty of, while he lives in the profeſſion of a pure and holy religion, are more ſcandalous and infectious than other men's; the wickedneſs of his life caſts alſo a blemiſh and reproach on that holy religion which he profeſſes; and gives great prejudice againſt it to ſuch as were otherwiſe well difpofed to embrace it." Such an one, who pretends to great piety and devotion and at the ſame time leads a wicked life, is unworthy of reſpect, or even of notice, unleſs it be to expreſs our deteſtation of his impiety. One can ſcarce conceive of a more contemptible object: and he often meets with the contempt he deſerves. Good men deteſt him as an enemy to God and religion. Bad men look upon him with contempt, as aſſuming a fictitious character, and pretending to be what he knows he is not. Every one loves an honeſt man who acts agreably to his profeſſion. Every one deſpiſes an hypocritical deceiver, who ſpeaks you fair while he hath no deſign to ſerve you. They who have no religion themſelves cannot but abhor a man who puts on a form of godlineſs, and lives in vice and wickedneſs. Many abandoned ſinners are ſeized with horror, when they ſee others, as bad as themſelves, take the covenant of God into their mouths, and aſſume the character of ſaints; or, when

when they see those who frequent the Lord's table running to all excess of riot and vice. Wicked as they are, they dare not mix religion with their crimes, or profess to know God while in works they impiously deny him.

But the contempt and reproach which hypocritical professors meet with in this world is but a light matter, when compared with the abhorrence and indignation of a holy God. We read of some who will " awake to shame and everlasting contempt." And who may more justly expect such a reception in the great day of accounts, than they who have professed the religion of Christ and lived in contradiction to his laws? Our Lord ever discovered a peculiar displicency with hypocrites; and repetedly pronounced the most terrible woes against them. Men who put on a shew of religion to deceive others, or to cloke their vices, that they may under this appearance practice the enormities of a vicious life, are among the most odious kind of sinners. The great God will cast them away from his presence; He will not admit them into heaven; He will cast them into outer darkness; He will consign them to the prison of hell, and to one of the hottest places there. Our Lord, designing to represent the misery to which a sinner of the first magnitude would be doomed, says, " The Lord of that servant shall cut him asunder, and appoint him his portion with hypocrites: there shall be weeping and gnashing of teeth."

This

This charge of hypocrisy was often brought by our Saviour against the scribes and pharisees, of whom he spake with unusual severity. They were not men, who had a concern for religion, and were careful to guard against vice and wickedness, but were under some mistake about their internal state.—They were not men, who went a great way in morality, and only wanted a holy principle. There might be some such among them. But the men against whom our Saviour denounces his woes were guilty of scandalous immoralities.—They devoured widow's houses, and for a pretence made long prayers.—They paid tithes of mint, anise, and cummin, but neglected the weightier matters of the law, judgment, mercy, and faith.—They made clean the outside of the cup and the platter, but within were full of extortion and excess.—They were men, to whom Christ sent prophets, wise-men and scribes, some of whom they killed and crucified, some they scourged in the synagogues, and others they persecuted from city to city.—These were the men, to whom our Lord said, " ye shall receive greater damnation." The like doom will be pronounced on wicked christians, on ungodly professors, on hypocrites, formalists, who hold the truth in unrighteousness; on apostates, men who once had some touches of religion, who seemed to have been enlightned, and to have tasted of the heavenly gift, and after that have fallen away into vice and profaneness. These are the men who are condemned by their own profession, who seal their
damnation

damnation at the Lord's supper, and make his table contemptible; and not those poor trembling souls, who have a serious concern about their salvation, and are seeking an interest in Christ; who are desirous to be what they profess to be, and to walk in all the commandments and ordinances of the Lord blameless. These latter, I say, are not the persons who seal their own damnation at the Lord's table, even though it should appear, that they were destitute of that principle of holiness, which only can render them acceptable to God in their attendance on any of the institutions of religion, or ensure to them a right to eternal life.

One who profanely trifles with divine ordinances is in a very incorrigible condition. By setting under the means of grace and not profiting by them; by erasing the good impressions which have been made upon his mind; by a course of formality and hypocrisy, he becomes insensible of guilt, and conscience grows quite callous. The recovery of such an one is an event hardly to be expected. The common means of grace have been used with him already and have proved ineffectual, and if God should see fit to go out of his common method, these are not the persons who are likely to be thus favored. 'Tis true all things are possible to the power and grace of God, and some of the vilest character have been reclaimed; but such instances are rare, and therefore can afford but little encouragement.

Thirdly,

Thirdly, Let not those who are without indulge prejudices against religion on account of the bad lives of those who profess it. It is not for want of precept that christians are not more circumspect in their walk. The gospel enjoins the greatest purity of heart and holiness of life. You find no defect there. And if you want example, we can point you to one in whom all the precepts of the gospel were perfectly exemplified, whose whole character was excellent, amiable, and spotless. I mean the great Author of our religion. If you meet with any defect in him, it is undoubtedly a just argument against christianity. But how unreasonable is it to find fault with the religion of Jesus Christ, because the lives of his disciples are not agreable to it! to despise the table of the Lord because all who come to it are not what their profession obliges them to be! Condemn them you may, and so doth the gospel they profess. You say it is a shame that men who make such high pretensions should allow themselves in deceit, injustice, uncharitableness, detraction, profaneness, intemperance, as these men do.—It is so—we join with you in censuring their evil practices. But why do you charge their crimes upon the gospel, which enjoins truth, justice, charity, sobriety, and every other virtue?—Is not christianity true because all men are not christians?—Is our religion an imposture because some men who pretend to embrace it are deceitful, and are not what they pretend to be?—Is this good reasoning?

reasoning?——Consider christianity as you have it in your Bibles—Was ever any thing more pure or more inviting? But after all, your objection is founded on an entirely false supposition. You say the lives of professors are not answerable to their profession—We own it as to some, too many. —But surely you will not bring this charge against all—Are there not christians to be found, who adorn the doctrine of God our Saviour; and exemplify, in some good measure, the precepts of the gospel? whose light shines in their good works? Why do you not, on account of these, glorify our Father which is in heaven? Take heed, lest, under a notion of testifying against the hypocrisy of some pretenders to religion, and because you would not be like them, you contract prejudices against religion itself—against the only method of salvation which infinite wisdom hath found out, or ever will find out; and thus plunge yourselves into eternal perdition.

Fourthly, Professors of religion should seriously consider of how great importance it is, that they walk worthy their profession. They in particular, who come to the Lord's table, should be very careful they do not by their wicked lives render it contemptible. The honor of God, the credit of religion, the salvation of others, as well as your own eternal welfare are very greatly concerned in your conversation. Every irregularity of your's does hurt

hurt to the cause of Christ; and you cannot so effectually injure him, as by a visible contempt of his laws. Whereas, if you live as his gospel teaches, you will have the comfort in your own breasts—you will honor God—you will be useful to the world—and you will do the greatest kindness to mankind. " Brethren, if any of you err from the truth, and one convert him; let him know that he which converteth a sinner from the error of his way, shall save a soul from death, and shall hide a multitude of sins." What a mighty incentive! How must every one feel the force of this motive, who hath the least degree of that benevolence which christianity ever recommends, and of which our Lord set us so amiable an example! How should such considerations influence christians to walk with the greatest circumspection and care, not as fools but as wise; to guard their lips, to take heed to their steps, that they may not give any just ground of offence to any, but may cut off occasion from those that desire occasion; and that they who have taken so cruel and malicious a part may be ashamed, having no evil thing to say of them. Great jealousy and watchfulness become us while we are in this present evil world, where we are surrounded with temptations, and exposed to continual dangers. And as an upright heart is the best foundation of a christian life, let us look to God to create us anew in Christ Jesus to good works, that we may walk in them. And after we are thus become his workmanſhip, let us not think we have apprehended, or that we are already perfect, but forgetting the things that are behind, let us reach to thoſe that are before, preſſing onward towards the mark, for the prize of the high calling of God in Chriſt Jeſus.

It is worthy particular attention, that though true grace cannot be loſt, the appearance of it may. One who is truly regenerate will not miſs of heaven, he is not therefore out of danger.—He may ſin—He may diſhonor God—and prejudice others againſt religion. This ſhould make a good man exceeding cautious. But a meer profeſſor of chriſtianity, even one who hath been brought near to the kingdom of God, may be left to total apoſtacy—may become a monſter of impiety and wickedneſs. Guard, my brethren, againſt every tendency to ſuch a ſtate. You may, by a wicked life, " ſay the table of the Lord is contemptible," you may lead others to think it ſo, but the contempt will in the end return upon yourſelf. Your hypocriſy will expoſe you to the ſcorn of men, it will make you abhorred by God, it will encreaſe your guilt, and dreadfully aggravate your future miſery.

SERMON XVII.

Practical Observations on the History of Judas and his tragical End.

MAT. XXVII. 3, 4, 5.

Then Judas, which had betrayed him, when he saw that he was condemned, repented himself, and brought again the thirty pieces of silver to the chief priests and elders, saying, I have sinned, in that I have betrayed innocent blood. And they said, What is that to us? see thou to that. And he cast down the pieces of silver in the temple, and departed, and went and hanged himself.

THE man, whose unhappy end is recorded in these words, had been one of the distinguished followers of our Lord. He was early called to be a disciple; was one of the twelve whom Jesus chose chofe to be his apoftles, and whom he fent forth to publifh the glad tidings of the kingdom.

My defign is, To give you fome account of Judas, the perfon whofe agonies of defpair and horror are exhibited in the text—And to lead you to fome fuitable reflections on the fubject.

We are not told when this unhappy man began to follow Jefus, nor what were his original motives. —He might be convinced, by the miracles our Lord wrought, that he was the Meffiah fo long expected, and might feel fome emotions of heart under his preaching. The wickednefs and treachery he was afterward guilty of do not prove that he was hypocritical in his profeffion of regard to Jefus at firft: Many believed the truth of our Lord's miffion, and were his profeffed difciples, who never felt the effectual power of religion on their hearts, and therefore in a time of trial fell away.— Poffibly, Judas had bad views from the beginning. There had been a general expectation of the Meffiah among the Jews: It is very plain but few of them thought of a fpiritual kingdom: By far the moft looked for a temporal Saviour, who would deliver them from the Roman power, and fubjugate all nations to the Jews. This feems to have been the expectation of our Lord's own difciples. He checked their ambitious fpirit when it difcovered itfelf, and affured them that his kingdom was

not

not of this world; and yet, even after his resurrection, they inquired of him, " Lord, wilt thou at this time restore the kingdom unto Israel?" It was not till the Spirit was poured out from on high, that they fully understood the design of his mission, and the nature of his kingdom. If the other disciples, who were men of honest minds, had such worldly and ambitious thot's, it may easily be supposed that Judas had; that he fixed his mind wholly upon the illustrious appearance our Lord was to make, formed pleasing imaginations of the state of dignity to which he should be advanced, and the large opportunities he should have of gratifying his avarice, which seems to have been the ruling passion; and that these were the views he had in becoming a follower and disciple of Jesus. But whether Judas had sinister intentions or not in his first professions, we are soon made acquainted with the badness of his heart, though he still appeared to adhere to his Master, and ventured to take on him the character of an apostle.

The first time we find him mentioned is, when our Lord constituted his twelve apostles, of whom Judas was one. ¶ It seems surprizing at first tho't, that our Lord, who undoubtedly knew what was in man, and who said of Judas † " Have not I chosen you twelve, and one of you is a devil," should invest such a wretch with so sacred a character. But if we examine the matter a little more closely,

we

¶ Mark 3. 19.   † John 6. 70.

we shall find, that he acted in this, as in every thing else, becoming the wisdom of God.

In the first place, By this the prophecies were fulfilled. There are several passages in the Psalms which the apostle Peter expressly applied to Judas, ‡ " Men and brethren, this scripture must needs have been fulfilled, which the Holy Ghost by the mouth of David spake before concerning Judas—for it is written in the book of Psalms, Let his habitation be desolate and let no man dwell therein, and his office let another take." These words could not have been so remarkably fulfilled in Judas, if he had not been called to be an apostle.

Again, By our Lord's calling one to be among his chosen twelve, who afterwards turned out a traitor, we are furnished with a very strong argument, that there was no secret scheme carried on between him and his followers. If there was, Judas must have known it, and had he known any collusion, he would undoubtedly have discovered it, and there had been no cause of that remorse of which our text gives an account.

Once more, This instance of Judas, chosen to be an apostle and becoming such a prodigy of wickedness, teaches us not to be surprized, if some among the professed disciples of Christ contradict their profession, and apostatize from his religion.

At

‡ Acts 1. 16, 20.

At the fame time, his defpair and the tragical effect of it afford a folemn warning to all, to avoid every approach to his crime.

When our Lord ordained his twelve apoftles, he " gave them" (Judas among the reft) " power over unclean fpirits to caft them out, and to heal all manner of ficknefs and all manner of difeafe." § This man, fo abandoned, was employed " to preach the kingdom of God," and had power of working miracles. He was raifed to a ftation of the higheft dignity and importance in the difpenfation which Chrift came to introduce, though under the government of the moft fordid paffions.—Even the extraordinary gifts of the Spirit were not an evidence of a fanctified heart. " Many will fay to me in that day, Lord, Lord, have we not prophefied in thy name? and in thy name have caft out devils? and in thy name done many wonderful works? and then will I profefs unto them, I never knew you, depart from me, ye that work iniquity." || One would be inclined to think, that fuch ftriking proofs of divine power would have influenced the hardeft heart; that no one could have ufed the name of Jefus in fuch an authoritative manner, and feen fuch wonderful effects accompanying this ufe of it, without heartily fubmitting to him as Lord and Chrift. But we fee Judas cafting out devils, who was himfelf a fervant of the prince of darknefs. We fee him ufing the name of Chrift with the authority of an apoftle,

§ Mat. 10. 1. || Mat. 7. 21, 22, 23.   and

and publishing the glad tidings of peace, while at the same time he was a stranger to the glory of his character as Mediator between God and man, and had never felt the power of that religion he preached. Some are ready to imagine, that they who have superior knowlege and gifts, especially, if their station in life calls them to study and speak of the excellencies of Christ and the glory of his kingdom, and to be conversant with the gospel which gives such an amiable view of him, must make great attainments in religion; that they have no difficulties, no struggles, no temptations which can at all endanger them; that they are always in a serious devout frame, always thinking of God, and of those subjects that tend to prepare them for the eternal world. But they have in this quite wrong apprehensions of things, and much too high an opinion of the privileges which these men enjoy. It is true, they have peculiar advantages, but these are only means, and the end is far from being necessarily connected with the means. No dignity of office in the church of Christ, no acquaintance with the truths of religion which arises from study and conversation, can secure us from sin, or from the awful doom of hypocrites. Many not only profess to know God, but do really know much of his nature and his works in speculation; they have great understanding in the scriptures, can discourse with propriety and judgment on the doctrines and duties of our holy religion, and deliver themselves with such life and energy, as to warm the hearts

and

and edify the minds of true christians, and yet know nothing as they ought to know, have no practical acquaintance with the truths of religion. They may be wife men after the flesh, and yet not be wife unto falvation. These considerations may serve to correct the sentiments of those, who have the persons of any in admiration, and form too high an opinion of men weak and imperfect as themselves. They are certainly very proper for the serious contemplation of those, who are employed in studying and discoursing on the great and important truths of christianity. But it is very unjust and unreasonable, because this may be the case, and sometimes hath been, to infer that it always is; or to argue that there is nothing in religion, because some professors are not what they pretend to be. It is hard to censure all as hypocrites who call Jesus Master and Lord, because some are; or to pronounce all who preach in the name of Christ strangers to him, because he will say to some who have been engaged in this imployment, "I never knew you." None have a right to " censure or condemn whole bodies of men for the faults of particular members." Methinks the instance of Judas, taken in it's connection with the sincerity of the other apostles, should rather lead to a more charitable conclusion. Of twelve, whom Christ called to be his select followers, one only proved false-hearted; eleven were honest in their professions of regard to him; and though these had their weaknesses and their faults, which were especially visible at the time of his last sufferings and death, yet their hearts were upright before God, and they were, in the end, glorious instruments of spreading his gospel through the world. Timid and irresolute as they were at first; they afterwards, with a noble fortitude, endured the greatest hardships and sufferings in the cause of their Master, and counted not their very lives dear when called to resign them for his sake.

We find mention made of Judas at another time, † When "many of his disciples went back, and walked no more with him. Then said Jesus unto the twelve, will ye also go away ? Then Simon Peter answered him," in the name of the rest, "Lord, to whom shall we go ? Thou hast the words of eternal life. And we believe and are sure, that Thou art that Christ, the Son of the living God." In these words Peter uttered the sentiments of his heart; and, as he supposed, the sentiments of all the rest : For Judas had carried himself with such decency and propriety, that there seems to have been no suspicion of his insincerity among the other disciples. But our Lord, who could not be deceived by any specious pretences, knew the hypocrisy of his heart. "Jesus answered them, have not I chosen you twelve, and one of you is a devil." Our Lord did not specify the wretch of whom he spake with such unusual asperity, that they might all be jealous of themselves, and might

† John 6. 66—71.

might suppress every tendency to such baseness and ingratitude. But the Evangelist tells us, "He spake of Judas Iscariot the son of Simon, for he it was that should betray him, being one of the twelve." Some suppose that Judas, finding, by our Lord's preceding discourse, that there would be nothing in his kingdom to gratify his carnal and ambitious views, now first entertained the thought of betraying him. If this was the case, it shows the badness of his heart, that so plain a proof of Christ's acquaintance with his secret thoughts and purposes did not alarm him, and deter him from proceeding further. It seems it did not. But surely it is a consideration which ought to awaken the mind of every hypocritical and false professor, that Jesus Christ knows the thoughts and intents of his heart. You may possibly preserve your reputation in the world, you may answer some sinister ends which you have in view; though this is not certain; Judas, as we find in the sequel, did not succeed in his worldly designs, he was detected and exposed. But if you should go on without discovery to the end of life, yet what will it avail when you stand before your Judge? Then the thoughts of your heart will be laid open; and you will appear, what you would not now on any account be thought, a deceiver and an hypocrite. Let me beseech you to prevent such an ignominious discovery by repentance. Become honestly that good man and real christian, which you would have the world think

you

you are. This is the only way to have peace in your own mind—to appear with confidence before the judgment seat of Christ—and to escape the wrath to come.

This discourse of our Lord is supposed to be more than a year before his crucifixion. So that the crime of Judas appears to have been a very deliberate act.—It was not a tho't which only passed thro' his mind, as good men have sometimes horrid suggestions, which, if immediately rejected, are not charged upon them as crimes.—It was not the effect of a sudden temptation, by which men are sometimes surprized into an action they abhor.—It was long premeditated.—Our Saviour gave him warning from time to time, but he did not attend to it. He retained the appearance of a disciple with a design to betray his Lord; and under the mask of friendship concealed the most cruel intentions.—How carefully should we guard against the first motions of sin, and suppress evil thoughts as soon as they begin to rise! Had Judas attended to our Lord's admonition, rejected the horrid suggestion when he first perceived it, and sought divine grace to overcome the temptation with which he was assaulted, he had not been that prodigy of wickedness he afterwards proved. But, unhappy man! he did not oppose the wicked thoughts which Satan put into his heart—he gave way to them—he indulged them. Possibly, there were

some

some feeble efforts. Conscience might be sometimes alarmed under the preaching of his Lord, and by the repeated admonitions which Christ gave him. Perhaps it was owing to this, that he did not attempt to perpetrate his perfidious design sooner. But he returned to his wicked meditations—pleased himself with the advantages he hoped to gain—His tenderness of mind gradually wore off—The Spirit of God forsook him—Satan took full possession of him—and he could, without horror, think of the blackest crime that ever was acted under the sun.——Take warning, you who have been hitherto under restraints, but find evil thoughts frequently coming into your mind; especially, if you are tempted to sin, and begin to be inclined to listen to the temptation: You are in awful danger of the greatest crimes. One who suffers his thoughts to run upon forbidden objects is not likely to keep long from wicked actions. Oppose therefore these beginnings of vice. Resist the tempter and he will flee from you. Maintain a constant sense of the being, perfections, and government of God—of your obligations to holiness—and the danger of sin. There is no so effectual a way to keep out bad thoughts, as to keep your minds continually stored with those that are good. If you have been led astray by the tempter, engage in the work of repentance, before you lose your tenderness of mind—before you are given up to your own imaginations, and are left to commit all iniquity with greediness.

"Can

"Can the Ethiopian change his skin, or the leopard his spots, then may ye also do good, who are accustomed to do evil."

The next place in which Judas is mentioned, is John 12. 3. We are told, "Then took Mary a pound of ointment, of spikenard very costly, and anointed the feet of Jesus, and wiped his feet with her hair, and the house was filled with the odor of the ointment." Who would not have supposed, that such an instance of zeal and respect would have met with the approbation of all, but to be sure of the disciples of Christ? that they would have applauded this generous expression of her gratitude and affection? Or if they could not approve the expence which Mary put herself to, yet so long as their Master was silent, and did not find fault, who had given so many instances of his wisdom and attention to the conduct of his followers, we might reasonably expect, they would not object or murmur; and it seems, most of them were possessed of so much modesty as not to express any dissatisfaction. Matthew indeed tells us, "When his disciples saw it they had indignation." Mark says, "They had indignation in themselves." But we may with reason suppose, that the plural is, in these evangelists, put by a usual figure for the singular; this is the more probable, as the speech, which the disciples are said to make, is expresly said by John to be made by Judas. However it was with the other
disciples,

disciples, he could not suppress his malignant sentiments, nor keep from uttering his discontent. As we are told in the 4th verse, " Then faith one of his disciples, Judas Iscariot, Simon's son, which should betray him, why was not this ointment sold for three hundred pence, and given to the poor ?" Had his heart been warmed with love to Christ, he would not have thought that a waste which was bestowed on him. A regard to the poor is a matter of great importance, but it is not to swallow up every other consideration. Every duty is to be attended in its proper place.——Some men think all religion consists in piety and devotion, and have no concern about good works.—Others imagine, that if they abound in acts of charity, this will atone for their neglect of other duties, that charity will cover a multitude of sins, even though they impenitently persist in them.—Both are wrong.—No pretences of regard to God can be sincere, where they are not accompanied with love to our brethren. Nor can any acts of liberality meet with the Divine acceptance, unless they flow from love to him, who, as he is the greatest and best of beings, deserves our supreme regard. A man may give all his goods to feed the poor and not have charity.

But the emotion of Judas did not proceed from his tenderness for the poor, it was the effect of a sordid avaricious temper. " This he said, not that he cared for the poor, but because he was a thief, and had the bag, and bare what was put therein." As he
was

was now meditating a defertion of our Lord, it grieved him that he miffed fo fine an opportunity of gain.——How ready are men to mifcall their conduct! and with what falfe pretences do they endeavor to deceive the world! Judas would fain conceal his avarice by pretending tenderness for the poor, which is a moft amiable and ufeful difpofition. So others will call their niggardly contracted fpirit, prudence, œconomy, or any thing but what it is. Who doth not deteft the hypocrify of Judas, who profeffed a concern for the poor, while he only meant, by the moft infamous robbery, to enrich himfelf? I cannot well omit the note of the pious Mr. Henry on this paffage. "They," fays he, "to whom the management and difpofal of public money is committed, have need to be governed by fteady principles of juftice and honefty, that no blot cleave to their hands, for though fome make a jeft of cheating the government, or the church, or the country, if cheating be thieving, and communities being more confiderable than particular perfons, if robbing them be the greater fin, the guilt of theft and the portion of thieves will be no jefting matter. Judas that had betrayed his truft foon after betrayed his Mafter." He who pretended fuch a vaft regard to the poor was, a few days after, contriving a fcheme of the moft horrid cruelty and perfidy to his great Lord and kind benefactor.

We

We have the account Luke 22, beginning. " Now the feaſt of unleavened bread drew nigh, which is called the paſſover, and the chief prieſts and ſcribes ſought how they might kill him, for they feared the people." The ſolemnity of the ſeaſon and the ſacred ſervices in which they were employed had no influence to reſtrain them from their wicked deſigns. They he'd their conclave in the houſe of Caiaphas the high-prieſt, and there conſulted how they might take Jeſus by ſome artifice, as they were apprehenſive of the people, who retained a reverence for one who had appeared in the character of a prophet, and to whom God had borne witneſs by ſuch a ſeries of miracles.

" Then entered Satan into Judas ſirnamed Iſcariot, being of the number of the twelve. And he went his way, and communed with the chief prieſts and captains, how he might betray him unto them, and they were glad and covenanted to give him money." v. 3, 4, 5. Matthew tells us, he made the propoſal himſelf ; " ſaying, What will ye give me, and I will deliver him unto you ? and they covenanted with him for thirty pieces of ſilver." Covetouſneſs ſeems to have been the great ſpring of Judas's conduct. The love of money is the root of all evil. This puſhed this miſerable man on to his ruin. How ought every one to guard againſt this ſordid—this unworthy paſſion—which hath brought many others beſides Judas to laſting ſhame and perdition. View the world as it is, incapable

capable of yielding you rest; guard against it's snares; and maintain a generous, a christian contempt of it. Think, how great, how good, how all-perfect Jehovah is, who reveals himself to you in the gospel! This God is your's, or he may be your's. How satisfying the rest! how transporting the joy which christianity affords! it begins here, but its duration hath no period. And will you, for any thing this world can afford, consent to miss this great—this inconceivable happiness? Alas! to the disgrace of human nature, multitudes have preferred the most trifling vanities to this infinite good.

Covetous as Judas was, yet he contracted with the priests for a very small sum. Providence so ordered it, that they should propose, and that he should accept just thirty pieces of silver, in order to the accomplishment of Zechariah's prophecy in which this sum was specified. † The fixing this particular sum might be designed by the Jewish rulers as an expression of their contempt of our Lord, it being the price at which a slave was set by the Jewish law. § " A slave," as one observes, " was rated by the law at thirty shekels of silver, which, if we reckon them at half a crown, which was something more than their real value, amounted to no more than three pounds fifteen shillings of our money; a goodly price that he was prized at of them."—What a stoop was it in our blessed Lord. to submit to this indignity and contempt! Such was his love to mankind! such was his desire to promote their best good!

† Zech. 11. 12. § Exod. 21. 32.   " And

"And he promised, and sought opportunity to betray him unto them in the absence of the multitude." He not only engaged, but he was steady to a contract which he ought to have broke, with detestation and abhorrence of his wickedness in making it. We never can, by any engagement of ours, make it right to do a thing that is in itself sinful. But it seems Judas was quite determined. We hear of no remorse—no hesitation. He sought to deliver him in the absence of the multitude. He knew his Lord's practice of retiring; and as He usually permitted the twelve to be with him, Judas knew the place of his retirement; there he proposed to seize him, as it might be effected without danger of a tumult.—How criminal is it to abuse the confidence of our friends and benefactors, and to betray them at those times, when they, generously relying on our honesty and fidelity, commit themselves to us. This aggravates guilt, and is to add treachery to baseness and ingratitude.

The next passage we are called to take notice of is, Mat. 26. 21. While Jesus was eating the paschal supper with his disciples, "he said, verily I say unto you, that one of you shall betray me." Our Lord made this declaration with a friendly design of alarming Judas; and, if possible, reclaiming him from his horrid purpose. He had in view also, by discovering his knowlege of this act of perfidy before it took place, to confirm the faith of his other disciples, which such an event was so likely to stagger. "Now I tell you before it come, that when it is come to pass, ye may believe that I

am

am he." * "And they were exceeding forrowful, and began every one of them to fay unto him, Lord, is it I?" v. 22. The declaration of Jefus filled his difciples with furprize and grief. A variety of melancholy reflections crowded into their minds. It was a thought they knew not how to bear, that their Mafter was to be taken from their head; to be told that he was to be betrayed and become a victim to treachery and wickednefs was an aggravation of their uneafinefs; to hear that the perfidy was to be from among them, while no one was fingled out as the traitor, compleated their diftrefs. They could not entertain any doubt whether Chrift fpake the words of truth and fobernefs—they had no reafon to fufpect their fellow difciples—they knew each one more againft himfelf than againft any of their brethren—and their averfion to the crime made them the more afraid left they fhould be left to commit it. "They began" therefore "to fay unto him one by one, is it I?" My heart, Lord, feels an abhorrence of the crime thou haft predicted, and I cannot entertain a thought of committing it; but when I hear thee declaring, that one of us fhall betray thee, I tremble at the apprehenfion of being that one.—It is an excellent fpirit which thefe difciples difcovered;—What charity were they poffeffed of towards one another!—What a fenfe had they of the corruption and treachery of their own hearts, that they fhould think it poffible for them to commit a crime, of which they could not feel the leaft traces within them; but which they held in the greateft deteftation!—How becoming is fuch

* John 13. 19. diffidence

of Judas and his tragical End. 405

diffidence in creatures weak and finful as we are!
—At the fame time one cannot help being furprized, that Judas, who was capable of fuch impiety and ingratitude, fhould have had the art to behave fo, as that, on fuch a declaration, every one of the difciples fhould fufpect himfelf rather than him.

" And he anfwered and faid, he that dippeth his hand with me in the difh, the fame fhall betray me. The Son of man goeth as it is written of him, but wo unto that man by whom the Son of man is betrayed." v. 23, 24. Dr. Doddridge hath the following note on thefe words, " As this paffage is not liable to the ambiguities, which fome have apprehended in Acts 2. 23. and 4. 28. (which yet feem on the whole to be parallel to it in their moft natural conftruction) I look upon it as an evident proof, that thofe things are in the language of fcripture faid to be determined, or decreed, (or exactly bounded and marked out by God, as the word moft naturally fignifies) which he fees will in fact happen, in confequence of his volitions without any neceffitating agency; as well as thofe events, of which he is properly the author: (and as Beza well expreffes it, qui fequitur Deum, emendate fane loquitur, we need not fear falling into any impropriety of fpeech, when we ufe the language which God has taught :) I fay, without any neceffitating agency, becaufe I apprehend that this text, among many others, muft entirely overthrow the fcheme, which fome laborioufly endeavor to eftablifh, That where God forefees an event, he always determines to render it neceffary, cessary, and so to suspend the moral agency and accountableness of the creature concerned in it. Were this the case, nothing could be more unjust, than to foretell punishments to be inflicted for such actions; which is plainly the case here, and indeed in most other places where evil actions are foretold." It would be unfit to threaten punishments, which it would be unjust to execute; to punish men for actions of which they are not the authors would be unjust; and therefore it would be impiety to assert this of the blessed God.

Matthew goes on, "Then Judas which betrayed him, said, Master, Is it I?" v. 25. He was the last that put the question: He put it now, not because he had any doubt whom Jesus intended, but lest his fellow-disciples should interpret his silence as a confession of guilt, and hoping that our Lord would conceal him as he had hitherto done. "He," (that is Jesus) "said unto him, thou hast said." Which was the same thing as if he had directly told him, thou art the man. All this did not awaken this hardened sinner. On the contrary, he became more furiously set upon the destruction of his Master. "After the sop," which seems to have been given as a private intimation to John, "Satan entered into him." He took more full possession of him. "Then said Jesus unto him, that thou doest, do quickly." † Our Lord knew he had a baptism to be baptized with, and he was straitned till it was accomplished. He knew the time was now come, in which it was determined he should enter on his sufferings, and he earnestly

† John 13. 27.

earneftly defired to meet them, however contrary they were in themfelves to his innocent nature. He knew, that after death, he fhould go to his Father and enjoy the glory he had with him before the world was, and he looked forward with joy to the time of his departure.———How happy they, who like their Mafter are always ready for fufferings, and can rejoice at the approach of the king of terrors ! This fhould be our defire and endeavor. To this end we fhould improve ordinances and providences. Death cannot be far off, it may be near. Let us work while the day lafts, the night cometh wherein no man can work.

" Now no man at the table knew for what intent he fpake this to him. For fome of them tho't becaufe Judas had the bag, that Jefus had faid unto him, buy thofe things that we have need of againft the feaft ; or that he fhould give fomething to the poor."—How much candor is difcovered by the apoftles ! Being innocent themfelves, they were not difpofed to think others guilty, and were ready to put any conftruction on the conduct of Judas, and what our Lord faid to him, than that, which if true, muft lead them to give up their fellow-difciple.— How amiable fuch a temper ! how engaging fuch miftakes ! how much better than a difpofition to cenfure, revile, and condemn all, whom our narrow minds incline us to think the foes of God ! May we ever have that charity which hopeth all things, which believeth all things, even tho' it may lead us fometimes to embrace thofe, who will in the end turn out hypocrites and traitors ! " He

"He then having received the fop, went immediately out, and it was night." Not all the warnings our Lord gave Judas had the leaft effect, unlefs to encreafe his rage; there appears no fign of repentance—no deliberation—no delay—As foon as he found he could conceal himfelf no longer, and perhaps finding the hour agreed upon by the Jews was at hand, he went out to accomplifh his cruel and wicked purpofe.

While Judas was gone to deliver him into the hands of finners, Jefus, with a more than philofophic calmnefs, went on to give his other difciples fuch inftructions and warnings, as he found neceffary to prepare their minds for the approaching great and folemn events. At the very time, when his enemies were about to execute the fcheme they had been fo long contriving, and his laft and moft amazing fufferings were juft at hand, this compaffionate Saviour, ever mindful of his great errand, inftituted the holy eucharift to be a memorial of his death. He as it were forgat his own forrows to promote the good of his church. "The Lord Jefus, the fame night in which he was betrayed, took bread." Surely this is a circumftance which muft have great weight with every ingenuous mind. With what readinefs ought we to obey the command of our dying Saviour, who hath loved us and given himfelf for us, and who never could command any thing but what is agreable to the higheft reafon! To him be glory for ever—Amen.

SERMON

SERMON XVIII.

Practical Observations on the History of Judas and his tragical End.

MAT. XXVII. 3, 4, 5.

Then Judas, which had betrayed him, when he saw that he was condemned, repented himself, and brought again the thirty pieces of silver to the chief priests and elders, saying, I have sinned, in that I have betrayed innocent blood. And they said, What is that to us? see thou to that. And he cast down the pieces of silver in the temple, and departed, and went and hanged himself.

THE solemn warnings and admonitions our Lord had given to Judas, as we have observed once and again, served rather to confirm him in his wicked purpose, than to produce any remorse in his breast. Finding that his treachery was known to his Master; and fearing that he should be exposed to his fellow-apostles; he as it were took Jesus at his word, who had said, "what thou doest, do quickly." He went out, to concert with the chief priests the immediate execution of that black and horrid crime he had undertaken to perpetrate. He went out, to betray his Master, of whose divine mission he could have no reasonable doubt, and of whose perfect character he had himself been witness. ——Jesus also soon went out, to enter on his sufferings, and to meet his betrayer. He retired to Gethsemane—there he passed thro' his distressing agony—there he had his bloody sweat—there his soul was exceeding sorrowful, even unto death. Having again given notice to his disciples of the near approach of their perfidious companion, he went forth, with a noble fortitude, to shew himself to the band that was sent to seize him. "Rise up, let us go; lo, he that betrayeth me is at hand. And immediately, while he yet spake, cometh Judas, one of the twelve, and with him a great multitude with swords and staves, from the chief priests, and the scribes, and the elders." ¶ St. John says, "Judas also which betrayed him, knew the place; for Jesus oft-times resorted thither with his disciples." ‖ There was, probably, at Gethsemane, some oratory, to which our Lord had been wont to retire after his public labors, in a more private manner to instruct his disciples, and to commit himself and them

to

¶ Mark 14. 42, 43.   ‖ John 18. 2.

to his Father in heaven. If so, no wonder Judas knew the place, who had so often been present with his Master at these sacred exercises. But it is truly astonishing, that the recollection of those tender scenes, in which our Lord had discovered so much regard to the human race and such a particular concern for his disciples, did not affect the mind of the traitor, and bring him to a pause. But we have no account of any thing like this: He had sold himself to do iniquity, and he was faithful to his infamous trust. To prevent any rescue, he took a company of soldiers, who were joined by a multitude made up of persons of all ranks and orders, compleatly armed, and determined to secure Jesus.

" And he that betrayed him, had given them a token, saying, whomsoever I shall kiss, that same is he; take him and lead him away safely. And as soon as he was come, he goeth straitway to him, and saith, Master, Master, and kissed him." † Kissing was the usual mode of salutation among the Jews, as among some other nations. "It is probable," as hath been frequently observed by commentators, " that our Lord in great condescension had permitted his disciples thus to salute him, when they returned to him after having been any time absent." Agreably, Judas, as soon as he saw his Lord, drew near to him with a shew of the greatest respect, as if he rejoiced to see him, and said,
Master,

† Mark 14. 44. 45.

Master, Master, and kissed him." Possibly, Judas persuaded himself that he could conceal his perfidy by this artifice, if not from Jesus, yet from his followers. He knew that he had been guilty of great dishonesty and wickedness while he had been their companion, and yet had been able to preserve his character, so that no suspicion had fallen upon him; and he had some hope that he might yet remain undiscovered. Such a hope was, indeed, groundless and unreasonable, after what had passed; but this doth not make it certain that he did not entertain it. It is no unusual thing for wicked men to argue absurdly, as well as to act foolishly. Lust and passion keep the nobler powers of the soul in an ignoble servitude; and hurry them on to a conduct as contrary to reason as it is to interest, which is not only unfit in itself, but tends to their certain ruin. It's dangerous tendency is evident to every one but themselves, who are most concerned to observe it; and the reason they do not see it, is because their foolish heart is darkened.

Our Lord well knew the treachery of Judas's heart, notwithstanding his pretended friendship and respect; and with a mixture of tenderness and indignation, Jesus said unto him, " Judas, betrayest thou the Son of man with a kiss?" § There is something inimitably fine and expressive in this answer. It shows that our Lord knew the man, and saw through his deceit. He calls him by name, and

§ Luke 22. 48.

and exposes his hypocrisy, treachery, and folly. Judas!—It is in vain to attempt to conceal your perfidy and ingratitude—You know that I am the Son of man—not only your Master and Lord, who have been loading you with favors, and to whom you have professed the warmest affection—but the promised Messiah, the King of Israel.—You have sufficient evidence that I justly claim these exalted titles—and yet, forgetting both your character and mine, you are come basely to betray me into the hands of those who have been long waiting for an opportunity to put an end to my life, and to overthrow the benevolent design upon which I came into the world.—Is not this crime attended with sufficient aggravations?—Why dost thou as it were strive to accumulate guilt, by adding hypocrisy to ingratitude, and insolence to treachery?—Know, unhappy man, that I penetrate your dark designs; that I am acquainted with your secret transactions; and am aware of the errand upon which you are come; and therefore cannot return your insidious salutation, nor own thee as a disciple; but must, from this time, consider thee as an enemy and a traitor.

It doth not appear, that our Lord designed to take any particular notice of Judas, till he attempted to accost him as a friend: Perhaps he would have treated him with silent contempt, and have left him to the horrors of his own mind. But the air of respect and affection the traitor put on vexed his
righteous

righteous soul, who never felt the least motion within him contrary to the most perfect sincerity. It filled him with holy indignation. Ill-treatment is hard to be borne from any person, or at any time: It is hardest of all when it comes from those who have pretended respect and friendship, to whom we have shewed kindness and affection, and from whom we expected answerable returns. It was this gave an edge to David's sorrow, " For it was not an enemy that reproached me, then I could have borne it; neither was it he that hated me, that did magnify himself against me, then I would have hid myself from him. But it was thou, a man, mine equal, my guide, and mine acquaintance. We took sweet counsel together, and walked to the house of God in company." † We cannot wonder then, that our Lord Jesus Christ, who had all the feelings of humanity, and the strongest aversion to every thing of moral evil, had the treachery and wickedness of this base dissembler in the highest detestation.

Judas made no return to this severe repulse—He was not capable of replying—guilt struck him dumb—He had not a heart to repent—and bold and wicked as he was, he had not the hardiness to mix with the disciples of Christ—He therefore shrunk into the enemies' ranks, and silently accompanied them in their execrable undertaking.——How this unhappy man disposed of himself afterwards, or what thoughts agitated his mind, while

Jesus

† Psalm 55. 12, 13.

Jesus was before the council, we are not told.—Probably, he was in some private corner about the court, anxiously expecting the event.

The next account we have of him is in the words I read to you at the beginning of this discourse. " Then Judas which had betrayed him, when he saw that he was condemned, repented himself, and brought again the thirty pieces of silver to the chief priests and elders." Expositors are not agreed at what time Judas had this interview with the priests and elders. Some, supposing that Matthew observes the order of time, fix upon that interval, when Jesus, being condemned by the great council, was led away to Pilate. § " But after this," says Dr. Doddridge, " the Jews were so intent on persuading Pilate to consent to his death, that there was hardly time for the Sanhedrim's adjourning to the temple, where this occurrence happened; before they had prevailed with Pilate to condemn him." He places this account of Judas at the time, when Jesus was condemned by the Roman Governor, when orders were given for his crucifixion, and they were actually leading him to the place of execution.

Till this time, Judas might have flattered himself, that Christ would deliver himself; either that he would strike some signal blow upon his enemies,

or

§ Vid. Grotius and Dr. Guyse in Loc.

or that he would escape from them by miracle, as he had done once and again; and so he should secure his money, and his Master receive no injury. But when he saw him condemned, and meekly submitting to the power of those who had him in their hands, a multitude of distracting thoughts crowded into his mind. He recollected what Christ had spoken of his death; and when Pilate sentenced him to be crucified, he could not but remember our Lord's frequent intimations that he should suffer that kind of death.—Now, his guilt appeared before him with all the black and horrid circumstances which attended it. He had betrayed his Master—his friend—his guide—his benefactor—one who had followed him with the kindest admonitions and most useful instructions—a prophet, yea and more than a prophet, the Saviour and Redeemer of men—He had put a stop to all his benevolent designs and gracious operations, and caused him to be treated as a criminal of the worst class. At the same time, Judas would naturally call to mind the dreadful doom which Christ had denounced against him, if he perpetrated the horrid crime he had just been guilty of. Instead of those high ambitious thoughts which he formerly entertained, of being one of the first in Christ's kingdom; he saw himself lost—undone—reserved and destined to eternal woe—without one glimmer of hope, or the most distant prospect of relief. Full of distress, horror, and despair, he repented of what he had done.—

done.—He repented, not with true godly sorrow, but with a gloomy furious remorse which only plunged him deeper into ruin. However, as the first effort to get ease, he carried back the wages of unrighteousness which he had received. The thirty pieces of silver for which he had sold his Master became now an insupportable load. Dearly as he loved money, he could not look upon this price of blood, of the most precious blood, without horror—he could not keep it without torment. Every piece of silver was like a dart striking thro' his liver, it was a sting to his conscience already tortured with a thousand severe reflections. He was distressed till he had got rid of that sordid gain, for which he had just now in a sense bartered his immortal soul. He carried the thirty pieces of silver back to those from whom he had received them, "saying, I have sinned, in that I have betrayed innocent blood." Thus did Providence order that our Lord should have a testimony even from the man who had betrayed him. He made a confession of his sin, when it was not possible he should have any temptation to prevaricate—a confession, which nothing but a pungent sense of guilt could have extorted from him.—He made it publicly, and in the presence of those who had been partners in his crime.—He made it before our Lord's crucifixion, that if possible he might prevent that awful tragedy.

It might reasonably have been expected, that when the priests and elders heard the confession, and saw the distress of this unhappy man, they would be struck with the deepest horror, and hasten to Pilate, in order to prevent the execution of the unjust sentence they had compelled him to pronounce. But no disposition of this kind appears. They expressed no remorse for their own guilt—no concern for an innocent person just going to suffer a cruel death—nor the least pity for a despairing wretch whom they had drawn into the crime which was the cause of his present distress. With a cool and determined countenance they answered him, "what is that to us? see thou to that."—" Is this," says one, " the language of rulers, yea, of priests? But they had cast off the fear of that God, whose ministers they were, and had devoted themselves to gain and ambition. They therefore felt no remorse, even when Judas trembled before them, and appeared almost distracted, under the sense of a crime, in which they had been confederates with him. But their consciences were seared as with a red hot iron, and all their familiar converse with Divine things served only, in such a circumstance, to harden their hearts, as tempered steel gathers strength from the furnace, and the hammer." Judas could not thus quiet his conscience. Their sedateness in wickedness afforded no relief to him. It rather increased the agony of his mind to find them determined to prosecute their plan. He found there was no hope from them of saving that innocent, that illustrious person whom he had betrayed: and frantic with rage, " he cast down the pieces of silver in the temple, and departed."—

ed."—Behold the deceitfulness of sin!—Not many hours before, Judas received this money from them, and was gratifying himself with the thought of improving and enjoying what he had so wickedly procured. But now, he throws it back with detestation and contempt. It was of no value when his conscience was awakened; it was nothing, less than nothing and vanity: Or rather, it was a burthen too heavy for him to bear.——So it is with sin at all times and of all kinds, it is treacherous and deceitful. Men fondly imagine they shall enjoy great pleasure in the gratification of their sensual or ambitious inclinations. They dream of continual delight and ease; but they find themselves deceived and disappointed. They miss of the delight they expected—They meet with an adder in the path—— "In the midst of laughter the heart is sorrowful, and the end of that mirth is heaviness." When conscience is throughly alarmed, they would readily resign all their honors, all their pleasures, however dearly purchased, if that would give ease to their distressed minds. Conscious of guilt, they wish they could recal the unhappy actions of their past lives; their hearts tremble for fear of God.—Happy for them, who mourn for sin with that " godly sorrow which worketh repentance unto life." This is not always the effect of convictions and awakenings. Some lose all hope, their distress like that of Judas ends in black despair—Others drown sorrow in their cups, or perhaps in the cares and amusements of life—They have not grace to repent, even when they are

are senfible of their crimes. Too many return with "the dog to his vomit," and with the "fow, that was washed, to her wallowing in the mire." It is impoffible men should act a more perverse and unreasonable part. If they were to live here always, or if death put an end to their existence, their conduct would not be so criminal. But taking things as they are, it is stupidity, it is distraction. "Madness is in their heart while they live, and after that they go to the dead." An awful found to the guilty sinner.!—They go to the dead—happy for them if this was all—Yes! Non-existence, gloomy as the thought is, would be happiness, when compared with that state of misery and sorrow which awaits them. Oh! then, think of your ways before it be too late—repent while repentance may be of advantage to you—" Turn ye, turn ye, why will ye die?"

But to return to Judas—He departed from the priests and elders lightened of his money, but not at all quieted in his mind. And now—what courfe should he have taken? What! but to have repaired to that Master he had betrayed—to have implored the mercy of that God he had so highly offended—and to have trusted to the merit of that blood he had been so impiously instrumental in shedding?— Who can say he might not have obtained mercy?— But instead of acting in this wife and rational manner, "he departed—and went and hanged himself."

—Tre-

—Tremendous alternative!—To precipitate himself into that misery which he dreaded!—and to hurry before the awful tribunal of a holy God, through fear of his vengeance!

Such a shocking inconsistency of conduct is every one guilty of who commits the horrid crime of suicide—a crime so contrary to all dictates of reason, and the very first principles of human nature, that some have supposed it impossible to be committed by any one, who is not deprived of the capacity of reasoning and reflecting. I am willing to make every allowance for those unhappy persons who have been left of God to put an end to their own lives—It is not to be doubted, that a great part of them have lost the possession of themselves, and therefore have not been moral agents, nor accountable for what they have done. But charity itself cannot conclude that this hath been the case with all who have laid violent hands on themselves. It is not sufficient to say this crime is to the highest degree irrational. May not this be said of every wilful sin? Men often break the laws of God, when they know and believe, that by their disobedience they expose themselves to the damnation of hell. They run with their eyes open into eternal perdition. They have reason, but they do not exercise it. They suffer themselves to be governed by their appetites and passions, when they know the consequence will be death; that their present conduct will accelerate the death of the body, and is

likely

likely to terminate in the second death. This may fitly be called madness and distraction, because men under the government of reason would not act thus. But it is voluntary madness, and which they might prevent; and therefore they are justly chargeable with their irrational conduct.—And this I fear is too often the case with self-murderers. They are themselves the causes of that discontent, that shame, that horror, that despair, which have this fatal end—They act irrationally when they have power to act otherwise—They will not repent—They will not implore the mercy and grace of God—But give way to their gloomy passions, till they precipitate themselves into an action, which is to the last degree criminal, and infinitely dangerous.—They rise up against the government of God—take his work into their own hands—and, while they are guilty of a most daring act of rebellion against their sovereign Lord, they put themselves beyond the possibility of repentance.—To get rid of their present misery, they plunge themselves into that, which is not only greater, but absolutely remediless—Let all, but especially those who are in great distress, whether of a temporal or spiritual nature, carefully arm themselves with the strongest resolutions against every temptation to this dreadful sin. Reject the first suggestion with detestation, it is both unnatural and diabolical, and doth not admit of the least deliberation. As the most effectual preservative, seek the Spirit and grace of God, to deliver you from such thoughts, as, if indulged, are likely to to end in perdition here and hereafter. It was despair of the mercy of the infinitely benevolent Jehovah that led Judas to destroy himself—a disposition of mind, which, after all God hath done for man, is most inexcusable and affrontive, and which we ought to resist with the greatest firmness and constancy—To think our case desperate is the most likely way to make it so.

You doubtless observe some difference between the account given in our text, and that which we have in Acts 1. 18. There, the apostle Peter, speaking of Judas, says, " and falling headlong he burst asunder in the midst, and all his bowels gushed out." Some, in order to reconcile these accounts, render the words in Matthew, that he was suffocated, namely, with grief, shame, and remorse; or, which is the same thing, died of a squinancy occasioned by it. And that he fell down on his face, and afterwards burst asunder, as is common to persons in that distemper. ¶ But the more usual conjecture, and which is not the less just for being common, is, that the rope or that to which it was fastened gave way, so that he fell on his face, and, being at the top of some precipice, his bowels gushed out by the violence of the fall. § These circumstances in the death of this wicked traitor more signally manifested the righteous judgment of God, to all who were witnesses of them. " And it was known unto all the dwellers in Jerusalem."

¶ Univ. Hist. vol. 10. p. 595.   § Guyse and Doddridge.

I should gladly embrace the charitable sentiment of those, who think that the repentance of Judas was sincere, and that he obtained mercy of God. But I cannot find any warrant for such a conclusion. And we may not pervert the scriptures, even to magnify the grace of God.

How great the difference between Judas and Peter! and how different the dispensation of heaven towards them!—Judas betrayed his Master; Peter denied him—The crime of Judas was the effect of deliberate malice; Peter's of a sudden surprize—Peter went out and wept bitterly; Judas departed and hanged himself—Peter was restored to his office; Judas was a son of perdition—Thus God "hath mercy on whom he will have mercy, and whom he will he hardeneth." We are not indeed to suppose that God ever acts without reason: and though sometimes the reason of his conduct is hid from us, yet in this case it was obvious. Peter had a good and honest heart, though he was guilty of a very great sin; Judas had long been a base dissembler, and had perfidiously embezzled the little stock with which our Lord had entrusted him.—Peter loved his Master, and followed him because he believed him to be the Christ the Son of God; Judas had no regard to his Lord, and followed him only from base and sordid motives.—Divine grace had made the difference, but the difference was made.—In all we see God's regard to holiness, and the perfect rectitude of his nature and of his conduct.

Behold also the sovereign distinction made between Judas and the thief on the cross.—Judas had long sat under the instruction of him who spake as never man spake; he had been a professor of religion, and was raised to the dignity of an apostle. The thief had lived in vice and wickedness, been an open enemy of God, and died a victim of justice.—He was taken and Judas left.—The thief heard from the mouth of the Saviour of the world, " this day thou shalt be with me in paradise ;" Judas went to his own place.—No appearance of religion, nor sacredness of character can avail us with a holy God, if we continue under the guilt of sin, and are deceitful in our religious professions. But on the other hand, repentance is never too late if it be sincere ; nor are any offenders excluded from a share in the merits of Christ and the mercy of the gospel, unless they exclude themselves by unbelief and impenitence.

I have now gone through this affecting history, and have made so many practical reflections as I went along, that there seems but little occasion for a particular application. There is one inference from the story of Judas which I have already mentioned, but which is of so great importance that it deserves a more particular consideration.

It is this, That Jesus the great Founder of our religion was no impostor, but was in truth the Son of God, the promised Messiah. Our Lord came to introduce a new dispensation of religion; to accomplish the things " which were written in the law of Moses, and in the prophets, and in the psalms," concerning an extraordinary person who was to come into the world to instruct and reform mankind. His religion was not, like that of Moses, to be confined to a particular nation; the kingdom of Christ was to be of large extent; according to the promise made to Abraham, " In thy seed shall all the nations of the earth be blessed."—Jesus himself was " not sent but to the lost sheep of the house of Israel;" his personal ministry was confined to the land of Judea; and even there he was to be seen on the public stage only for a short time. In this time he was to lay the foundation of that kingdom which the God of heaven was to set up according to the ancient prophecies, a kingdom which was never to be destroyed.—He was to prove himself to be the Messiah promised to the fathers—and to give such evidences of his divine mission, as might be a sufficient ground of a rational faith, not only in his day, but in all ages of the world.——It was, therefore, not merely expedient, but necessary, that there should be a number to testify and bear witness of the great facts upon which the truth of christianity rests, and to publish them to the world. Accordingly, Jesus first " ordained twelve, that they should be with him, and that he might send them

forth

forth to preach, and to have power to heal sick-
nesses, and to cast out devils." He afterwards sent
out seventy others on the same errand. But the
first twelve were the persons whom he admitted to
the greatest intimacy—they were with him in all
his retirements—they followed him in all his jour-
nies—they received such marks of favor, that, a-
greably to the carnal and ambitious notions of his
kingdom which they at first entertained, they expected to be his ministers of state, and to sustain the
highest employments under him.——His view in
calling them and keeping them near his person was
indeed very different from their's : It was to prepare them for the glorious work of preaching the
gospel, and that they might be able to declare to
the world the things that Jesus had done and taught.
Nothing could be more wisely ordered, upon the
supposition of the truth of christianity, and the
reality of our Saviour's divine mission. The
apostles were authentic witnesses of facts which
they had "seen and heard," though they did
not at first understand the great consequence
of those facts, or of their testimony about them.
By the marvellous descent of the Spirit on the day
of Pentecost, the whole scheme of the christian religion was committed to them, and they were endued with power from on high ; they then preached the gospel with all boldness, and wonderful was
the success of their preaching. By the apostles, or
by their means, and during their lives, christianity
had a swift and extensive spread, not only thro'out
Judea,

Judea, but through a very great part of the world.

    Let us now suppose, on the other hand, that Jesus had some secret design different from that which he professed, that he intended to propagate a falshood, and upon this falshood to erect his kingdom. His design must have been communicated to those chosen followers who were to be employed in carrying it on: Or they must have discovered it themselves. ———As they were with him at all times, and in all places, they must have had opportunity to observe his retired actions, and the most secret parts of his life: They must have known whether his private conduct was answerable to what openly professed. He called himself the Son of God, and publicly declared that he came to correct the false notions of religion and morality which had obtained, and to set an example of perfect virtue. There was reason to expect a person of such an extraordinary character would be eminent for his devotion, his purity, his charity. They who were continually with him could not but see, whether there was any thing in his behavior, when retired from the view of men, inconsistent with these pretensions, any thing that looked like art and collusion, or like one who designed to deceive them, and to impose on the world. It was impossible that a person with whom they were conversant in all situations, and for a number of years, should carry on such a scheme, without giving them some suspicion of his sinister views; or that they should be deceived in the miracles

racles which he pretended to work, and which were of such a nature as not to admit of a deception, where those who were witnesses of them had only a common share of understanding; it follows therefore that if he was an impostor, his twelve disciples at least were confederate with him.

As Judas was one of our Lord's select followers, one of the twelve who were his constant companions, if there had been any such secret design as we have supposed, he must have been made acquainted with it; if there had been any confederacy he would have been in it. There is no appearance of a distinction between him and the other apostles. In two or three instances, Jesus took Peter, James, and John to be witnesses of some transactions in which he chose to be more private than common. But he did not raise these to any higher station, nor allow them to assume a superiority over their brethren. Nor did the notice he took of them give any offence to the other disciples; any more than the particular regard he shewed to John, who lay in his bosom, and was by way of eminence stiled the beloved disciple, did to Peter and James. As to Judas, it is plain he was upon a par with his brethren. He was constituted an apostle at the same time; he attended on our Lord as they did; he was sent forth as they were; he was endowed with the same extraordinary gifts; a particular trust was committed to him; he had the care of whatever sum his Master was at any time owner of; it was left to him to provide necessaries for the

little

little company our Lord always had about him; and to distribute to the poor according to his Master's direction. Whatever obliquity there was in his heart, he appeared to the other disciples honest and faithful, they had no suspicion of his integrity, nor did his Master by any neglect or rebuke give him any occasion of disgust. If there had been any particular difference in the conduct of our Lord to Judas, or in that of Judas to his Master, any neglect, any coldness, or indifference, on the one side or the other, it would have raised suspicions in the minds of the eleven, and when Christ said "one of you shall betray me," they would have immediately fixed upon him as the person; whereas each one was more ready to mistrust himself, "and they began every one of them to say unto him, Lord, is it I?"

When Christ sent out his apostles to preach the gospel, and professed to give them a power of working miracles, Judas was sent forth with the others. The evangelist tells us, that Jesus gave his twelve disciples "power and authority over all devils and diseases." And we are told how fully they executed this commission; ‡ "And they went out and preached that men should repent; and they cast out many devils, and anointed with oyl many that were sick, and healed them," Now Judas could not but know, whether he had this power or not; whether he had in fact, by invoking the name of Jesus, healed diseases and cast out devils.

Here

‡ Mark 6. 12, 13.

Here was a fair trial of his Master's character and authority. If these miracles were wrought by power derived from him, and in confirmation of that religion he came to introduce, there was no room to dispute his divine mission, or to doubt whether he was the Messiah. On the contrary, if Judas found that Jesus professed to give him a power, which he did not receive; and that he pretended to vest him with authority over diseases, of which notwithstanding he did not find himself possessed, he must conclude Jesus was not that extraordinary person he declared himself to be, but was a deceiver and impostor. If this was the case, Judas ought to have exposed such a mere pretender; he would have done right in disclosing any wicked secret which had been committed to him, in joining with the scribes and pharisees in undeceiving the people, and in using his utmost endeavors to bring such an offender to condign punishment, and irritated as he was, no doubt he would have done it.

Did Judas make any such discovery, even when he confederated with the priests and elders to betray his Master? Did he bring the least charge against him of any secret wickedness? How eagerly would his enemies have catched at such a confession! How diligently would they have propagated such a fact! What a triumph would it have afforded them over him who had set himself up as a Prophet, if one of his own disciples had opened any private scheme, or had only suggested that he had

had pretended to more than he had been able to perform! How exactly would an infinuation of this fort have anfwered their views! and what ufe would they have made of it to undeceive the people who had conceived a high opinion of his perfon and character! What a principal evidence would he have been againft Jefus on his trial before Pilate, when they were obliged to pick up every one who would alledge any thing that would ferve the turn, whether true or falfe! But is there the leaft hint of any thing of this kind? No, they feemed willing to keep him out of fight during the trial, as one that would injure rather than help their caufe. Judas, abandoned as he was, did not dare to prevaricate to fuch an awful degree, to affert any thing againft his Mafter, or to charge him with the leaft crime. He was convinced of his perfect rectitude, and had been witnefs of the power which Jefus had exerted himfelf in innumerable inftances, and which he had fometimes communicated to others, even to Judas himfelf; and this traitor moft probably thought, that he who could " ftill the noife of the feas, the noife of their waves," would quiet " the tumult of the people," and deliver himfelf out of their hands. This was no unreafonable conjecture after the much greater exertions of his divine power which Judas had been witnefs of.—When this miferable man found himfelf difappointed in this his expectation, he was feized with the greateft horror and diftrefs from the

thought

thought of what he had done; and, as the only expedient to obtain relief, he made a public declaration of his Master's innocence and his own perfidy and guilt to the Jewish rulers; that if possible, he might prevent the injustice and cruelty which were like to be the consequence of his treachery. And when, to his utter confusion, he found that he could make no impression on their obdurate hearts, he put an end to his own life, as not able to bear the horrid tragedy which was going to be acted. Doth this look like a man who knew Jesus to be a deceiver? Could there be a stronger evidence of his full conviction of his Master's integrity, and of the justice of his pretensions? It seems impossible to account for the behavior of Judas in this last period of his life, upon any other supposition; and taking it in this view, it is a strong confirmation of the truth of the christian religion. And this serves to illustrate the wisdom of God in appointing him one of the twelve.

God over-ruled this awful act of wickedness, as he more eminently did the death of that just one who was thus cruelly and ungratefully betrayed, to the purposes of his own glory; but this did not extenuate the crime, nor should it lessen our abhorrence of it. We see here a miscreant, betraying his Lord and Master—a Master who had treated him with the greatest affection, and had raised him to the highest honor—one, of whose divine mission he had the most convincing evidence, and whom he knew to be the Son of God, and the Saviour of men—one, whose preaching he had long sat under, and whose holy life he had particular opportunity to

observe

obferve!—We see him deliberately contriving the ruin of this illustrious person; pretending friendship while his heart was full of malice and deceit!—What crime so black, that human nature is not capable of it!

Let us not wonder, if our friends forsake, betray, and abuse us. Let us look for such things in this deceitful wicked world. " The disciple is not above his Master, nor the servant above his Lord."

While we tremble at the awful destruction of Judas, let us carefully avoid every approach to his sin. Our Lord's person is indeed above any injurious attempt of our's, but men may have the same disposition of mind that was so fatal to this ungrateful traitor, and may commit sins that greatly resemble his.——The day will come, when the ungodly sinner, and the concealed hypocrite, must appear before his impartial tribunal. Then, all their dissimulation, all their wickedness, will come to their remembrance, and fill them with remorse and horror. How earnestly doth Judas, that son of perdition, wish, that he had not been guilty of the impious deed which brought him to such a dreadful end, or that he could recall his base and wicked treachery! The best way to prevent such fruitless wishes is to do nothing we should desire to recall. He who would not repent of betraying Christ, must take care not to betray him. Whatever present advantage any one may gain, by calling Christ Master and Lord, and at the same time betraying his cause and interest in the world, it will be as certainly true of him as it was of Judas, that " it had been good for him that he had never been born.".

SERMON XIX.

Man doomed to return to the dust from whence he was taken.

GENESIS III. 19.

Dust thou art, and unto dust shalt thou return.

THERE is no subject which men are more loth to meditate upon than their own frailty and mortality. They shrink back at the thought of death, it spreads a melancholy gloom over their minds, and they wish to put far away the evil day. They live pleasantly with their friends; they have many agreable enjoyments; and they cannot bear to think of leaving them. Especially, they cannot think of entering into an eternity, which the most, it is to be feared, find themselves unprepared for. They, therefore, avoid these gloomy reflections, and when they intrude, endeavor to dissipate them

them amidst the cares and pleasures of life. This is too much the temper and conduct of mankind; and in nothing do they more evidently discover the folly which is bound up in their hearts. If, indeed, by forgetting death we could prevent it, if by inattention to this disagreeable subject, we could lengthen out our time on earth; or, if serious contemplations on mortality had a tendency to hasten a dissolution, their conduct in suppressing these thoughts might admit of some excuse. But is this the case? Can any one propose this advantage? or indeed, can he propose any advantage which ought to influence a reasonable mind? It is a duty to think of death because we must die; because death concludes our time of probation; and fixes our state forever. "It is appointed unto men once to die, but after this the judgment." Nothing can justify, nothing can excuse our inattention to such an interesting, such an important subject. If we do not often and seriously meditate on this great change, it is not likely we shall ever be prepared for it. But if we live under a constant apprehension of the shortness and uncertainty of life, we shall soon learn to apply our hearts unto wisdom.—This would cure us of our fondness for worldly objects. We should immediately perceive the vanity of all things here, if we duly considered that in a short time we must leave them.——This would lead us to acquaint ourselves more with the state into which we are going

ing, and would make us follicitous to secure that eternity of happiness which the gospel reveals and offers. The christian, who hath a lively faith in things future and invisible, cannot feel a reluctance when called to leave the world; he will rather desire earnestly to be with Christ, which he must esteem to be far better than the most comfortable situation in this life. The consideration of our frailty and mortality would cause us to think soberly of ourselves and as we ought to think: It would make us less follicitous about the body, and more careful about the soul which is incomparably the superior part of man. Instead then of suppressing such thoughts, we should with the greatest care cultivate and cherish them—we should attend to the calls of God in his word and providence to get ready for our departure—we should suffer nothing to divert us from that which is the great business of life—we should not allow one day to to pass without remembering the sentence pronounced on the first Adam, and virtually on all his posterity, "Dust thou art, and unto dust shalt thou return."

These words teach us what was our original, and to what we shall be reduced. It will not be time ill-spent, if I lead you to some serious reflections on both.

In the first place, we are led up to our original, "Dust thou art." In the account which Moses gives

gives of the creation of man, we read, that " the Lord God formed man of the duſt of the ground." He put the particles together, and gave them that ſhape and form in which we now behold them. How much of the wiſdom and goodneſs of God is ſeen in this formation of our bodies!— How admirably is the whole frame contrived to anſwer the purpoſes for which it was deſigned; ſo that we cannot ſee how any part could be ſpared, or conſtituted better than it is; and are bound to ſay with the devout pſalmiſt, we are " fearfully and wonderfully made!" Every limb, every veſſel is placed ſo as to be moſt uſeful and convenient.— And how great is his power who could make theſe curious bodies out of the duſt of the earth, who could ſo exactly faſhion and modify that which is in itſelf quite vile and contemptible; and conſtitute a variety of uſeful organs from ſuch unpromiſing materials.

We are not to ſuppoſe man was wholly made up of duſt, " there is a ſpirit in man, and the inſpiration of the Almighty hath given him underſtanding." We read therefore, that when God had formed man of the duſt of the ground, " he breathed into his noſtrils the breath of life, and man became a living ſoul." 'Tis this ſoul which gives life and motion to the body, and which alone is ſenſible of pleaſure and of pain—'Tis this which thinks and reaſons, which chuſes and refuſes—This only is capable

pable of moral good and evil—It is a myſterious union which ſubſiſts between two ſuch different ſubſtances. It is wonderful, that matter and ſpirit ſhould be ſo cloſely connected as to make but one perſon, and yet each remain the ſame; that is, matter not become ſpirit, nor ſpirit become matter: That there ſhould be ſuch a near and intimate ſympathy between them, as that the ſtate of the one ſhould greatly affect the ſtate of the other. We are ſenſible of the fact, we feel the connection, but we know not how it is effected; we can form no idea of their mutual impreſſions or operations on each other.

'Tis obſervable, that our text ſpeaks in the preſent tenſe; not, duſt thou waſt, but " duſt thou art." This form of expreſſion intimates, that the body of man is eſſentially the ſame that it was at firſt. 'Tis the ſoul that diſtinguiſhes it from other matter; and renders it agreable, active, and uſeful. Let the ſpirit or ſoul withdraw, or be ſeparated from it, and the body will preſently fall into duſt, as mean and ſordid duſt as ever; which ſhews what it is in itſelf. It was duſt at firſt—it is now only a maſs of animated earth—and it will at length return to the duſt as it was.

But this leads us to conſider, Secondly, To what man will be reduced. " Duſt thou art, and unto duſt ſhalt thou return." We juſt obſerved, that the body of man was duſt originally; and if ſeparated

rated from the soul it would fall into dust again. But our bodies were nevertheless designed for immortality. If man had kept covenant with God, he would have been preserved from death by the divine power. Had not man sinned, there would have been no separation between soul and body; and consequently the body would have been always animated and capable of action. The threatning which God denounced as a sanction of his law, and to deter man from the violation of it was, " In the day thou eatest thereof thou shalt surely die." When he had sinned, what was before only a threatning, was turned into a sentence of condemnation; the sentence was pronounced by God, his Sovereign—his almighty Judge. " Dust thou art, and unto dust shalt thou return." Nor was this designed to be the case with Adam only, to whom it was immediately spoken: He acted for his posterity, so far at least, as that they are by a righteous constitution of heaven, involved in the consequences of his apostacy. This is the account the apostle gives us, " By one man sin entered into the world and death by sin, and so death passeth upon all men, for that," or, unto which, " all have sinned," or are dealt with as sinners. It may admit of dispute, whether the sin of Adam is imputed to his posterity so as to transfer his guilt to them, but it is certain they all feel the effects of it—They are bro't by it into a sinful imperfect state—The mind is weakened and depraved, the passions and appetites have an undue influence, so that there

is

is none capable of moral action who doeth good and finneth not. Our bodies are mortal; we are haftening to the grave, where the duft will return to the duft as it was. This is the unalterable decree of that God in whofe hand our breath is; and in whofe power it is to continue us in life, or to reduce us to our primitive nothing. " In Adam all die," the great and the rich, as well as the poor, and the low: There is none can retain the fpirit, or fecure it from the ftroke of death; "there is no difcharge in that war." This is fo plain a point, that you would all wonder if I fhould labor to prove it, nor am I capable of bringing any more conclufive arguments, than offer themfelves to your thoughts without any help of mine.

When we look into our Bibles and read of the antediluvian patriarchs, that they lived eight and nine hundred years, yet the account of them is fummed up with this at laft, " and he died." After the flood the time of the life of man was gradually fhortened, till it came to be limited to threefcore years and ten, an age which few furvive.— One generation goeth and another cometh.—Our Fathers where are they?—They reft from their toils and labors. If we look back to the firft fettlement of New-England, not one is to be found who was then alive. Of thofe who laid the foundation of thefe rifing colonies it would be hard to find even the duft. There are none now on the ftage who have feen or known them. What was once vifible of them is forgotten—The memory of these excellent men still remains—Their names, their love to God, his truths and ways, will, we trust, be had in everlasting remembrance, and be an incitement to their posterity to imitate their virtues.

But why do I speak of the first settlers of New-England? If we have only retrospect to our own time; how few are there that were on the stage of action within our remembrance! How many that a few years ago had parents to help, advise and protect them, are risen up to be parents themselves, and are called to do the same kind offices for their children.—Our progenitors are gone, and we are going after them.—How many of our friends, our relatives, our neighbours, have been laid in the silent grave, within the compass of a few years! If we have been on the public theatre only twenty or thirty years, or even less, and look back and think of those with whom we first contracted an acquaintance, we find that there is but here and there one remaining—They are gone—the places that have known—the persons that have seen them—we that have had agreable society with them,—shall know,—shall see,—shall converse with them no more.—And it will be said of us in a short time as it is of them—They are dead!—Some daily feel the decays of nature; they find their tabernacle of clay tottering and ready to fall. Such as these may well think of a dissolution as not far off; they have the sentence of death in themselves. But
whether

whether we have such premonitions or not, death may be nigh, even at the door. How many who could boast as firm a constitution as our's have been numbered with the dead! and that before they have been wasted with sickness, or enfeebled by age! " One dieth in his full strength, being wholly at ease and quiet: His breasts are full of milk, and his bones are moistened with marrow. And another dieth in the bitterness of his soul, and never eateth with pleasure. They shall lie down alike in the dust, and the worms shall cover them." " Man that is born of a woman, is of few days, and full of trouble."

We know that we must die, but we know neither when nor how. We may have years to live; or, God may say to us, " this night thy soul shall be required of thee." Thou dost, perhaps, feel at present in perfect health; but, before the light of another day, thou may'st be seized with dying agonies—Thy body may be covered with a cold sweat—Thy pulse may tremble and intermit—Thy breath may grow short—and every part of the vital frame may cease to perform its proper function. That body which is now so hale and vigorous, may be a lifeless corpse, and hastening to the dust from which it was taken. These are things which do not admit of dispute. They are truths which at once strike the mind with conviction. None can deny them; and yet few attend to them as they ought.

ought. Were they mere speculations, you might disregard them without danger; it would be of no importance whether you attended to them or not. But since they are truths in which you are so nearly concerned; it becomes every friend of mankind —It becomes every christian—It especially becomes one who is appointed to watch for souls, to do what he can to rouse you out of your criminal insensibility.

I must therefore observe, that nothing is to return to dust, but that which was dust before. The sentence pronounced on man is, " Dust thou art, and unto dust shalt thou return." i. e. That part which is constituted of dust must return to what it was at first. But the wise man assures us, that as "the dust returns to the dust," so "the spirit returns to God who gave it." The soul of man was not formed out of the earth as the body was, but was brought into existence by the immediate act of the Deity, without the use of any materials already created. It is a spiritual substance. It hath no dependence on the body for life. It can exist and act without it; at least no one can determine that it cannot. We may not with any certainty conclude, because the body is without life and motion, that the soul ceases to exist, or to be active. He who formed the spirit of man within him can undoubtedly unmake it; and if there is any thing in that revelation with which he hath favored us, which makes it evident that this is his design, we ought to receive it it as the truth, however contrary it is to our preconceived notions, to what we have expected or defired. But it is certain there is no declaration of this fort, nor the leaft intimation that the death of the body terminates the exiftence of the foul. So far from this, the whole current of fcripture fets the other way. We have many intimations, that the fpirits of men furvive the body; that they not only exift, but are in an active ftate.—Why elfe did Paul "defire to depart to be with Chrift;" when he could have greatly promoted the Redeemer's kingdom, and increafed his own happinefs, by remaining longer in the prefent world?—Why doth our Saviour fay to the thief on the crofs, " this day fhalt thou be with me in paradife?"—Why are we told in the parable of the rich man and Lazarus, that when Lazarus died, he " was carried by the angels into Abraham's bofom," by which the Jews expreffed the higheft ftate of happinefs in another world? But that the rich man, who is faid to be buried, " lift up his eyes, being in torments?"—We read of the " fpirits of juft men made perfect."—And why fhould this thought of an intermediate ftate feem incredible, fince the foul in the prefent ftate often acts, when we are not fenfible that it makes any ufe of the body? Certainly this fuppofition implies no contradiction, nor doth it involve us in any abfurdity. But I am not called to enlarge on this point, it was fit to mention it when I was fpeaking of our returning to duft. I proceed to the

I M.

IMPROVEMENT.

In the first place, Must these bodies return to dust, this should lead us to look upon them as they are, frail, fading, and perishing. Nothing is more certain, than that our bodies will soon be food for worms, and reduced to the most sordid dust. This we have a most sure and certain persuasion of; and yet how sollicitous are we about them!—How curious in adorning them!—How elated with any little circumstance in which they either do, or we imagine they do, excel others. Poor vain wretch! What is it you are so pleased with? What is it you value yourself upon? Upon a vile body—upon a body of humiliation—which ought, every time you think of it, to give you the most low and abasing thoughts of yourself! That body is only dust, kept together at present by the power of God; but it will soon be without life or motion—a mere lump of putrefaction—more ghastly and odious, than now it is beautiful and agreable. Your surviving friends will be as careful to cover it and bury it out of their sight, as you are to display the beauty of it. It might answer a valuable purpose, if our gay young people would now and then visit the repositories of the dead, that they might see to what they shall soon be reduced, and might learn not to think more highly of themselves than they ought to think. Where is that fine skin—those beautiful features—that exact proportion—which vain minds meditate upon with so much pleasure?—Canst thou see any

distinction?—do not all appear alike sordid and frightful?—You chuse to retire from a sight so disagreeable—an object so offensive.—Just such will you be after a few days and months are passed—Just so spectators will retreat from your ghastly visage—or rather, from your polluted dust, and naked bones!—'Tis a disagreeable picture I am obliged to draw—but it is a true likeness—it answers to the original.—Should I tell you that, after death, you would remain such as you now are, you would not give credit to the report, you would know that it was only foolish flattery. And should not such vain creatures have a true mirror sometimes set before them, that they may have a view of themselves, and learn a lesson of humility from the sight?

Secondly, How absurd and irrational is it to spend all our time about our bodies, and to neglect our immortal spirits!—You see what your bodies are, how mean the materials of which they were composed at first, and how despicable their end is like to be.—Your souls have a more noble original. They are produced by the inspiration of the Almighty; and they have some resemblance of their Creator. They are not to die with the body; but are, in a separate state, to enjoy compleat happiness, or sink into inexpressible misery, according to the things done in the body. And, upon this view of things, I am willing any man should be judge in his own cause. Who can pretend to justify,

tify, or even excuse his own conduct, in pursuing after wealth, honor, sensual pleasure, or any kind of happiness, which terminates in the body, and must cease with it; while he neglects his soul, which is designed for immortality?——We blame not your care about the world, and to secure things that are convenient for the body, provided it do not degenerate into anxiety; if your love of the world is not inordinate, and you are not immoderate in your pursuit of earthly things. We only urge you to place your affections on things according to their true worth and importance. Earthly things are good, so far as they answer the end for which they were designed; this end is to support life, and to make your situation here agreable. But they were never designed to be your portion; they ought not to engross your attention; they cannot make you happy in this world, and they will not follow you into another. " Naked," says Job, " came I out of my mother's womb, and naked shall I return thither."——We blame you then, if you set a higher value on the things of this world than they deserve; if you look for more good from them than they are capable of yielding you.—We condemn you, as acting a most weak and unreasonable part, if you take greater care of your bodies, than of your souls, which are so much superior, and upon the care of which your eternal state depends —if you labor for the meat which perisheth, and not for that which endures to everlasting life— if you seek to be rich and great here, and are not
sollicitous

follicitous to be rich towards God, and to fecure eternal glory. " What will it profit," my brethren, " if you gain the whole world, and lofe your own foul." ? All the happinefs which you can enjoy in this world is unfatisfying in it's nature, and momentany in it's duration : But the mifery of the future world is awful, is dreadful, is permanent.

Permit me to put a cafe to thofe who are feeking a portion in this life and forget another ; let confcience give the anfwer and make the application. There have been, it is to be feared, many great and rich men, who have been able to command every earthly enjoyment that their hearts could wifh for ; but they have been ftrangers to religion, have indulged to luxury and vice, and are now in a ftate of punifhment.—There have been others, low in their worldly circumftances, deftitute of the comforts and even the neceffaries of life ; but they have been rich in faith, heirs of the kingdom, and are now entered on their reward.—Is there a wretch, think you, in the place of torment, let his fituation on earth have been ever fo exalted, who would not be willing, taking both worlds into confideration, to change ftates with any one in the kingdom of heaven, even with one who had gone through the moft afflicted and trying fcenes here, and who had the loweft place there ?—But on the other hand, do you think the leaft faint in the kingdom of glory would confent to take the place of any one in the regions of the damned, though, previous to such an exchange, he might enjoy the highest degree of prosperity that any one ever arrived at in this world.—What glorified saint would not prefer a life of poverty and distress, considered in connection with the happiness that hath followed, to a life of the greatest affluence and glory which must terminate in extreme misery ?—What damned spirit would not chearfully endure all temporal sorrow, if he might escape everlasting destruction ?—Oh ! how would a condemned sinner leap with joy, to hear that he was again to be put on his probation ; or to have the least glimmering of hope, that God would entertain thoughts of mercy ! You, who are yet on this side the eternal world, have not merely a glimmering of hope, you are favored with the invitations of the gospel ; it is an accepted time, it is a day of salvation. But after this life, you will have no more calls, no more invitations; as the tree falls so it will lie ; as your moral state is when you die, so will your eternal state be fixed.——— What we urge you to is, to live and act now, as you yourselves are convinced, you shall wish you had acted, if you leave the world in a state of impenitence and unbelief.

Thirdly, When we see others expiring and returning to their dust, it should put us in mind of our dissolution. Such sights we often see in this dying world. Our relatives and friends are continually leaving us. We have frequent occasion to sigh

sigh out that mournful complaint, " Lover and friend haft thou put far from me, and mine acquaintance into darkness." They are laid in the grave; death feedeth upon them, and their beauty is consumed. As they are, thou wilt soon be; thy body like their's will moulder in the grave. But—where will thy soul then be? This is an enquiry you ought often to make. If God should see fit to loose the vital band, in what state would my soul be? I am assured this will not return to dust, because it hath not, it never had any thing earthly in it's constitution, unless earthly desires and inclinations are a part of it. I am taught in the scriptures, that my " spirit will return to God," will return—not to be annihilated ; but to receive a sentence of absolution or condemnation, according to the things done in the body. Which of these sentences should I receive, if God should this night require my soul of me?—And who knows but he may?—Have I submitted to Christ?—Am I a new creature?—Do I possess a christian, a heavenly temper?—Have I led a holy life?—Am I not rather a stranger to religion?—under the dominion of my lusts?—Do not my works prove, that if I should leave the world as I am at present, I should sink into everlasting perdition?—Shall I continue in such a state of awful danger?—Shall I not immediately repair to that Saviour who is the only hope set before me?—Shall I not without delay accept the gracious invitations of the gospel?—Lord, assist me by thy grace, and work in me both to will and to do of
thy

thy good pleasure.——Some such thoughts as these we ought always to have when we see others dying or dead: Especially when they are those who were near to us in one way or another. Such providences ought to lead us to serious reflections on our own mortality; if they do not, it looks as if nothing would.

Fourthly, From what hath been said, we learn the evil of sin. Tho' our bodies were but dust, and therefore not immortal in their own nature, yet they might have been preserved in life by the power of God. If man had not sinned, he would not have died; the union between soul and body would never have been dissolved. But no sooner had Adam eaten the forbidden fruit, than he became a frail dying creature. Thus did God testify against the sin of man. Every time, therefore, we see any cut off by the king of terrors, we have a clear proof of the malignant nature of moral evil, which introduced sorrow, frailty, and mortality into the world.— Nor is the death of the body the only bad effect of the disobedience of the first parent of the human race. Man is, by means of the first sin of Adam, brought into such a state, that all who are capable of moral action do actually sin against God their Maker and Lord. The appetites and passions gain the ascendant, and prevail against all remonstrances of reason and conscience. How such a depraved nature is conveyed from Adam to his posterity, it is difficult for us to say; as it is to reconcile it to

the

the perfections of God, that there should be such a connection between the first man and his descendants, or indeed to permit the introduction of moral evil at all. The latter none will deny, and that this unhappy event is the consequence of Adam's apostacy from God seems plain from the sacred oracles of truth, " By one man sin entered into the world." Every deviation from the law of God defiles us more and more ; it incurs the displeasure of a holy God ; and exposes to that punishment which is denounced against the sinner in his word. —How clearly doth all this evidence sin to be the worst of evils ! 'Tis evil in the sight of God, or he would not punish it with such severity. And it is the greatest evil to man since it hath brought upon him death in this world, and exposes him to perdition in another. Is sin so great an evil ? how carefully should you watch against every tendency, and avoid every temptation to it !—What folly ! what madness ! to cherish a serpent that carries such a sting ; and whose fatal venom you have so sadly felt ! Let no enticement prevail with you to act contrary to the rules of reason and religion ; and devoutly implore his aid and assistance whose grace alone can keep you from falling.

Fifthly, What hath been said may serve to vindicate God from injustice, or even from hardship, in sentencing man to death. By this he put man into no worse state than he was originally in. He was dust, and God determined that he should return

return to dust again. Had the Creator given him life and then taken it from him, without default of his, I know not that it would have been contrary to any rule of justice or equity. He hath a right to take what he gave. But how perfectly just and equitable is his proceeding, when we consider him as acting in quality of a judge! Death was the threatning denounced ; it was the sanction with which God had guarded his law ; it was a punishment no way disproportioned to the demerit of the crime ; and therefore the inflicting it when man had sinned, seemed to be not merely an act of justice, but of wisdom, that the creatures of God might have a testimony of his aversion to sin, and a discovery of his rectoral holiness. As to the other consequences of the apostacy, the entail of so many evils and distresses on the posterity of the first man, the state of depravity and sin into which mankind are bro't, and that future misery which will be the portion of a great part of the human race ; without pretending to remove all the difficulties in which this subject is involved, it may be sufficient to say, that however mankind have reason to regret and mourn the original apostacy, as it is the cause of so much sin and distress ; yet every hard thought of God must vanish, when we consider the provision which a wise and good God hath made for our relief and deliverance. Thro' the mediation of Christ man may not only escape the misery of which he seems in danger ; but may attain the perfection of his nature in holiness and happiness. And to this end the

evils

evils of life are made subservient. So that God hath over-ruled even the apostacy of man, as to his own greater glory, so to our advantage. Our bodies turn to dust, but they will be raised; our souls are defiled, but they may be renewed by the Spirit of God; we are brought into danger of everlasting ruin, but we are by Christ raised to the hope of a blessed immortality. All this blessedness is set before us in the gospel, if we do not obtain it the fault will be our own. Instead then of complaining of hardship, we have reason to admire the wisdom and goodness of God, who hath by Christ brought man into better circumstances than he could have been in merely by the law of his nature. This leads to another reflection.

Sixthly, How thankful should we be that life and immortality are brought to light by the gospel? It is an unhappy situation to which the apostacy of man hath reduced the whole human race. But what a different scene doth the gospel open to view! Here we behold an offended God seated on a throne of grace; reconcilable to his fallen creature; kindly ready to deliver him from the sorrowful effects of his apostacy; willing again to stamp his image on the soul; and to admit him to glory and happiness. Nor are our bodies beneath his notice. The gospel doth not, indeed, promise deliverance from death; but it promises a restoration to life; that this corruptible shall put on incorruption, and this mortal shall put on immortality.

Thus

Thus hath the second Adam retrieved what we lost in the first, "As in Adam all die, so in Christ shall all be made alive." How much reason is there for gratitude to him who hath pitied us in our low estate, and sent his Son to redeem and save us! What condescending goodness doth it discover that he should take so much care of these tabernacles of clay, which were made of dust, and which sin hath rendered so sordid and frail!—We are often called to attend the burial of our friends, we see the triumphs of the king of terrors; at such times, let us turn our thoughts to that glorious day, when "the Lord himself will descend from heaven with a shout, with the voice of the arch-angel, and with the trump of God; and the dead in Christ shall rise."—How doth this glorious prospect scatter the horrors of the grave!—How reasonably may we comfort ourselves and one another with these words, when we are called to part with friends who died in hope! Their souls are now happy with the Lord; and those bodies which are returning to the dust, will be awakened out of their graves, and shall be fashioned like to Christ's glorious body.—How may this consideration give us courage in an hour of death! Of what consequence is it what becomes of our bodies when we die, if our souls are safe. That sordid dust to which we must return will be preserved by God for the most happy purposes, it will change its humiliating appearance, and will be as shining and glorious as now it is mean and vile.—This will be the happy

portion

portion only of those that have an interest in Christ, who is the resurrection and the life.—Although a state of blessed immortality is revealed to man; yet we may not from thence think, that all the children of Adam will certainly be admitted to happiness. No, the gospel hath its terms and conditions as well as the law; and unless we comply with them, we shall be more miserable, than if Christ had not come to redeem and save men. The grace of the gospel will increase our condemnation. Let us therefore embrace that Saviour whom God hath provided, and submit to him in his whole character. Let us make a business of religion, and suffer nothing to take us off from the care of our souls. It ought to be a mighty incentive to us to be diligent in this great work, that this is our only working time; as death leaves us, so judgment will find us, and so our future state will be determined. None can tell how short this time may be. We have constant admonitions of our frailty in the deaths of others, and in our own weaknesses and infirmities; let us therefore work while the day lasts, the night of death cometh wherein no man can work.

Well may the guilty determined sinner tremble at the thought of appearing before the tribunal of Jesus Christ. There is something awful in the thought of eternity. The righteous man shudders when he thinks of going into a separate unknown state.

state. Hath not he reason to fear who hath no prospect but of a miserable futurity? Attend then to the voice of reason and of conscience which is the voice of God. If any thing deserves attention, this doth. "Endeavor," as one speaks, " to make sure work for dying and for eternity, that you may die well, and not miscarry in that great and last change. An error here is fatal and cannot be corrected, consequently the utmost caution is due in order to avoid it. It was a good answer to one who asked why the Lacedemonians were so slow in passing capital judgments, why so many examinations taken; so many defences permitted to the accused; and after conviction and sentence such a space of time before execution; because, saith he, a mistake in this case is incorrigible, they may destroy the living, but cannot revive the dead. And thus it is in the affair before me; when the sentence of death is passed and executed, it cannot be reversed: my state is determined for ever. 'Tis appointed for all men once to die, once and but once, they do not live again, have no further opportunity to repent of what was ill done, of what was undone. Help me, therefore, Oh my God, to secure this main point, this greatest point, to get ready for dying, dying with safety and comfort!" ¶

¶ Mr. Grove.

SERMON

SERMON XX.

The Blessedness of those who have not seen and yet have believed.

John XX. 29.

Jesus saith unto him, Thomas, because thou hast seen me, thou hast believed. Blessed are they, that have not seen, and yet have believed.

OUR Lord had often, during the course of his ministry, predicted his death and resurrection in such plain terms, that we, in these days, have no difficulty in understanding him; and yet, it is evident, the apostles did not expect his death, and were greatly shocked when that event took place. They had no notion of his rising again, and were very slow in believing it, when it was affirmed by those who had seen him.

These good men had very dark and contracted notions of the Messiah's kingdom, till the Holy Ghost

Ghost was poured out.—Then they understood, that the Messiah was not to be a temporal Prince, as they before expected; but was to reign in the hearts of men.—Then, they found they were not to be raised to earthly grandeur, to live a life of ease and splendor; but were to encounter the most fierce opposition, to suffer the most cruel persecution, and to be, were it not for the hopes of immortality, of all men the most miserable.——And their disposition was so entirely changed, that they had no desires after that magnificence, the idea of which had before taken full possession of them. They were willing to suffer, and even to die for the name of the Lord Jesus. They went about —not to enlist men under his banner, and to subdue the Romans and other nations to the Jews—not to make themselves rich and great in this world.—But to turn men from these vanities; to set up a spiritual kingdom; to make known the doctrine of forgiveness through a Mediator, and to teach the certainty of an immortal state of happiness in another world.—To this benevolent employment they devoted themselves; in this they chearfully spent their lives: And, through their indefatigable labors, the word of God grew mightily, and prevailed against all opposition. By means of their preaching, and the precious remains they have left in the sacred records, the weakest christians have now more just notions of the Messiah's kingdom, and comprehend more fully our Lord's meaning, when he spake of his dying and rising again; than did even these chosen vessels, while their Master was with them. We

We are ready to wonder that the apostles did not remember, as well as the Jewish rulers, that Jesus had said, "while he was yet alive, after three days I will rise again." But they were so affected with his unexpected death, that it is plain they did not remember this prediction, so as to receive any consolation from it. His crucifixion put an end to their hopes, and left them in a state of dejection and distress. They did not know what to make of the first reports of our Saviour's resurrection; and it was not till they had sensible demonstration of the certainty of this event, that they dismissed their doubts, and gave full credit to this great and fundamental article of our holy religion.

Jesus first appeared to Mary Magdalene—Then to the other women who were going from the sepulchre: But the disciples to whom they related what they had seen did not believe them. "Their words seemed to them as idle tales."—Afterwards, he appeared to Simon—Then to two disciples as they went to Emmaus. When they told this to the residue, they believed them not, at least they had their doubts and suspicions. They would not admit the truth of this important fact, till they had the testimony of their senses.—Our Lord therefore condescended to give them this evidence. " The same day at evening, when the doors were shut, where the disciples were assembled for fear of the Jews, came Jesus and stood in the midst of them."

Even

Even then, it is said, " they believed not for joy." They were so criminally incredulous, that their Lord " upbraided them for their unbelief and hardness of heart," after he had given them such manifest proof of his being risen.

Now, it seems, they were in general satisfied. " But Thomas, one of the twelve, was not with them when Jesus came. The other disciples therefore said unto him, we have seen the Lord. But he said unto them, except I shall see in his hands the print of the nails, and put my fingers into the print of the nails, and thrust my hand into his side, I will not believe." After the evidence Thomas had of the resurrection of Jesus, there seems to have been an unreasonable obstinacy in this determination. He knew his brethren to be honest men; and after the united testimony of so many to a fact in which they could not easily be deceived, his incredulity could not be justified. If men were to insist on sensible demonstration in all cases, there would be an end of testimony, and endless confusion would be introduced.

However, our Lord condescended to the weakness, or if you will, the perverseness of Thomas, though he left him a considerable time in a state of anxious uncertainty. He knew the honesty of his heart, and therefore would not leave him in unbelief. He overlooked what was amiss, and kindly gave him the evidence he desired. " And after eight

eight days, again his disciples were within, and Thomas with them: Then came Jesus, the doors being shut, and stood in the midst, and said, peace be unto you. Then saith he to Thomas, reach hither thy finger, and behold my hands; and reach hither thy hand, and thrust it into my side, and be not faithless but believing." This is a tender but very plain rebuke of Thomas's incredulity. He lets him know, that he was well acquainted with his unbelief, and the manner in which he had expressed it. But without upbraiding or reproaching him with his obstinacy, (in which perhaps there was a mixture of resentment, because Christ had not given him the same evidence he had given his fellow-disciples) instead of upbraiding him with this faulty disposition, our Lord invites him to receive the very proof he had insisted upon. Thomas, struck with the condescension of his Master, and ashamed of his backwardness to believe, proceeded no further, sought no other means of conviction, but cried out with surprize and joy, My Lord! and my God! —He not only received him as risen, but in the strongest terms acknowleged the dignity of his person and character.—I say Thomas proceeded no further;—for, as it is not said that he attempted to search for the wounds, according to his former declaration, we ought to suppose that, convinced by what he had seen and heard, he immediately owned the truth of our Lord's resurrection, without a particular examination of his body. This is especially probable, as in our text it is implicitly asserted, that

his

his faith was founded in sight. "Jesus saith unto him, Thomas, because thou hast seen me, thou hast believed. Blessed are they, that have not seen, and yet have believed." These words are not to be taken in so strict a sense, as if every one who believed without the evidence of sight, would be more blessed than they who saw Jesus after his resurrection; in which case, every one who believed after our Lord was taken up into heaven, would have a superior degree of happiness to the apostles themselves. The words can only imply, that the blessedness of those who have not seen is superior, where all other circumstances agree or are equal. Or that where a man yields to rational evidence without seeing, he is in a more happy state of mind, than another, whose assent rises only to the same degree, and is founded on the evidence of sense. "It was in effect, telling Thomas, it would have been much more acceptable, if he had not stood out so long; and it was doing it in such a manner, as would be most calculated for the comfort and encouragement of believers in future ages, to whom, in many of his speeches to the apostles themselves, our Lord expressed a most obliging and affectionate regard."

Possibly Jesus might intend, in these words, to express his particular approbation of John, the writer of this gospel, who seems to have been the first that believed the truth of his Lord's resurrection. We are told in the beginning of this chapter,

ter, that when Mary Magdalene had informed Peter and John that they had " taken away the Lord out of the sepulchre; they ran both together, and the other disciple did out run Peter, and came first to the sepulchre." Being naturally timid and cautious, he did not enter in : " But stooping down, saw the linen cloaths lying ; yet went he not in." " Then cometh Simon Peter," and being of a more bold and forward disposition, he " went into the sepulchre, and seeth the linen cloaths lie ; and the napkin that was about his head, not lying with the linen cloaths, but wrapped together in a place by itself." The other disciple, encouraged by Peter's example, ventured to go in after him, " and he saw and believed"—Saw what?—He saw what Peter had seen—" The napkin that was about his head, not lying with the linen cloaths, but wrapped together in a place by itself." He saw all things disposed in such regular order, as shewed that the body of Jesus was not hastily hurried away, as if it had been stolen, but that there was rather the appearance of calmness and leisure.

" He saw and he believed," that is, say most commentators, he believed what Mary Magdalene had reported, that they had taken away the body of Jesus. How jejune a sense ! and what reason is there for departing from the common sense of the word *believed* in the new-testament ? which is an assent to the truth concerning Jesus Christ ; or a belief of his general character as Messiah. It had hardly

hardly been worth mentioning, that John believed the body was not in the sepulchre, when he saw it was not there. It is much more probable, that this is, as Dr. Doddridge understands it, " a modest intimation, that John first indeed of all others believed the truth of Christ's resurrection; inferring it, as he reasonably might, from the order in which he found the sepulchre. These words" says he, " have a force, and a grace, on this interpretation, which no other can give them." ¶—Nor do the words immediately following at all militate with this sense, " For as yet they knew not the scriptures, that he must rise again from the dead."—These words may be considered as an excuse for their not believing that Christ was risen, till this time: Or, they may intend, that none of the disciples (not even John, though he believed that Christ was risen) fully understood the scriptures which referred to this great event, and how great good was connected with it; which was undoubtedly true. If this sense of John's believing is just, we may reasonably suppose, his Lord designed, in our text, to express his approbation of his faith, who believed that Christ was risen, before he saw his Person; which was what no other had done.

But, upon the supposition, that our Lord had this in view, when he said, " Blessed are they who have not seen, and yet have believed;" the words

¶ See also Mr. West's admirable observations on the resurrection of CHRIST.

words are by no means to be confined to this instance, but are to be extended to all who believe in all ages, through the word of thofe who had feen Chrift rifen. Bleffed are they in time! and blefled throughout eternity!

From the words of our text we obferve,

Firft, That though we have not fenfible demonftration of the refurrection of Chrift, yet there is fufficient evidence to produce a rational belief of this great and important fact. There can be no doubt that Chrift arofe from the dead, if the account given by the evangelifts is true. It is afferted in the moft exprefs terms. And how fuch an hiftory could be obtruded on the world, if it was not true, cannot eafily be conceived. There is not only the teftimony of a number of honeft fenfible men, that they faw Chrift after he was rifen, converfed with him, faw him eat, felt his body, or might have handled it, were invited to fatisfy themfelves as much as they pleafed. There is not only this direct teftimony, but the refurrection of Chrift was followed with a remarkable effufion of the Holy Ghoft, whereby the difciples were enabled to fpeak with tongues, and to perform the moft extraordinary miracles. Thefe powers, they exprefly declared, were in confequence of the refurrection and afcenfion of Jefus. The miracles they performed were of fuch a nature, that it was fcarce poffible they who were prefent fhould be deceived. Efpecially they who were continually watching to
enfnare

enfnare them, and who conftantly oppofed and reviled them.—If they were wrought, they were an indubitable evidence that Chrift was rifen, and confequently was the promifed Meffiah.—If they were not wrought, no man could have had the infolence to fay they were. Inftead of being attended to, and of converting any to the faith of Chrift, all would have rejected them as bafe impoftors; it had been right to treat them as fuch; and they themfelves muft have had the confcious horror of fuffering the juft demerit of their crimes. Whereas the gofpel preached by them had free courfe, ran, and was glorified. Multitudes believed. Some of fuperior character, with refpect both to their ftation and abilities; and even fome who had with cruel zeal oppofed their Mafter, and with wicked hands had crucified and flain him.

The apoftles could have no worldly inducement to affert or propagate a falfhood; they amaffed no riches; they were advanced to no places of dignity; they endured hardnefs; they were abufed, fcourged, and treated with all kinds of ignominy and cruelty. They could expect nothing but perfecution, fufferings and death, if they profeffed to own Chrift as their Mafter and Lord.

The backwardnefs of the difciples to believe the refurrection of Chrift, however faulty, is an argument of the reality of the fact. It was a demonftration that they were not willing to be deceived;

ed; that they were cautious in yielding their affent; and confequently that they had the fulleft evidence that Jefus was rifen, before they believed it. They would not believe the teftimony of their companions, whom they knew, and of whom they could have no reafonable fufpicion. They had repeated atteftations, and yet infifted on the evidence of their own fenfes. Then, and not till then, they fubmitted. They did not believe till the evidence was irrefiftible. Which circumftance, though it leffened the virtue of their affent, yet renders it more convincing to thofe who come after. Their unbelief for fo long a time, joined with the effufion of the Holy Ghoft, and the power with which they were endued from on high, renders the truth of our Saviour's refurrection indubitable.

In this refpect, we have the advantage of his immediate followers. They had not thofe proofs of his divine miffion which we have, in his refurrection, and the great events confequent upon it and connected with it. Thefe are the greateft and the higheft evidence of the truth of chriftianity. And therefore many are of opinion, that our Saviour refers to them, when he fays, " All manner of blafphemy fhall be forgiven unto men; but the blafphemy againft the holy Ghoft fhall not be forgiven unto men; and whofoever fpeaketh a word againft the Son of man, it fhall be forgiven him; but whofoever fpeaketh againft the Holy Ghoft, it fhall not be forgiven him, neither in this world, neither in

the

the world to come." † Even thofe, who rejected Chrift when on earth, might be brought to conviction and repentance, and fo obtain forgivenefs of their fins, when they faw the power of the Holy Ghoft accompanying his apoftles and followers. But our Lord warns his hearers, that if they fhould blafpheme the Holy Ghoft in his moft fignal gifts and operations, by which he would bear witnefs to the truth of chriftianity, and fhould refift this higheft evidence, which God would ever vouchfafe to give; they muft be left in impenitence and unbelief, and be excluded forgivenefs. A confideration which may well alarm the infidels of the prefent day; and fhould make us all careful, not to contract their guilt, nor expofe ourfelves to their punifhment!

Secondly, There may be doubts about the truths of religion, where there is real fincerity of heart. What more important truth than the refurrection of Chrift? and yet the difciples, who had followed our Lord with fuch affection and diligence, were hardly perfuaded to believe it. Thomas's doubts might proceed from the great defire he had that the refurrection of Chrift might prove true, and his fear of being difappointed. This was a right difpofition in itfelf, though it degenerated into unreafonable diffidence, and even a perverfe obftinacy. Should not this teach us charity towards thofe, who may not immediately embrace truths which we apprehend

† Matt. 12. 31, 32.

prehend of great importance? Things may not appear to them in the fame ftrong light they do to us. They may have difficulties which we have not. —It feems ftrange to us, that the apoftles did not fooner believe that Chrift was rifen; but we have not their prejudices, their difappointment, and wrong notions to combat with; we cannot realize them. We believe they were honeft good men long before. And may not others be under miftakes when they err from the truth, as we think? Every error doth not proceed from a wicked mind, and it is not for us to fay, how far a good man may fall into wrong fentiments in religion. God may have wife ends in permitting fuch miftakes; as he had in permitting the difciples to be fo unreafonably backward in believing Chrift was rifen, viz. to give others ftronger reafon to believe this important fact. This we may be fure of, that God will not fuffer a fincerely good man to continue in an error which would prove fatal. "If any man will do his will, he fhall know of the doctrine whether it be of God." It becomes us to be very cautious, how we determine any point to be fundamental, which God hath not determined to be fo.

I may properly add here, That a truth may be fundamental under fome circumftances, which is not under others. The refurrection of Chrift, tho' plainly taught by him, was not a fundamental doctrine before his death: The belief of it was not neceffary

ry to denominate the apostles good men, when they denied it. And yet the apostle Paul tells us it was afterwards. "If Christ be not raised, your faith is vain, ye are yet in your sins."‖ The reason is plain: Their circumstances and our's are very different. We have not their pre-conceived notions to oppose; and we have means of conviction which they had not.—A further argument this to mutual candor and forbearance. As we cannot exactly tell the circumstances and prejudices which other men are under, it is best not to judge or censure our brethren; but to leave them to Him, who "is a God of knowlege, and by whom actions are weighed."

Thirdly, We observe, that to yield our assent, when we have proper moral evidence, is more commendable, than to insist on the evidence of sense. We all think Thomas, and indeed all the disciples faulty, in being so backward to believe, when they had such evidence of our Saviour's resurrection. Our Lord severely rebuked the two disciples, with whom he walked in the way to Emmaus, "O fools, and slow of heart to believe all that the prophets have spoken! ought not Christ to have suffered these things, and to enter into his glory?" † There is no doubt but we may have sufficient moral evidence of the truth of facts, where we have not the evidence of sense. We continually act upon this supposition—We go upon the testimony of others—We reason from things we know; and are convinced, by such rational deductions,

‖ 1 Cor. 15. 17.   † Luke 24. 25, 26.

ductions, of many truths, which we should otherwise be ignorant of—We argue from principles that are self-evident. On this foundation we raise our superstructure. We think any conclusion just, which is properly deduced from premises that are true. We yield our assent to truths which appear to follow from other truths.—And we do right.—. If we determine to believe, only where we have sensible evidence, we shall deny a God, a Providence, and almost every truth of natural and revealed religion. According to this rule, we must reject all those facts which are conveyed to us in history, and involve ourselves in endless confusion and absurdity: One born blind must deny that the sun ever rises and sets; or that there is any such thing as light: The eastern monarch who lived in a warm climate, was quite right in refusing to believe the first relations concerning the effects of frost; and we could not have blamed him for putting the priest to death, who affirmed that in the country from whence he came the waters were congealed into solid ice, as he would certainly have done, if the testimony of others had not corroborated the declaration of the priest, and the Prince had not been favored with understanding enough to yield to their united testimony, and to believe a thing he had not seen, though at first he thought it impossible.

A man who yields to rational evidence without seeing, shews greater simplicity, candor, and wisdom, than he who infists on ocular demonstration, after sufficient evidence of another kind hath been propoſed to him. Where there is an attentive candid mind, open to rational conviction, it argues a love of truth, which is a virtuous diſpoſition. Whereas when we believe only what we have ſeen, there is ſcarce room for the exerciſe of virtue at all. We aſſent becauſe we cannot help aſſenting. Such a rational faith, or a faith founded on proper moral evidence is more virtuous, and conſequently more acceptable to God, in proportion to the difficulties it ſurmounts, and the temptations it meets with to infidelity.

God ſaw fit to afford ſenſible evidence of the reſurrection of Chriſt to but few comparatively; but their teſtimony, in connection with its concomitants and conſequences, is a ſufficient ground of a rational belief; and the nature of the thing admits of no other proof. In order to give every one the evidence of ſenſe, which ſome ſceptical men urge as neceſſary, Jeſus muſt have left the realms of bliſs and glory, where his preſence is ſo much needed for us: He muſt have been continually dying and riſing from the dead: And in that caſe, it is much to be queſtioned, whether the commonneſs of the event would not have rendered men leſs attentive to it. So we obſerve the conſtant riſing and ſetting of the ſun, moon, and ſtars, with much leſs attention,

tion, than we do the appearance of a comet. Tho' the constant regular motion of the former, affords a much stronger proof of the power and goodness of God, than the unknown wanderings of the latter.

There is no end of gratifying the perverse humours of men; they insist on one thing after another; and some will never be satisfied. They raise objections contrary to all reason and common sense; and if they can but persuade others to disbelieve christianity, they give themselves no concern, tho' they are left without any religion—any principles at all. What advantage these men can propose to themselves or to the world, if they should gain their point, it is hard to say; or what good end could be answered. Such a state of absolute uncertainty and doubt would be most uncomfortable to individuals, and greatly prejudicial to society. It can hardly be supposed, that persons of such an unhappy cast of mind, would be influenced by any evidence, which it would be agreable to the character of the all-wise God to give them. They who reject the testimonies we have of the truth of the facts recorded in the new-testament, would scarce be convinced by any other. Men who are not influenced by the standing means of religion, would not be influenced by any rational methods at all. " If they hear not Moses and the prophets, neither will they be persuaded, though one rose from the dead." † The infidelity of the most proceeds

† Luke 16. 31.

not from any defect in revelation, or in the evidences of it, but from the perverseness and obstinacy of their own minds.

Fourthly, We observe the blessing which our Saviour pronounces on those who have not seen, and yet have believed. It is matter of unspeakable joy, that there is a Saviour born into our apostate world... That he "was delivered for our offences, and raised again for our justification." They were blessed, who saw Christ's day and embraced him as their Saviour and Lord, but the foundation of their blessedness was not their seeing Christ with their bodily eyes; it was their belief of things which were not seen. Those things in Christ which were the proper reason for their trusting and rejoicing in him, who lived in the time of his dwelling with man upon earth, were always invisible, and entirely matters of faith to them, as they are to us. They had much greater reason to rejoice on account of those truths, which were revealed concerning Christ, and which were not objects of their senses, than on account of what they saw and heard.

It was a reasonable foundation of joy, that one was come into the world who taught the will of God in so perfect a manner, and who gave such full demonstration of his divine power: But it was, even

even then, a matter of greater joy, that he came—To save them from their sins by the power of his grace—To make atonement for their offences—To assure them, that God was through him reconciling the world to himself, not imputing their trespasses to them—and to give them the hopes of a blessed immortality. And these doctrines were proper objects of faith. Though Christ wrought such stupendous miracles, which were seen and known; yet none could see, with their bodily eyes, the dignity of his person, or the excellency and importance of his character. These were things proposed to their faith; and were to be argued from the testimony which God gave in those great and visible effects.

Nor was faith in Christ the necessary or certain effect of seeing what he did, or of hearing what he taught. Many who heard his doctrines, and were witnesses of his miracles, refused to own him in the character of the Messiah, they treated him as an impostor, and ascribed the supernatural works wrought by him to the power of Satan. When Peter made that noble confession, " Thou art Christ, the Son of the living God. Jesus answered and said unto him, Blessed art thou Simon Bar-jona, for flesh and blood hath not revealed it unto thee, but my Father which is in heaven." ‡

They

‡ Matt. 16. 16, 17.

They who rejected him were without excuse, after the evidences he gave of his divine mission, in not believing the testimony of God concerning him. But is not the case the same, with those who reject him now? Though we are not eye-witnesses of his miracles; though we do not hear the gracious words which proceeded out of his mouth; yet they are transmitted to us, from those who were witnesses of them, with such marks of authenticity, as are sufficient to afford matter of rational conviction to every upright and attentive mind. We have enough laid of Christ in the word of God, and that with such divine attestations, as will command an assent, so far as means can go. The disadvantage, therefore, which we lay under, with regard to those who lived in our Saviour's day, is not so great, as we are apt to imagine. Since we have sufficient moral evidence of the truth of what was then delivered and done; and those things in Christ which are of the greatest importance, were then as well as now, the immediate objects of faith, and not of sense; and are of such a nature, as that a sight of him, and an attendance on his personal ministry, would not certainly produce a belief of them. We are as capable of attending to the evidence we have, and of assenting to these truths, as we should have been if we had lived in that day.

It is by faith only, we can view him as appointed by the Father to the work of redemption—It is
by

by faith only, we can see his fitness to be a Mediator and Saviour—It is by faith, we see that he hath paid the price of our redemption—It is by faith only, we can survey the promises which are great and precious, and that we can have a prospect of that future state of immortal life and happiness which the gospel reveals and offers. When a good man is persuaded of these truths, and at the same time is satisfied from himself that he hath an interest in the promises, he may rejoice with exceeding great joy, though he doth not see Christ with his bodily eyes, or hath not sensible evidence of his resurrection. " Whom having not seen, ye love : In whom, though now ye see him not, yet believing, ye rejoice with joy unspeakable and full of glory." §

Instead of finding fault that we did not live in Christ's day, that we had not ocular demonstration of his miracles, and were not favored with his personal instruction, let us be thankful for the great advantages we have, and which we enjoy without fear or molestation. Let us improve the means which God vouchsafes us, of attaining to the perfection of our nature in holiness and happiness. " Let us fear, lest a promise being left us of entering into his rest, any of you should seem to come short of it." ‡ If we miss of immortal life and glory, it will not be owing to a defect of means, but to our own perverseness and obstinacy.

§ 1 Pet. 1. 8.   ‡ Heb. 4. 1.

"They shall come from the east, and from the west, and from the north, and from the south, and shall sit down in the kingdom of God;" when many who have eaten and drank in Christ's presence, who sat under his gracious instruction, and some who were employed by him to preach the gospel of the kingdom, who prophesied in his name, and in his name have cast out devils, and in his name have done many wonderful works, will be rejected in that severe language, " Depart from me ye that work iniquity." BLESSED ARE THEY THAT HAVE NOT SEEN, AND YET HAVE BELIEVED.

www.ingramcontent.com/pod-product-compliance
Lightning Source LLC
Chambersburg PA
CBHW021423300426
44114CB00010B/621